BEYOND TRANSCENDENCE IN LAW AND PHILOSOPHY

BEYOND TRANSCENDENCE IN LAW AND PHILOSOPHY

Louis E Wolcher BA JD
Charles I Stone Professor of Law
University of Washington School of Law

Birkbeck
LAW PRESS

First published in Great Britain 2005 by
Birkbeck Law Press, The Glass House,
Wharton Street, London WC1X 9PX, United Kingdom
Telephone: + 44 (0)20 7278 8000 Facsimile: + 44 (0)20 7278 8080
Email: info@cavendishpublishing.com
Website: www.cavendishpublishing.com

Published in the United States by Cavendish Publishing
c/o International Specialized Book Services,
5824 NE Hassalo Street, Portland,
Oregon 97213-3644, USA

Published in Australia by Cavendish Publishing (Australia) Pty Ltd
45 Beach Street, Coogee, NSW 2034, Australia
Telephone: + 61 (2)9664 0909 Facsimile: + 61 (2)9664 5420
Email: info@cavendishpublishing.com.au
Website: www.cavendishpublishing.com.au

Library of Congress Cataloging in Publication Data
Data available

Hardback ISBN-10: 1-85941-988-7
Hardback ISBN-13: 978-1-859-41988-5
Paperback ISBN-10: 1-85941-985-2
Paperback ISBN-13: 978-1-859-41985-4

1 3 5 7 9 10 8 6 4 2
Printed and bound in Great Britain

For Susie, Sarah, and Edward

Acknowledgments

The author has previously published portions of certain chapters in this book in article form. Permission to use and modify various passages from the following texts is therefore gratefully acknowledged.

In Chapter 2, with kind permission of Hart Publishing: Wolcher, L (2004) 'Thought's prison: an image of images', in Lippens, R (ed) *Imaginary Boundaries of Justice*, 21–50, © 2004 Hart Publishing.

In Chapter 3, with kind permission of Kluwer Academic Publishers: Wolcher, L (2003) 'Ethics, justice, and suffering in the thought of Levinas: the problem of the passage', 14 Law and Critique 93–116, © Kluwer Academic Publishers.

In Chapter 4, with kind permission of Kluwer Academic Publishers: Wolcher, L (1998) 'A meditation on Wittgenstein's *Lecture on Ethics*, 9 Law and Critique 3–35, © Kluwer Academic Publishers.

In Chapter 5, with kind permission of Kluwer Academic Publishers: Wolcher, L (2002) 'The third mountain: a meditation on chaos and order', 15 International Journal for the Semiotics of Law 25–52, © Kluwer Academic Publishers.

Preface

This book is the result of nearly two decades of thinking about Western philosophy from a standpoint that has been deeply influenced by the teachings and practices of Zen Buddhism. Most Zen philosophers who are known in the West – DT Suzuki and Kitaró Nishida, for example – write works that tend to westernise Zen; they *adapt* and *modify* Zen by bringing it closer to the problems that preoccupy Western thought, and by dragging its notoriously obscure texts into the open air of rational intelligibility. Without suggesting that I despise rationality and intelligibility (a dangerous thing for an author to do), I would like to reverse this traditional relationship between Zen and Western thought: to 'Zenise' Western philosophy, as it were, by writing a book that is meant to be philosophical in form, but ultimately koan-like in content. Although the book aspires to attain a clear perspective on the interrelated and allegedly 'rational' themes of *being*, *ethics* and *language*, the perspective itself is neither rational nor irrational. However well-reasoned they may appear to be, my words are ultimately intended to be the philosophical equivalent of a description of the sound made by one hand clapping. To this end, I have chosen three of the 20th century's greatest philosophers as my principal interlocutors concerning these important categories of thought: Martin Heidegger (being), Emmanuel Levinas (ethics), and Ludwig Wittgenstein (language). Many other thinkers will come up in the course of discussion – most notably Anaximander, Aristotle, Leibniz, Kant, Schelling, Hegel, Schopenhauer, Nietzsche, Husserl, Benjamin and Derrida – but I care less about the various 'philosophies' of these individuals than I do about the *matters* that called them to think in the first place: namely, what they took to be the (ponderously) profound themes of being, ethics and language.

Since the foregoing paragraph does not contain the name of anyone who explicitly styled himself a philosopher of law, I should probably issue a disclaimer to any reader who expects something 'legal' from this book just because Birkbeck Law Press has published it, or because I am a law professor. This volume is not 'about' law or legal theory in any normal sense of these words. There are, to be sure, certain passages and sections dealing explicitly with problems of law and justice: for example,

I discuss legal formalism and the problems of interpretation and lawfulness in Chapter 1, law-and-justice in Chapter 3, and rule-following in Chapter 4. However, the book as a whole is preoccupied with matters that include law and justice without being narrowly about them in any traditional way. As I see it, a philosophical work that limits itself to 'law' in the popular or academic sense has already sold its soul, as it were, to conventional ways of thinking. At the risk of offending many people by saying it, I believe that any thinking which adheres to the form 'the philosophy of X' is *a priori* unphilosophical. Such a work lets ossified and arbitrary divisions and distinctions control its paths of thinking, rather than the other way around. To put it all in a nutshell, one might say that this book is highly relevant to law and justice, but only because it aspires to be highly relevant to just about everything.

From the Zen point of view that is exhibited in this book, the essence of being, ethics and language is ultimately the same as the essence of law and justice. At the heart of them all is the mind's supine surrender to a kind of reassuring *movement*. The movement goes from one idea or term to another idea or term that depends on the former as its cause, origin or ground. In this movement, the mind creates the illusion of a difference between terms that are abidingly linked in such a way that they are taken to be elements of a larger sameness. The illusion makes it seem that the grammatical pairs 'cause and caused', 'origin and originated', and 'ground and grounded' refer to non-linguistic beings or essences that, like Siamese twins, are born separate but conjoined. In truth, however, these pairs are more like the illusion of two connected bodies that appears when a single body is reflected in a funhouse mirror. In this respect, a judge's decision to pass judgment on someone for doing something that violates the law is no different in principle than a philosopher's decision that beings are grounded in being (Heidegger), that ethical responsibility comes from our encounter with the face of another human being (Levinas), and that language is a logically bounded medium that makes certain matters, such as metaphysics and ethics, unsayable (Wittgenstein). In this book, 'highfalutin' philosophy, divine justice, and mundane law all dwell on the same level, inside an endless hall of mirrors.

In each of the foregoing cases the thinker lets his curiosity and his judgment obey what is essentially a norm of representation – a mere rule of grammar, as it were, that passes itself off as an unquestionably natural datum authorising the mind's movement from antecedent to subsequent, from A to B. I call this norm *logical transcendence*, represented symbolically as $A \Rightarrow B$. I call it logical transcendence, rather than *logical necessity* or the *principle of sufficient reason*, because I want to emphasise its contingency. The principle of reason, for example, says *nihil est sine ratione* ('nothing is without reason'), as if reasons were there to be found and described, rather than made; logical transcendence, on the other hand, says that things only have those 'reasons' that our minds let them have. People sometimes speak metaphorically about their 'train of thought' – one that they find and follow, or else lose – ignoring the fact that a moving train travels from point to point on iron rails that cannot take it along any other axis of direction than the one in which it is heading. Instead of comparing their thoughts to a train, people really ought to speak in terms of the *rails of thought* that they themselves lay down by the very act of thinking them. And why is it that the mind lays these rails of thought down, only to forget this fact and pretend that it is merely following them from A to B, like a train? From the standpoint of Buddhism (and this book), the answer to this question is simple and obvious, but difficult to accept. We *let* logical transcendence happen because of our attachment to the possibility of enduring solutions for the problems that are created by our own suffering, and by the sufferings of other beings about whom we care.

Unfortunately, there is no enduring rational solution to the problem of craving desire – and hence suffering – *as such*. This kind of desire ceaselessly yearns to transform the given (*thusness*, in Zen thought) in accordance with the formula 'A ⇒ B', and therefore always finds itself in the regrettable position of feeling dissatisfied with the results of its own efforts to achieve satisfaction. 'Everything disappoints', says Kierkegaard: 'Hope, the hoped for does not come, or the hoped for comes – and disappoints' (1993: 62). Hegel calls the human tendency *always* to be dissatisfied with given conditions 'negativity'; Zen calls it a manifestation of suffering that is born of a delusion. In letting logical transcendence have its way with us, we enter a circle of self-frustrating effort that Buddhists call *samsára*. This Sanskrit word names the cycle of birth and death and, in its most profound sense, it does not refer to some sort of flaky New Age doctrine of reincarnation, but rather to the birth of each new moment of suffering out of the death of the moment before. In a word, the norm 'A ⇒ B' is not an eternal truth: it is an artefact of desperate minds that find themselves adrift on a sea of impermanence.

Despite what has just been said, this book is not an argument against law, science and philosophy, all of which produce a plethora of results (some good, some not so good) according to the stipulation 'A ⇒ B'. It would be better to say that the book is an argument against *attachment* to the ideas that lead to results, including especially the idea of logical transcendence itself. Since attachment to ideas creates a kind of blindness to anything that the ideas do not authorise, this book is also an argument against the shameful indifference to universal suffering that always seems to accompany attachment to definitive solutions, even the best of all possible solutions. For as Levinas puts it, there are tears that the civil servant does not see, tears of the other that are all the more terrible because they proceed from the necessity of a reasonable order (1996: 23). The point that I want to make is *not* the Sartrean one that human beings are all *a priori* existentially free, and therefore that the feeling of necessity is an illusion. Rather, this book explores the possibility of an awareness that goes beyond the categories 'freedom' and 'necessity', and beyond the choice between them – a kind of awareness that lets go of what made us become obsessed with freedom and necessity in the first place.

The warring concepts of freedom and necessity are both yoked like oxen to the idea of logical transcendence, even if they do pull in opposite directions. The idea of necessity is intelligible only because it projects a sort of hardwired passage between causes and conditions (A) and human thoughts and deeds (B). However, freedom, too, relies on the norm 'A ⇒ B' for its very intelligibility, projecting a passage between an unconditioned will or other human faculty (A) and the thoughts and actions that are supposed to depend on it (B). Uncritical adherence to the norm of logical transcendence is thus prior to the opposition between freedom and necessity, just as it is prior to every other opposition within language. To borrow an image from TS Eliot's poem *The Love Song of J Alfred Prufrock*, I want to suggest in this book that we unthinkingly let the norm 'A ⇒ B' fix the world, including human beings, in a formulated phrase that leaves it sprawling on a pin, like a bug. However, whatever else it may be, the world is not like a dying bug – indeed, it is not *like* anything at all.

To paraphrase the 9th century Chinese Zen master Lin-chi, the rule of logical transcendence allows thought to create understanding from the fingers of an empty fist (Schloegl 1976: 60): although we are constantly grasping at truth with the fingers of language and images, all we ever really hold in our fist is emptiness. At its most basic level, this book is an extended meditation on the possibility of letting go of our obsession with language and images, in philosophy and in life, and getting beyond logical transcendence to a way of being that combines, paradoxically enough, both detachment and attachment. In this state of affairs, which is ruled impossible by the standards of conventional logic, a radically detached and indifferent insight into what Zen calls thusness goes hand in hand with a radically compassionate and involved concern for the suffering of others – *all* others. Compassion for universal suffering is impossible so long as we continue to let 'A ⇒ B' divide the realm of suffering into the right and the wrong, the lawful and the unlawful, the just and the unjust. A compassion that is this large would require both *detachment* from the obsession with divisions, and *attachment* to the unbearably sad plight of a suffering humanity. The tone of the book is therefore simultaneously cold and warm, remote and near, severe and kind. Unfortunately, a preface can no more tell you what the foregoing remarks mean than the label on a bottle of wine can put the actual taste of the wine in your mouth. You must drink the wine to taste it, and you must read the book to experience the possibility of letting go of craving attachment to logical transcendence. Having made this point as well as I can, it would still be both possible, and useful, for me to give a brief outline of the book's structure here.

Chapter 1 ('A Zen Beginning') introduces certain fundamental Zen ideas that are relevant to all subsequent chapters, including craving desire, attachment, thusness, and what I call Zen's deflationary view of language and knowledge. The chapter then turns to the famous 'mountains and rivers' koan, goes on to analyse the three primary conceptions of transcendence in philosophy, and then ultimately traces all of Western thought, from the pre-Socratic to the postmodern, to the root phenomenon of craving desire for answers to the questions that the norm of logical transcendence, 'A $\Rightarrow$ B', beguiles us into asking. Chapter 1 also openly admits the formal contradiction at work in the book's use of statements that take the form of logical transcendence in order to criticise logical transcendence, only to say 'So what?' to this allegedly shocking inconsistency. Those who treat contradictions like vampires, to be avoided at all costs, can never achieve insight into why they cling so obsessively to the law of non-contradiction; they cravenly accept it as their master, rather than attempting to reverse the relation, don the master's robe and pick up its bowl and staff, and transform themselves into *its* master. A master of this type understands that the self-conscious *saying* of a contradiction, employed as an expedient means to achieve insight, is never the same as asserting, rather ridiculously, that the contradiction contains a logically valid *said*, or even that it conveys some sort of mystical or poetic profundity.

Chapter 2 ('Heidegger's Groundless Ground') continues to expose the problematic character of logical transcendence by bringing out Heidegger's fundamental evasion of it; here I focus on certain Heideggerian texts, written both before and after his so-called 'turn', about the principle of reason and the unity of ground in Kantian philosophy; I trace Heidegger's lifelong obsession with the priority of being over beings to his uneasy adherence to the norm of logical transcendence, which manifests itself in an unresolved tension or contradiction in his philosophy between being-as-ground and freedom-as-ground.

Chapter 3 ('Levinas's Problem of the Passage') considers two important theses advanced by Levinas, namely, that a radical kind of ethical responsibility is born of the intimate sociality of the relation between two people, and that ethics, as he defines it, provides a superior kind of passage to justice in the social and political spheres; I enact a phenomenology of distress in the moment of justice to show how these arguments manifest a kind of pitiable collapse into a linguistic 'feel-good' solution that would sanction the violence and suffering that always attend worldly attempts to rectify injustice.

Chapter 4 ('Wittgenstein's Noisy Silence') takes the form of a meditation on Wittgenstein's *A Lecture on Ethics*, an extraordinary text in which this most intense of all modern philosophers expresses the thesis that metaphysical and ethical statements are nonsense, and makes a kind of personal announcement to the effect that he could not speak, and would remain silent, about the questions that arise in these ineffable spheres; this chapter investigates the plight of a thinker who grew so afraid of the rule of logical transcendence that he got captured by it on the rebound, as it were, by allowing himself to ground a legible kind of silence on the dogmatic belief that language is only good for expressing the mundane.

Finally, Chapter 5 ('The Third Mountain') reappropriates the metaphor of a three-part journey in the 'mountains and rivers' koan to investigate the relation between chaos (no A, no B, and no passage between them) and order (A ⇒ B) in Western thought, and to bring the book to an end that is meant to represent or suggest the possibility of a new kind of beginning.

It is hard to know how to classify this volume. Heidegger famously maintains that traditional Western philosophy is *onto-theology*. Philosophy is *ontology*, he thought, because it questions beings as such about the manner of their being, and it is *theology* because it questions beings as a whole, that is, being and its ground. Although Heidegger's description of philosophy has much to be said for it, I feel compelled to deny that this book is onto-theology in his sense, for it is not so much concerned with questioning beings and being as it is with questioning the very practice of questioning-and-answering itself. This does not mean that it is no kind of philosophy at all, however, for the book concerns itself with a large number of philosophical problems and texts. On the other hand, it also seems to dispute or contradict the very thing that motivates philosophers and makes philosophy possible: the movement from ignorance to truth. What philosopher would ever cite with approval, as I do here, the Buddha's thesis from the *Visuddhi Magga* that '*there is no difference between stupidity and wisdom*'? (Bancroft 2000: 110).[1]

---

1 A note about style: Throughout this book, all italics are my own stylistic addition, unless noted otherwise.

If it is fair to characterise this book as both philosophical and not philosophical, one could also say the same kind of thing about its relationship to theology. The book is theological, at least in the conventional sense of the word, because it occupies a Zen Buddhist point of view, and Buddhism is usually taken to be one of the world's great religions. But then again it is not theology, because it has nothing to do with God, faith or revealed truth, and because it does not have what Heidegger calls a 'religious intention' (1985: 24). Quite the contrary: revealed truth, whether religious or philosophical, is one of the ideas that it tries to expose as a pernicious illusion. What theologian would cite with approval, as I do here, Deshan's radical devaluation of the allegedly inspired language contained in religious texts: *'The whole canon is old paper for wiping filth'*? (Cleary 1998: 192).

If some kind of classification were required, I would prefer to jettison all ordinary labels and classify this book as a kind of journey. Writing it has certainly taken me on a long journey. But as far as its readers are concerned, of *what*, exactly, is it a journey, and *where* does the journey lead? These are fair questions, and I will try to give a brief sketch of the answers to them here. Let me begin by referring to a Chinese character, *xin*, that appears quite frequently in ancient Zen texts:

In English translations of Zen works, this character is normally rendered as 'mind'. However, the word *mind* is conventionally associated with the intellectual side of human beings, as opposed to their affective side, whereas the Chinese term at once denotes the intellect and connotes feelings and emotions, or rather, refers to the heart as the common site of both the intellect and the emotions. Indeed, *xin* is in fact a pictographic representation of the human heart: at the top an open pericardium, in the middle the organ, and at the bottom a summary delineation of the aorta. Hence, some translators have taken to putting the word 'heart' in place of 'mind' (Schloegl 1976: 11). I think this is a mistake. The traditional

Western distinction between mind and heart, reason and emotion, is unsupported by the phenomenal facts of the case, for our immediate feelings always come pre-clothed in the garb of some kind of rational interpretation from the very first moment that we notice them *as* 'feelings'. More importantly, language does not rightly support any dualism between reason and emotion in *Zen* thought. In response to the first question, therefore, I will simply say that this book aspires to be a journey of the mind-and-the-heart *together*.

As for the question of where the book leads, I would ask you to notice that the idea of 'leading' (from here to there, from A to B) is the very thing that I want to make into a problem in these pages. Logical transcendence, $A \Rightarrow B$, is a leading that we *let* happen because of our craving attachment to solutions for the problems that bother us. To let go of attachment to logical transcendence is therefore to let go of attachment to the fetish of 'leading' and being led. One might say that the journey we will be taking in this book leads *backwards*: to the beginning of 'leading', and thus to a kind of beginning that has nothing to do with the ideas of cause, origin, or ground. It is a beginning that we are always already at, whether we know it or not. Dissolving all distinctions between discourse that is trivial and discourse that is profound, this beginning is amazingly simple, ordinary, and easy to see. It is as ordinary as a sneeze, a bottle of passable wine, or a passing cloud. And precisely because it is nothing special, it turns out that this beginning is unbelievably difficult to grasp.

Contents

List of Illustrations

Chapter 1: A Zen Beginning

'Beyond Transcendence'

The idea of transcendence, in one form or another, lies at the very heart of philosophy. In its most basic sense, transcendence is the metaphor of a passage applied to the human condition. Formally speaking, this metaphor depicts a movement of someone who transcends (however this one may be characterised) to something or someone else called the 'transcendent'. Concretely, the possibility of transcendence in Western philosophy is usually expressed as a theme or problem in the fields of epistemology, ontology, and theology. It is also embedded, albeit obscurely, in the idea of logical necessity and in the principle of sufficient reason, and even more obscurely (and primitively) in the ubiquitous practice of giving explanations or accounts of philosophical problems. This is because the one who explains or accounts also makes a transcending passage: from the idea (A) of an antecedent cause, ground, or origin to (⇒) the idea (B) of a caused, grounded, or originated. Law, too, proceeds on the basis of transcendence, first moving from a state of uncertainty about the case before it to knowledge of the facts and the relevant legal rules, and then from this self-certain knowledge to an outcome in which public force is either applied or withheld. As these examples suggest, even thinking itself can be characterised as transcendence, at least to the extent that thinking is defined as one idea somehow 'leading' to another in the mind of the thinker.

It might appear, therefore, that the title 'Beyond Transcendence' suggests this book is about how to transcend transcendence, and perhaps philosophy itself, towards some sort of super-transcendence or super-philosophy. It is not. Trying to write such a book would be like trying to write an impossible treatise on how to get wetter than water, for as Levinas says, 'no one can speak of a "beyond the ultimate" or "pre-original" without their becoming, by that very beyond or beneath, ultimate or original' (2003a: 51). The Japanese Zen master Hakuin (1689–1769) once remarked, in the middle of writing an 18,000-word text, that even a superior person will make at least one mistake if he uses 1,000 words; but he also went on to say, rather hopefully I think, that an inferior person given the same amount of words will manage to say at least one good thing (Waddell 1999: 45). Therefore, if I may be permitted to distil a great fog of language to a tiny droplet of truth, the idea of 'Beyond Transcendence' in the title means that instead of reaching an end in these pages – some kind of meta-transcendent theory or point of view on being, ethics and language – we will discover that there is no beginning. Or, if you will, we will discover that we are always at the beginning in contemplating and acting in these spheres, and not a single step we might take could ever lead us away from this beginning. In conventional speech the idea of a beginning is linked to progress towards some sort of end, whether realised or not. However, the beginning that is indicated by the words 'Beyond Transcendence' is not ends-oriented in this sense. Instead, the beginning to which I refer is one that we are always already *at*, in the sense of being on the verge of, but never *in*: a sort of beginningless beginning, if you will.

It follows that we will not be abiding by Augustine's mystic injunction to 'descend, so that you may ascend' (Alighieri 1994: xiv). Although descending to the mundane surface of things in order to prepare a foundation for thought's subsequent flight to the sublime sounds liberating, this procedure is really a trap: Augustine's *dictum* wrongly implies that there is a fundamental difference between the beginning and the end of thought. The solution to a genuine philosophical problem always reproduces the problem in a new form the very moment it is articulated; indeed, the solution itself now becomes the problem. The metamorphosis of solutions into problems is what distinguishes philosophy from production, and thinking from consumption. Philosophical thinking is always on the verge of something that it pursues with the enthusiasm of a hungry greyhound chasing a mechanical rabbit around a track. However, unlike the perennially frustrated racing dog, we will not try to catch the impossible rabbit of transcendence in this book. Instead, we will punch through the crust of academic tradition in an effort to catch sight of a singularly benign possibility: *letting go* of the problem of transcendence and the craving desire that leads us to wallow in it.

I do not offer this possibility to the world as a sort of new Absolute Knowledge at the end of history. On the contrary, I do not claim that it is any kind of *knowledge* at all. Nor does the possibility of which I speak spell the end of philosophy for those who seize it. Certain human beings are inclined to philosophise – that much is clear – and I have no desire to ridicule or negate this inclination, especially since I have it myself. If one were able to let go of all craving attachment to the problem (or device) of transcendence, philosophy would look exactly the same as it did before, when transcendence seemed to loom so mightily as a theme or core assumption. But while philosophy itself would not have changed one little bit, the philosopher who managed to let go would have changed considerably. And that, to paraphrase Robert Frost, would make all the difference.

What these admittedly obscure introductory statements mean will take the rest of the book to bring into view. One thing, however, is clear enough at this stage: since this book leads *from* the beginning back *to* the beginning, its point of view on the nature of philosophy is decidedly non-utilitarian. There is no such thing as progress or authority in philosophy, for a thinker must always begin at the beginning no matter how many times other thinkers, however great, have already travelled the same path. This is true not merely because it is a grievous mistake in philosophy to follow the paths of others' tongues. Far more significant is the fact that any thinking worthy of the name is always about the journey, and never about the destination. Mere scholarship transcends its theme like a jail surrounds a prisoner, enclosing it in a cage of 'correct' statements. The scholarly clarification of existing concepts and the construction of new conceptual systems constitute a kind of quasi-mathematical calculation with symbols and, however useful this procedure may be to the pre-existing projects of law and politics, it is not thinking. In fact it verges on what Marcuse, no friend of analysis, calls the 'liquidation of philosophy by analytic philosophy' (2001: 55). Indeed, no less an authority for analytic philosophers than Wittgenstein has declared that the nimbus of philosophy has been lost, and that the only judgment we can make about philosophers these days is whether or not they are skilful (2003: 342).

Although this book does not take issue with Marcuse's and Wittgenstein's diagnoses of the current state of analytic philosophy, it does maintain that there is a more enlightening kind of philosophising available to us. True thinking always thinks *with* and *inside* the matter thought, aspiring only to understand it and not to place it behind the bars of a description or theory. Understanding of this sort is like the centre of a circle around whose circumference 'yes' and 'no', 'true' and 'false', chase each other endlessly. The view from this centre allows one to recognise that words are but traps for images, images are but nets for ideas, and ideas are but cages for dead thoughts. Like soft-hearted hunters who catch game by means of traps, nets, and cages, and who subsequently let go of these devices in order to retrieve and release the living game within, we must try to perform the daunting task of using words to unlock and penetrate what words, ideas, and thoughts have trapped and nearly annihilated.

Alain Badiou has written that if poetry is seduction without concept, and authority is legitimation without idea, then philosophy interrupts both poetry and authority by removing the veil of mystery that surrounds them (Badiou 2003: 93–94). This is laudable: those who sing to us and those who rule us should not be allowed to deceive us. In this book, however, the objects to be desacralised are not poetry and authority, but the concepts and procedures of philosophy itself. Thus, while the problems of law and justice will figure in our journey, this work is no more 'about' law and justice, at least in the conventional sense, than it is about the so-called 'philosophies' of those whose names appear in three of its chapter headings: Martin Heidegger, Emmanuel Levinas, and Ludwig Wittgenstein. For just as a journey is not a destination, so too a *conversation* with great thinkers is not the same as giving an academic interpretation of their theories.

A Sketch of the Journey

The conversations that we will have with Heidegger, Levinas, and Wittgenstein quite naturally proceed from a sustained engagement with their work. The particular texts we will consider include primarily (but not exclusively) Heidegger's pronouncements on the unity of ground and the principle of reason, Levinas's statements about the relationship between ethics and justice, and Wittgenstein's remarks, in *A Lecture on Ethics* and elsewhere, about the impossibility of expressing the absolute in language. It turns out that these three thinkers share with all of Western thought an addiction to the most important idea of transcendence: what we will call *logical transcendence*. Roughly speaking, logical transcendence is the belief that one fact, idea, or term 'leads to' another fact, idea, or term – a belief that at once valorises truth and determines it as a kind of passage. Since a clarification of the idea of transcendence *as such* will prepare us better to understand the West's addiction to this belief, we will consider the various forms and pathologies of the norm of logical transcendence, $A \Rightarrow B$, later in this chapter. Afterwards we will turn our attention to the concrete and subtle manifestations of attachment to this norm that are displayed in the work of Heidegger (Chapter 2), Levinas (Chapter 3), and Wittgenstein (Chapter 4).

An initial indication of Zen

Apart from what lies on our Western bookshelf, the meditations and conversations in this book have been co-equally influenced by certain Eastern texts, most of them rather ancient, written in the Zen (*Ch'an*, in Chinese) Buddhist tradition of philosophising. I hasten to say that this is not meant to be a work 'about' Zen, although I will try to give certain basic information about it as we go along. Instead, this book aspires mainly to be a work *of* Zen, albeit a rather intellectual kind of Zen.

Without meaning to delve too deeply into the history of Zen, I should indicate that I have received inspiration for the ways of philosophising that are manifested in this book from methods employed by the Rinzai sect, including primarily the use of koans.[1] Rinzai was founded in the 12th century, and is today one of the two primary schools of Zen in Japan (the other being Sōtō).[2] Since Zen is easy to see but difficult to know about, as the Chinese Zen master Chao-chou[3] (778–897) famously put it (Green 1998: 38), the notion of a book attempting to enact 'intellectual Zen' would seem to be a contradiction in terms. Indeed, it would be both futile and wrongheaded of me to deny the ultimate truth of Wu-tzu's observation that talking about Zen is like looking for fish tracks in a dry riverbed (Schiller 1994: 370). Nevertheless, the world has heard of such a thing as *Zen philosophy*, and we shall see in the next chapter that even as thoughtful a thinker as Heidegger once expressed interest in a koan. There is no single right way to do Zen, and Zen practice does not categorically exclude any particular method in principle. Indeed, for people who are tempted to read books like this, intellectual Zen may be a particularly expedient means – a 'turning word', as Zen masters sometimes put it (Schloegl 1976: 95), that can allow the reception of philosophical language to go in new and surprising directions.

The term *expedient means* (*upāya-kauśalya*, in Sanskrit) can be broadly defined as what answers as appropriate for achieving penetrating insight in the particular situation that confronts us. The use of expedient means should not be confused with Western pragmatism, for a Zen master is not beholden to any *doctrine* that rejects dogmatism in favour of 'what works': if being dogmatic, doctrinaire and inflexible happens to be an expedient means for the situation, well then, that is what a Zen master will be. Expedient means are the product of a radicalised kind of compassionate concern for the suffering of others. For example, one of the best-known Zen koans is the word *Wu* (*Mu*, in Japanese), meaning 'no', which Chao-chou uttered in response to the question whether a dog has Buddha nature (roughly speaking, enlightenment). But Chao-chou did not *always* say 'no' when he was asked this question – there were

---

1 The Japanese word *koan* comes from the Chinese *gung-an*, the literal meaning of which is 'public case'. A koan is a short text, sometimes in the form of a riddle, which certain Zen masters employ to advance and test a student's level of attainment.

2 Damien Keown describes the difference between Rinzai and Sōtō as follows: 'whereas Sōtō emphasizes the practice of "just sitting" in the conviction that human beings are already possessed of an enlightened nature that needs only to be realized, Rinzai actively pursues the goal of enlightenment through the use of tools such as kōans and strenuous practice' (Keown 2003: 238).

3 *Joshu*, in Japanese.

times when he said 'yes' (Pine 2001: 380). The difference in circumstances determined which means was more expedient. Chao-chou said that a dog does have Buddha nature to confound, challenge, and enlighten people who believed that humans are 'special', and always take priority over animals; but then again, he would deny that a dog has Buddha nature to confound, challenge, and enlighten those who were attached to believing in some mystical and ineffable union of all beings. 'Standing beyond all alternatives', as the Zen philosopher Keiji Nishitani says, Chao-chou 'embodies absolute freedom and can give to the dog or rob it of its essential "Being" (namely the Buddha-nature inherent in it) as he likes' (Parkes 1987: 151). Speaking colloquially, one could say that an *expedient means* is the compassionate use of different strokes for differently deluded folks.

As a form of Buddhism, Zen is connected, however loosely, to certain observations about and prescriptions for the human condition known as the 'four noble truths' (Van de Weyer 2000: 1/7). These are roughly as follows: (1) life is suffering; (2) the cause of suffering is craving desire and the illusions it spawns; (3) the cessation of suffering comes from letting go of our craving desires; and (4) there is a path[4] that one can take to the cessation of craving desire, and hence of suffering. Since Buddhism has nothing to do with God or an afterlife, it would be misleading to call it a religion in the Western, or theistic, sense of the word. In Buddhism, the great repose called *nirvana* signifies living as an awakened one in *this* world, not transcending to some 'other world' that we fancifully conceive to be a sort of ever-blissful *doppelganger* of our own. Be that as it may, to imagine the previous outline of the four noble truths as a dogma, creed, or programme is completely to misunderstand *Zen* thought. For one thing, Zen, unlike so-called Hīnayāna ('lesser vehicle') forms of Buddhism,[5] does not make the attainment of personal enlightenment the ultimate end of all practice. The figure of the *bodhisattva*[6] who returns to aid others, prominent in Zen and other forms of Mahāyāna ('greater vehicle') Buddhism, indicates that compassion towards the suffering of

4 Sometimes called the 'eightfold path' of right vision, right purpose, right speech, right action, right livelihood, right effort, right awareness and right concentration.

5 These forms are prevalent in Southeast Asia, where practitioners classify their various styles of Buddhism under the name Theravāda, from the Sanskrit word *Thera* ('elders'). The term 'Hīnayāna', meaning *lesser vehicle*, is used primarily by Mahāyāna ('greater vehicle') sects as an appellation for their competitors. As the metaphor of relative size indicates, the latter term carries a somewhat derisive connotation.

6 A compound of the Sanskrit words *bodhi*, meaning enlightened, and *sattva*, meaning being. A *bodhisattva* is someone who resolves to attain enlightenment in order to liberate others.

others is inextricably linked to enlightenment. And lest anyone is beginning to get worried on account of my failure to define the word 'enlightenment', or about the arrogance that seems to lurk behind its use, permit me this brief disclaimer: if I *knew* what 'enlightenment' meant I would tell you right now; but I don't *know* what it means, and if I did, this book would not be worth a tinker's damn.

Now I confess that I was tempted to withdraw the word 'compassion' from this book for the same reason that Toni Morrison deleted the word 'love' from her most recent book: because overuse has cheapened it, and because in a text like this it has less to do with squishy feelings than with hard work and thinking it through (Morrison and West 2004: 20). But I decided that a work of Zen without compassion is like a book without pages: impossible to write. Zen compassion is not infinite, but rather completely unconditional, a point to which we will return with a vengeance, so to speak, in Chapter 3. This and other Zen ideas and texts important for our journey will be brought forward as needed. But, for now, let me say that the notions of suffering (*dunkha*), craving desire (*trsnā*), letting go, and compassion (*karunā*) will figure very prominently in our journey, including even the apparently impossible prospect of letting go of these very notions themselves. One has to enter thinking somewhere, and whether we begin with Plato's sense of wonder (the Western spur to philosophising) or the Buddha's attention to suffering (an Eastern spur), it will ultimately make no difference to where we wind up – namely, at the beginning.

An initial indication of being, ethics and language

Heidegger, Levinas and Wittgenstein: why did I choose these three thinkers in particular as our interlocutors, and as this book's principal points of contact between Zen and Western philosophy? While their importance for modern Western thought is undeniable, they were chosen not for their fame, but rather for what they had to say about the themes that preoccupied them. At the risk of greatly oversimplifying their rich and variegated bodies of work, *primarily* Heidegger is the quintessential philosopher of *being*, Levinas is the quintessential philosopher of *ethics*, and Wittgenstein is the quintessential philosopher of *language*. What is more, Heidegger's lifelong passion for the utter simplicity of the question of being, the irremissibility of Levinas's concern and compassion for the suffering of others, and Wittgenstein's radically deflationary view of language and philosophy resonate with three of the most important themes in Zen thought: thusness, suffering, and enlightenment. Being (and thusness), ethics (and suffering), and language (and enlightenment): what else of importance is there to think and talk about in philosophy?

All three thinkers claim, albeit each in his own way, that there is a domain or sphere that lies beyond the everyday experience and interpretation of being, ethics and language, and beyond the ham-fisted pretensions of academic philosophers, not to mention legal academics and scientists. In this particular context, I am using the word *beyond* in the strong sense of something that transcends the ordinary. In his concept of the 'ontological difference', Heidegger says that being (as opposed to beings) escapes the net of representation and objectification, even if he does also maintain that language is the 'house of being' (1998: 239); Levinas says that the ethical relation between self and other is 'beyond being' – infinite (in the sense of unlimited), and therefore ineffable; and Wittgenstein says that the most important things in life, including being-as-a-whole and ethics, transcend our capacity to express them, and that the job of philosophy is merely to clarify the mundane things that can be said, while keeping silent about all the rest. Heirs of Plato, despite their rejection of traditional metaphysics, Heidegger, Levinas, and Wittgenstein all claim or aspire to a vision that transcends the comprehension of the vulgar and unenlightened.

All three thinkers also object to the dimming down of the light of life and experience by the managerial techniques of modern technology, broadly understood as the extension and intensification of human control and exploitation of natural and social processes. In our fast-paced, result-oriented, and hyper-technological world, the twin idols of efficient production and utility stand on the highest altar of values. Reason has been reduced to a mere technique for achieving individual and social wants and needs, while affective life is carefully co-ordinated, controlled and exploited by the culture industry, all according to what Marcuse calls the 'frightful science of human relations' (1964: 70). As for the law, it offers the window-dressing of 'justice' while managing and producing case results and social order in the way that a factory produces widgets. The idea of the 'beyond' in the thought of Heidegger, Levinas, and Wittgenstein represents a desperate effort to resist the flattening out of thought and experience that progress in the natural and social sciences, as well as in law and politics, seems to have brought with it as an unintended (or is it sometimes intended?) consequence. The word *progress*, as used here, does not mean a movement from worse to better, but rather what someone such as Foucault (2003) might call an ever-increasing and autochthonous tendency towards the perfection of strategies and techniques for management, control and resistance. Irrespective of what has just been said, this book is not a critique of contemporary culture and politics, nor is it interested in analysing philology or intellectual history. The monumental philosophical efforts of Heidegger, Levinas, and Wittgenstein are journeys of the human spirit that lead to a perspective. Despite the many differences among them in terms of style, substance and temperament, there is a level at which their various paths of thinking lead to *a* perspective, not three different perspectives: the perspective of transcendence *as such*. The idea of transcendence as such underwrites the belief that, in spite of all the misery of the world, it is still possible to be enlightened, or even happy, by living a life of knowledge, or at least a life of intellectual insight. This perspective is what is important, for it allows us to contrast an alternative perspective, informed by Zen, that is (or allows for) the emancipation of human thought and practice from the chains of prejudice, doctrinal orthodoxy, self-importance and illusion. In Western thought, at least since Plato, knowledge stands opposed to instinct, and reason to emotion, in a dualism that leaves knowledge and reason in control. In Zen, however, *original mind* stands beyond the pairs knowledge/instinct and reason/emotion. As the Zen saying goes, the perspective that I want to bring into view here allows us 'to be master *of* mind rather than mastered *by* mind' (Schiller 1994: 337). This perspective does not reject language, knowledge and truth so much as it puts them in their proper place – namely, far, far below us.

The Deflationary View of Language

Hui-neng tears a Sutra scroll

All fanaticism and violence, all indifference to the suffering of others and all impediments to personal enlightenment can be traced ultimately to the worship of texts: to being in thrall to texts, to being the slave of texts, to meekly doing what texts 'tell' us to do, to following the written and unwritten expectations of institutions and creeds the way sheep follow a Judas goat. The obsequious deference displayed by many (or most) academic philosophers to 'great personalities', living and dead, is another example, as is the seemingly endless academic practice of parsing famous texts and arguing about whether someone's interpretations of them are well founded. Trapped in a grim kind of neo-scholasticism, academic thought loses itself in the inessential and binds itself without a rope. If, as Nietzsche claims, the will to truth is the will to illusions, then the truth of texts must be deflated by anyone seeking to shed his illusions. One might justly call this insight the *deflationary view of language*. The close connection between language and illusions explains why Zen artwork tends to be deflationary in this sense, as in Liang-K'ai's 13th century drawing *The Sixth Patriarch (Hui-neng) Tearing up the Sutra* (Figure 1.1), which depicts a great Zen master desecrating a holy text.

Figure 1.1

The Sixth Patriarch (Hui-neng) Tearing up the Sutra
Liang-K'ai (early 13th century), hanging scroll, ink on paper, 73 x 31.7 cm
Collection of Mitsui Takanaru, Tokyo

It also explains why Zen commentary, unlike Western biblical hermeneutics, frequently expresses a level of disdain towards Buddhism's founding documents that sounds shocking to Western ears. To pick one of many possible examples, consider the answer of Bodhidharma (d 535), the Indian founder of Zen in China, to Emperor Wu's question 'What is the highest meaning of the holy truths?' 'Empty, without holiness', he is said to have replied (Cleary 1992: 1).

The recent political and religious controversy over the Brooklyn Art Museum's decision to exhibit British artist Chris Ofili's elephant-dung-spattered collage *The Holy Virgin Mary,*[7] not to mention the earlier brouhahas surrounding the display of Andre Serrano's *Piss Christ*, a photograph of a crucifix submerged in urine,[8] are symptoms of a strident Western attitude towards iconography that is the exact opposite of Zen's. When describing important Buddhist texts, Zen commentary is more likely than not to say things such as '*The whole canon is old paper for wiping filth*' (Cleary 1998: 192), or to call the Buddha a '*dried shit stick*' (Schiller 1994: 30), or to compare those who claim enlightenment to '*insects in manure*' (Cleary 1988: 247). Rather than being symptoms of minds that are fixated on the scatological, these sayings are meant to be *turning words* that intentionally play on the shock effect that can come from hearing scatological terms applied to what the reader may regard as sacred. The point is not that the West tends to think that books and icons are 'important', and Zen does not. The point is that, in field after field, including law, religion and philosophy, the West reveres and bows down to texts and icons, while Zen reckons them to be occasionally useful, but always dangerous, means that can all too easily become fetishes and impediments.

Chao-chou wrote that a golden Buddha cannot pass through a furnace, a wooden Buddha cannot pass through fire, and a mud Buddha cannot pass through water, thus reminding those who are inclined to revere symbols that at bottom even the most sacred of objects is just an impermanent hunk of mundane material (Cleary 1992: 525). Consider the Taliban's destruction in 2001 of the Great Buddhas of Bamiyan, carved from a cliff in Afghanistan some 1,500 years ago. While it is undeniable that this act of barbarism was an archaeological and cultural tragedy, it is important to understand that, from a Zen standpoint, it was neither a

---

7 The exhibit took place in 1999. The then mayor of New York City, Rudolph Giuliani, was quoted as saying that Ofili's collage was 'sick'. Reacting in part to popular outrage over the piece, Giuliani announced that public funding for the Brooklyn Art Museum would be cut off – a decision that was later reversed when a federal court ordered the city to restore funding. For one account of this affair, see http://www.renewal.org.au/artcrime/pages/c_ofili.html.

8 A Google search of the terms 'controversy over Piss Christ' yielded nearly 5,000 hits. For an account of the particularly heated controversy in Australia, see http://www.renewal.org.au/artcrime/pages/serrano.html.

religious tragedy nor a desecration. Taking these images of the Buddha seriously and reverently as symbols of the possibility of salvation or enlightenment: *that* would be the real desecration. This short explanation of Zen's relentless desacralisation of everything 'holy' will probably not satisfy those Western readers who cherish the symbols of their own religions. However, it does explain why the Japanese monk Ikkyā (1394–1481) wrote that *'a stone Buddha deserves all the bird shit it gets'*, and why his remark was judged sufficiently important to be included and preserved in the canon for over 500 years (Schiller 1994: 117). In a nutshell, the practice of deflating the sacred to the profane – and deflating the pretentious to the ordinary – lies near and dear to the heart of Zen. The question is, why?

Dethroning the god of texts

In the West, it is not enough to bow down to a specific and widely accepted expression of law and morality – one also feels the need to pledge allegiance to the general principle that self-subordination to *some* text, any text, is better than the radical alternative of freeing oneself completely from the dominion of texts. We call this pledge of allegiance 'being principled', and we praise those who take it when we say things such as 'I hate what she did, but at least she was acting on principle'. Thus, it comes to pass that humans have put a sort of god above their particular texts – a god of **texts** that is itself a **TEXT**: 'The Rule of Law', 'Ethics', 'The Word of God', and so forth. It is as if ostentatiously maintaining our attachment to being principled were more important than showing compassion, or even doing the right thing. This god of texts is not dead, as Nietzsche might have put it (1968: 45), but very much alive: it takes the form of certain images – sometimes pretty, sometimes awe-inspiring – to which we have become cravenly attached. Living in a dream (or nightmare) world in which books have little mouths to speak with, little feet to get from here to there, and little hands to push our bodies this way and that, we hardly ever notice that, strictly speaking, the 'The Rule of Law' has never decided a single case, no 'Ethics' has ever behaved ethically, and 'The Word of God' has never once lifted even as much as a finger. Those who follow the way of Zen, on the other hand, *do* notice these plain truths – *all the time.*

Consider the 97th case of the *Blue Cliff Record,*[9] for example, which has to do with the Buddha's Diamond Cutter Scripture – a document that

9 The case is as follows: *'The Diamond Cutter scripture says, "If one is scornfully reviled by others, this person has done wicked acts in previous ages which should bring him down into evil ways, but because of scorn and vilification by others in the present age, the wicked action of former ages is thereby extinguished"'* (Cleary 1992: 532). The implicit question is: what on earth does this mean?

we in the West might call a holy text. The commentary, written by Yuan-wu (1063–1135), refers to the 'ordinary ways' of interpreting the text, and especially to certain scholastic schools of Buddhism then prevalent in China. The practitioners of these schools recited the scripture out loud, over and over, and called this practice 'upholding the scripture'. With consummate skill, Yuan-wu undermines this kind of formalism by defeating the superstition that a text has or could have even as much as an ounce of spiritual power in itself. He does this by asking his readers to perform what people today would call a thought experiment: If you think a holy book is powerful, Yuan-wu writes, *'take a volume and lay it in an uncluttered place; see if there is any effect or not'*. (There will be no effect.) Later, he quotes another Zen master's words to similar effect: *'Pile up several cases of scriptures in an empty room, and see if they emit light'* (Cleary 1992: 535). (There will be no light.) Yuan-wu invites us to experience the radical implications of a very basic phenomenon: no matter how long you stare at a book lying on a table, or even at a whole library full of books, you will never see it *doing* anything on its own.

Pieces of paper and the images they evoke simply do not decide cases or feed the hungry. Although we often pretend that they do, I ask you take a look at the world and say honestly what you see there: all the while, is it not *our* mouths that speak, *our* bodies that move, *our* hands that sign legal papers and deliver groceries? If we want to let go of our self-defeating attachments to the illusory, we must *completely desacralise* the god of texts. *Desacralise,* not destroy: to deflate language is not to cast it aside, but rather to adopt an attitude towards it that somehow manages to steer between the Scylla of servility to texts and the Charybdis of contempt for them. Since the attitude of which I speak is by definition pre-linguistic, it can only be hinted at in words, as in the famous koan of the bamboo staff:

> Master Shou-shan held his bamboo staff up before his assembly, saying, 'Oh monks! If you call this a staff, you're clinging to the fact. If you don't call it a staff, you're ignoring the fact. What do you call it?' (Foster and Shoemaker 1996: 192)

If one of Shou-shan's monks had tried to answer this question in words, Shou-shan probably would have punched or kicked him on account of his ineptness. But since no one will do that to me here, let me give (with some trepidation) one possible 'answer' to the koan: *'When I want someone to bring my staff to me, I call it my "staff", and otherwise I don't – what's the big deal?'* This answer suggests that we must learn to put words like 'bamboo staff' in their proper place: we must kick them out of our minds and hang them on the wall of our tool shed. We must say to texts, as it were, 'You're not my boss!' No one in his or her right mind would choose to bow and scrape to a hammer. Why then do we ooh and aah over words like 'freedom', 'democracy' and 'Thou shalt not kill'? However much (or little) these words are used, *it is the manner of their use that matters,* and not the words themselves.

To imagine otherwise is to fall prey to one of the most pernicious illusions in philosophy: the belief that words *as such* can and do stand for or evoke something on their own. In Chapter 4 we will come back to this belief when we discuss Wittgenstein's critique of the *Bedeutungskörper* ('meaning-body') theory of language. For the time being, however, I would merely like to identify the root cause of the illusion that language 'means': raw fear. I am referring to the fear that if words do not *mean* something on their own, then nothing would stand between us and the abyss of meaninglessness. But ask yourself: how *could* belief in a formula such as *'Language always means; therefore "X" means Y'* save us from nothingness if we did not already understand how to use the symbol '*Y*'? And if we do already understand how to use '*Y*', does this not suggest that we are saved from the abyss not by language alone – not by the symbols '*"X" means Y*' – but rather *by ourselves*? The Zen path through language carefully *negotiates* the scary distinction (and choice) between meaningfulness and nothingness. As in the case of the bamboo staff, Zen steers between these two extremes, arguing that it is '*better you should give rise to a view of existence as big as Mount Sumeru,*[10] *than you produce a view of nothingness as small as a mustard seed*' (Cleary 1992: 474). Zen's deflationary attitude towards language does not create a 'void' that can only be filled, so to speak, by inflating the idea of nothingness. In brief, Zen is just about as far from wild-eyed nihilism as it is from naive realism, and just about as far from idealism as it is from both. As the Buddha would say, it is a *middle way*.

Having said that, please indulge my stridency as I declare, with the most compassionate of motives, that there can be no more falling down and genuflecting to the *logos*, no more feeling that this or that bit of text is our master or our saviour, or, for that matter, our mortal enemy. By way of illustration, consider the allegedly interesting philosophical question of whether there exists an 'external world' that is independent of our minds. If Zen does not assert a truth-claim that the world actually exists, neither does it assert the contrary truth-claim that the world does not exist. Zen is neither world denying nor world affirming. People who make the latter sorts of claims are *attached* (usually passionately) to the words and ideas that express their philosophical positions – hence the age-old 'battle' between realism and scepticism – whereas in Zen there is an almost

10 Mount Sumeru is the highest mountain and the centre of the world in Buddhist mythology.

bemused absence of attachment to either pole of the dualism 'real/not real'.

As an example of this last point, consider the interview between Yunju and Lord Liu that is described in the following koan from the *Book of Serenity*:

> Lord Liu Yuduan asked Yunju, 'Where does the rain come from?' Yunju said, 'It comes from your question'. The lord was delighted and thanked him. Yunju asked back, 'Where does the question come from?' The lord said nothing (Cleary 1988: 314).

Yunju's first answer draws attention to what Heidegger would have called the 'as'-structure of rain: it says, essentially, that rain comes from questions that ask (according to the questioner's fore-conceptions) where something that is merely *called* 'rain' comes from. So far so good: Lord Liu thinks he has learned something profound – hence his delight in the master's answer. What happens next, however, does not delight him. Although Yunju could have continued 'educating' Lord Liu by asking him why he had asked a question about rain in the first place, Yunju did not do so. Instead of attempting to conduct a sort of medieval Chinese seminar on the hermeneutic circle, Yunju violently reversed Lord Liu's question by asking where the question *itself* came from. To question questioning in this way is to annihilate the possibility of an answer. What *could* Lord Liu say in response to a question that devours both itself and all possible answers to it, leaving only Master Yunju's smile in the air, like that of the Cheshire Cat in *Alice in Wonderland?* People fall in love with the sound of their own voices, and do not look at things just as they are: *completely ordinary from top to bottom*. Rain is just rain. A question is just a question. The hermeneutic circle is just the hermeneutic circle. Seen from Yunju's point of view, rain, questions and the hermeneutic circle all stand on exactly the same level.

I said earlier that we must *completely* desacralise language, and the time has come to consider how complete this 'completely' is. It is important to recognise that Zen's kind of desacralisation is not the same as disillusionment in the sense that Marx uses the term. If putting texts in their proper place is an aspect of enlightenment, this should not be confused with the sort of Marxian critique of ideology that wants man to regain his reason so that he may at long last 'revolve about himself as his own true sun' (Marx 1964: v). The sunlight of reason is a pretty but dangerous metaphor, for the sun shines on horrors, too, and emancipation and beauty can also be found in dark places. As Georges Sorel so acutely observed in commenting on the French Revolution: '*During the Terror the men who spilt the most blood were precisely those who had the strongest desire to let their equals enjoy the golden age of which they dreamt and who had the greatest sympathy for human misery*' (Sorel 1999:10).

Unfortunately, bitter experiences such as the Terror have taught us again and again that those who obsess about 'reason' and 'abstract humanity' are always among the first to act inhumanely in concrete situations. This helps explain why Sheng-yi (b 1922) says that to fall in love with a teaching is the worst folly that anyone who compassionately seeks to liberate others (a *bodhisattva*) can commit (Pine 2001: 288).

The all-too-common paradox of a hyper-rational humanism that winds up being anti-humanist in its actions brings to mind Levinas's thesis that there is an almost inverse relationship between attachment to linguistic norms and compassion for suffering: the more there is of the former, the less there is of the latter. We will return to this theme in Chapter 3, where we will explore it in much greater detail. For now, though, I would like to borrow a metaphor from Wittgenstein to bring home the full measure of Zen's idea that language must be *completely* desacralised: the metaphor of a ladder that must be thrown away after one has climbed up it (Wittgenstein 1974: 74). If, with Marx, we define alienation as the historical process whereby humans allow themselves to become the objects of their objects, then the *complete* desacralisation of language requires even letting-go of attachment to the concept of alienation itself. We must throw 'alienation' away, as it were, after having climbed up it. Speaking more broadly, this suggests that we must strip away anything calling itself Marx*ism* along with all the other bloodsucking isms that have attached themselves to our minds like leaches. We can make progress only if we treat the great teachings we cherish like *'born enemies'*, as Dongshan puts it in the *Book of Serenity* (Cleary 1998: 343). The time has come to put an end to our domestication by official themes, including even (or rather, especially) the official themes that we have unreasonably lifted above ourselves in the form of our 'belief systems' and creeds.

'All humanity has books', writes Levinas (1998: 109), and this is true. However, he unjustifiably projects a Western fetish with the word onto humanity as a whole when he characterises the universal subject as *zum-Buch-Sein* (being-toward-the-book), at least insofar as the subject's relationship to the 'inspired word' is concerned. To receive a book believingly, lovingly even, and to tell oneself that one does not take the book to be a historical or logical report for the intellect, but rather as a ground or source of faith for the soul: this is the sort of thing that Levinas has in mind when he interprets the Talmudic simile *'the words of the sages are like glowing embers'* to mean that sagacious words can become a flame only if one knows how to blow on them (Levinas 2001b: 77). However, even granting the profundity and accuracy of this simile as a description of certain forms of religious faith in the West, it does not even come close to describing the kind of awareness that I want to bring to the surface in *this* book. When asked to describe the teachings of a whole lifetime, for example, the Zen master Yun-men (864–949) said simply *'An appropriate statement'* (Cleary 1992: 94); he thus signified what can only be called a sort of profound indifference to whether his words of wisdom are compared with glowing embers or dead ashes. For a fully articulated 'appropriate statement' is actually more dangerous than an inappropriate one: the wiser it is, the more likely it is that people will surrender to it and transform it into a talisman.

According to the Zen way of thinking, *'the name "sage" and the label "ordinary man" are merely empty sounds'* (Te-shan (780–865)), and *'sage is just a word,* sage' (Lin-chi[11] (d 867)) (Foster and Shoemaker 1967: 106). Thus, a certain action may be the right thing to do at the right time, despite the fact that all the arguments against it are wiser than wise, just as it can be the wrong thing to do even if all the sagacious arguments in its favour are irrefutable. In other words, one can truly penetrate words of justification or condemnation to their would-be theme only if the words themselves are treated as entangling vines:[12] neither affirmed nor negated, neither grasped nor rejected. Inasmuch as Zen first arose in China as a sort of synthesis of Buddhism and Taoism, permit me to borrow a Taoist insight to further the point I am trying to make by employing the Zen metaphor of entangling vines: *'The search for right is not search for truth, but search for those who agree with oneself; it is not a departure from wrong, but a departure from those who disagree with one's feelings and ideas'* (Cleary 1999: 214). From the standpoint of Zen, anyone who remains preoccupied with either grasping or rejecting words of justification makes simple awareness and attainment impossible. One might say that such a person mistakes the postage stamp for the delivery.

Thusness

Justification, the now-time, and thusness

There is, of course, an important sense in which a particular course of action can never be justified in advance, a point that Western philosophers like Jacques Derrida have made a career of noticing, albeit in different terms and with different motives. The simplest proof of this proposition takes the form of an existential truism: an act of justification (a common enough practice, especially in law) does not and cannot

11 *Rinzai,* in Japanese.

12 In Chinese, the term *tangled (or entangling) vines* is used colloquially to mean complications, and in Zen practice it is often used to refer to language itself, including the words of a koan (Cleary 1992: 329).

justify itself. Self-justification, like all forms of self-reference, is like a finger attempting to point at itself: impossible to accomplish. At best it simply *is* its spectral self for a fleeting moment – just another *saying* always fated to haunt the hither side of what is *said* (Derrida 1990: 941-45). The sentence *'I am presently justified in what I do'* immediately flies away with the saying or the writing of it, leaving only the dry husk of what-was-said, in the form of certain transient memory images or inky inscriptions on paper. Take the famous Zen trope of a finger pointing at the moon, an ostensive gesture that is the most primitive form (and symbol) of the event of saying. If, as the saying goes, *'the finger is what points at the moon, but it is not the moon'* (Foster and Shoemaker 1996: 149), then when the finger is withdrawn, so too is the event of pointing. What could be simpler to understand? On the other hand, what could be more difficult to *grasp*?

An ancient Chinese Zen master named Judi gave the ultimate proof, as it were, of the impermanence of the event of pointing (and hence saying) as such. The 84th case of the *Book of Serenity* (a 12th century collection of koans) reads: *'Whenever Master Judi was asked a question, he would just raise one finger'*, without any further explanation (Cleary 1998: 356). According to the text that follows this koan, Judi said on his deathbed that he had used his 'one-finger' Zen all his life without exhausting it. However, because he succumbed in the end to the desire to *characterise* a lifetime full of events of pointing, the commentary asserts that he should have had his finger cut off or broken on his deathbed. To similar effect, the text also tells the famous story of a servant boy of Judi's who was asked by people on the outside, 'What does your master teach?' In response, the clever boy simply held up a finger. The story continues:

> When [the servant boy] returned, he reported this to Judi, and Judi cut off that finger with a knife. The boy ran out screaming: Judi called to him, whereat the boy turned his head; Judi then held up one finger – the boy suddenly attained enlightenment. (Cleary 1998: 356–57)

One might say that Judi's servant learned the hard way the difference between *saying* (the finger that he lifted up to outsiders, *when* he lifted it up) and *said* (the mere memory image of this event of saying that he tried to 'report' to Judi).

All fingers aside, I will gesture verbally and formally at the important distinction between saying and said: the live event of saying or writing *'X'* is one kind of thing, and the trace that this event leaves of itself, in the form of the naked sign *'X'*, is an altogether different kind of thing. Distinguishing between the event-of-saying and what-was-said is not just an academic exercise. It gives us the means to observe two different but interrelated phenomena: *interpretation* and *reception*. Strictly speaking, the phenomenon of interpretation is explicit, and it happens only sometimes.

In interpretation, what-was-said (the textual object *'X'*) first shows itself to us as ambiguous or mysterious. We then proceed to subdue this text by performing a spate of work on it that culminates in an event-of-saying that takes the form *'"X" means Y'*. The phenomenon of reception, on the other hand, is both implicit and never-ending. In reception we unreflectively receive things 'as' what is already clear and familiar to us, either without feeling the need for interpretation, or after all explicit interpreting is said and done. Thus, either reception straightaway receives an un-interpreted *'X' as Y*, or else it receives the expression of its previous interpretation (*'"X" means Y'*) *as Z*, without further ado.

The terms *Y* and *Z* in this last formulation of the phenomenon of reception represent the unrealised possibility that the text in question *could* have been received differently, as not-*Y* or not-*Z*. Thus, the expression '2 + 2 = 4' *can* be received as 2 + 2 = 5 (as merely saying this proves), even if it is also true that this kind of reception, if generalised, would make accurate counting difficult or impossible. We must carefully distinguish between reception as a phenomenon and the consequences of a particular reception, just as we must distinguish between a particular reception and any subsequent attempts to justify it. The point is that even the most natural and obvious of receptions is nonetheless contingent on the event of our letting it be what it is. As we shall investigate more fully in the next chapter, Heidegger called the phenomenon of reception the *'as'*-structure of beings, according to which humans always receive beings in the first instance on the basis of their pre-theoretical fore-conceptions and fore-understandings. Long before Heidegger wrote *Being and Time*, however, Pascal alluded to the importance of the difference between reception and interpretation in the *Pensées*. Commenting on the impossibility of 'explaining' the law, he anticipated the deconstructive turn in Western thought by four hundred years when he wrote that custom *'is the mystical foundation of its [law's] authority; whoever carries it back to first principles destroys it'* (1941: 101).

To put Pascal's insight the way someone like Wittgenstein would have done, no expression of custom – no mere symbol – can possibly ground anything without being itself wordlessly *received* by those who accept it in just the way they do. You can keep on adding symbols that explain and justify other symbols of justification for as long as you want, Wittgenstein said, *'but adopt whatever model or scheme you may, it will have a bottom level, and there will be no such thing as an interpretation of that'* (Wittgenstein 1960: 34). The point is not that linguistic symbols always lead to an infinite regress of interpretations: '"X" means Y', '"Y" means Z', and so on *ad infinitum*. The point is just the opposite: we only interpret *sometimes*, and even when we do, sooner or later all of our interpreting comes to an end in the all-too-familiar phenomenon of reception. One might reformulate Wittgenstein's insight into a metaphor of thinness: what we happen to receive *right now* as 'justification in advance' and 'that which is justified' both stand on a narrow ledge that is thinner than even the thinnest razor. The Zen name for this super-thin ledge is 'thusness' or 'suchness' (*tathatā*, in Sanskrit). Just as thusness no longer contained the event of the servant boy's having lifted his finger to outsiders when he told Judi what he had done, so too thusness does not contain any of our earlier attempts to justify things in advance. The point is simple: none of these events of saying are here any more. Buddhists refer to this kind of simple but disconcerting fact as 'impermanence' (*anitya*, in Sanskrit). Wittgenstein conveyed much the same idea in a more colloquial and forceful way in one of his most insightful aphorisms: 'What the eye doesn't see the heart doesn't grieve over' (1983: 205).

This last statement is not meant to be either mysterious or dogmatic. It is offered as a turning phrase to reorient thought towards a truth that is as plain and obvious as the nose on your face: *when it comes to justification, the past has only the amount of standing that we* let *it have in the now-time.* The compound 'now-time' anglicises Walter Benjamin's term *Jetztzeit*, from the 14th thesis of his *Theses on the Philosophy of History*: 'History is the subject of a structure whose site is not homogeneous, empty time, but time filled by the presence of the now [*Jetztzeit*]' (1968: 261). It seems to me that Benjamin's interpretation of the 'now-time' in terms of history, fullness, and presence conveys a tone of *frenzied plenitude* that blander words such as 'present' and 'moment' do not; at the same time, his use of the word 'site', and his rejection of the phrase 'homogeneous, empty time', connote a kind of *concentration* of the now-time that nicely complements our metaphor of its super-thinness. In any case, this shows why I have chosen to use the term 'now-time' in connection with our meditations on thusness, even though thusness really has nothing to do with time or history as such, as we shall see. One might say that the now-time is the Benjaminian 'site', so to speak, for all images and attachment to images, and within which all liberation and mindfulness is possible. Still, it would be wrong to conclude that thusness is 'contained' in the now-time, as if the latter were like a huge box or meta-milieu that is fundamentally different from thusness. For the time being, let us just say that the now-time and thusness are more or less equivalent terms, or better still, names for different aspects of what is always the same.

Production and reproduction

Having said that much about thusness, I would like to return to the assertion I made, at the beginning of the previous paragraph, that if we do let the past control us, this event of letting always occurs in (or rather as) the now-time. Is it not obvious that nothing that was written or said in the past *physically* compels us to ratify or condemn anything now? Since texts do not twist our arms or hold a gun to our heads, this can only mean that when we justify or condemn something on the basis of what-was-said, we must be *permitting* the dry husk of what was once justified or condemned in advance (the mere symbol of these, I mean) to justify *right now, in the now-time.* I admit that it usually does not strike us that way, but that is how it is. A phenomenology of reception, like the phenomenology of sleep, is primarily the task of noticing what does *not* happen in the conscious mind. The phenomenon of reception explains how it comes to pass that a mere symbol (the 'law') can seem to sentence a man to death, despite the fact that the pages of a law book have never once declared someone guilty, and how a mere symbol (a 'rumour') can seem to ruin a person's life, despite the fact that an unspoken slur has never once besmirched anyone's reputation. In brief, we *permit* these things to happen by continuing to plod along inside familiar and comfortable ruts, like blinkered mules.

Of course, we often feel direct or indirect pressure from other people to let these things happen – a phenomenon that Duncan Kennedy aptly calls the 'double objectivity' of texts (1986: 521) – but no amount of social pressure can elide the fact that in the end it is our *own* mouths that say 'yes' or 'no' to the outcomes that we justify. This fact constitutes a kind of ghost in the machine that can haunt our feelings of necessity, even when everything appears to be perfectly in order. On those occasions, when it seems that we have no choice but to receive or interpret 'X' as Y, every now and then we may catch sight of the fleeting impression that we are like sleeping giants – that everything depends on our innate power of *letting be.* In these situations, the memory of past interpretations can give us the vague but well founded suspicion that texts do not secure their own meanings in advance, and that we must always perform *some* kind of work on them in the now-time if we want to put them into the harness of a deed.

Unfortunately, most of the time this suspicion is suppressed or defeated by the counter-phenomenon of reception, which remains the ever-fruitful source of the illusion that texts always already *mean* what they mean on their own, so to speak, and that they require nothing more from us than passively bearing witness to their meaning. I say 'unfortunately' because the differences between interpretation and reception are trivial when compared with their most important similarity: they are both manifestations of what the West calls *freedom*. I have much more to say about this similarity in the next chapter, where we will encounter Heidegger's interpretation of freedom as freedom-for-ground. For now, however, I will content myself with uttering the following neo-Clausewitzian epigram: reception is interpretation by other means.

Reception is freedom's way of letting things continue to be what everyone else ('they') says they are.

If we think of interpretation as a kind of production, in which we actively transform texts *into* other texts ('X' *into* 'Y'), it becomes possible to imagine reception as a kind of *re*-production, in which we passively let texts *be* other texts ('X' *as* 'Y'). As any competent social theorist will confirm, individual human beings are constantly reproducing their world, including even those things about it that they most despise (Berger and Luckmann 1967). Chipmunks, stones and sunbeams do not prostrate themselves before texts in order to declare war or justify greed: humans do. The intelligible world, the world of order and law, is a sort of vast conspiracy made up of countless individual sayings and doings. Since reproduction is merely another kind of production, it is possible to conclude that each of these phenomena makes us *responsible* for what we produce – responsible not just in the narrow ethical or legal sense, but also in the Zen sense that all deception is ultimately *self*-deception. We delude ourselves, for example, when we imagine that the law stands above humans, rather than the other way around, for we do not recognise the simple truth that the law is nothing at all without people constantly receiving it *as* 'the law'. However, there is a puzzling complication here: from a Zen point of view, we also delude ourselves when we cling to the 'simple truth' that humans always stand above the law, for even the desire to shed all of our illusions is a form of self-deception. As Yung-chia (665–713) put it, *'rejecting illusion and holding on to truth, the discriminating mind becomes falsely clever'* (Foster and Shoemaker 1996: 27). In short, even the mightiest of truths is *merely* true, as far as Zen is concerned – a useful but mundane text that is always less than a hair's breadth away from being false and disastrous.

Let me be clear about something: as the foregoing remarks may suggest, Zen draws no hard distinction between the phenomena of interpretation and reception. For one who follows the path of Zen, reception is a form of *yielding*, interpretation is a form of *overcoming*, and both are merely variations on the ubiquitous phenomenon of *being-ordinary*. Seen from this point of view, justification is an accomplishment that must be *constantly renewed* – either expressly or by acquiescence – if it is to have any consequences at all. Is it not the essence of conventional law and morality that we always bring to life what would be a dead letter without our constant complicity in the now-time? Does not the past in general always play the role of a dead Lazarus, unless and until *we* resurrect it in the form of our decisions and obsessions? How very hard it is to appreciate the following exceedingly simple fact: *what is going on in the now-time is all the occasion we will ever have to do and be anything*. The amazing collapse, in the now-time, of justified into justification, received into reception, and interpreted into interpretation, is what the medieval Zen master Yunju meant when he said that *'if you want to realise such a thing, you must be such a person; once you are such a person, why worry about such a thing?'* (Cleary 2001: IV, 173).

The great Japanese Zen master Dōgen (1200–53) hinted at why people have such difficulty understanding the event of collapse in the now-time: 'People only see time's coming and going, and do not thoroughly understand that the time-being abides in each moment'. It is not that time fails to pass between this time and another time, Dōgen said, *but that it never arrives in the first place* (Tanahashi 1999: 72–73). I have always thought that the following two lines from TS Eliot's poem *The Love Song of J Alfred Prufrock* describe the phenomenal facts of the case perfectly: *'In a minute there is time / For decisions and revisions which a minute will reverse'* (1930: 13). Notice that there is no apparent textual basis for distinguishing between the first 'minute' that Eliot mentions and the second: he calls them both 'a minute'. The radical indifference of Eliot's 'a minute' provides a clue that is absolutely essential for a proper understanding of Dōgen's statement that time does not 'arrive': *the now-time of thusness is never different from itself.* For no matter how many times we ask the questions 'Has the past returned yet?' and 'Is it the future yet?' the correct answer is always 'No. It is still the now-time'.[13]

Thusness and time

Eliot's poetic iteration of 'a minute' will take us only so far, however. It is important to understand that the now-time of thusness is not a 'minute' or a 'moment' – indeed, it is not a primordial temporal duration of any kind. It is not a lived and experienced Husserlian 'edge-point' (*Randpunkt*) of an interval of time characterised by the retention of the immediate past and the protention of the immediate future (Husserl 1991). Nor is the 'edge' of thusness the ground of all subsequent modifications of lived time into world or objective time, as in Husserl's philosophy. Rather, it is the site of a sort of *falling away* into emptiness on both sides of it. In Zen thought, the perception of duration does not presuppose the duration of perception: a paradox that I can best illustrate by means of the well known flag-and-wind koan. Two monks were arguing about a temple flag waving in the wind. One said it was the flag

---

13 I borrowed this formulation from Steven Appleby's cartoon, published in the *New York Times* at the close of the millennium, showing two partygoers. The one asks, 'Is it the future yet?', to which the other replies, 'No. It's still the present'. New York Times, 30 December 1999, at A2, cols 2–3.

that moved; the other disagreed, saying it was the wind that moved. Hui-neng (638–713) intervened with a remark that left both monks speechless: *'Gentlemen! It is not the flag that moves. It is not the wind that moves. It is your mind that moves'* (Schiller 1994: 332). The mind of which Hui-neng speaks – what Zen calls the *original mind* – does not move 'in' time. Nor is the structure of linear time 'in' the mind as a condition of all of the possibility of experience, as Kant would have it. But enough with privation: so far, I have only said how Hui-neng's 'mind' does *not* move. Is there some way of saying how it *does* move?

In answering this question, perhaps it would be best simply to say, as Ta-hui (1089–1163) does, that the mind's restlessness creates the *illusion* of what Zen calls the 'three realms': the forms of past, present and future (Foster and Shoemaker 1996: 189). Although this sounds better, it is still evasive and imperfect, for the word 'illusion' loses all meaning if it has no antithesis, such as 'reality'. So let me illustrate the difficulty of expression that I am encountering here by telling a little story about the Zen master Te-shan (782-865). Te-shan began his career as an itinerant lecturer expounding the Buddha's *Diamond-Cutter Sutra* all over China. One day he met an old woman who was selling cakes at the side of the road, and he asked her for some refreshment. She agreed to give him a cake only if he could answer a single question. Te-shan said smugly, 'just ask'. The old woman quoted a verse from the *Diamond-Cutter Sutra* – *'past mind can't be grasped, present mind can't be grasped, and future mind can't be grasped'* – and then pointedly asked him, *'which mind does the learned monk desire to refresh?'* The commentary reports that Te-shan was rendered speechless by this question, whereupon the old woman directed him to the monastery of Lung-t'an, where he eventually realised enlightenment and became a Zen master (Foster and Shoemaker 1996: 104). If only he had wordlessly snatched a cake from the old woman's hand, or answered her question by saying *'The mind that is hungry needs refreshment'*! If he had done something like this, Te-shan would have both had his cake *and* shown the old woman that he was not in need of any further training.

I realise that the import of this story is obscure (as it should be), so let me try to be as philosophically blunt as I can: it is fine to have the illusions of past, present and future – recurring images of temporal forms are not nothing, after all. Problems arise and begin to accumulate only when the mind lets itself become cravenly attached to the forms that pass before it. As Sheng-yi puts it, *'Form itself contains no suffering; it is attachment that contains suffering'* (Pine 2001: 385). By way of illustrating Sheng-yi's remark, look at the painting *Kanzan and Jittoku Laughing at the Moon* (Figure 1.2), attributed to the Japanese artist Shohaku (1730–83).

Figure 1.2

Kanzan and Jittoku Laughing at the Moon
Ink on silk, 6′ 3″ x 17½″, Attributed to Shohaku (1730-1783)
Colby College Museum of Art, Waterville, Maine, Gift of Helen Warren Cummings, 1962.099

This picture shows the sage Jittoku and his companion Kanzan[14] laughing at a mere *image* of the moon in a pool of water, and not at the moon itself, for the latter floats above them behind the trees. The reflection of the moon on water, when taken as a phenomenon in its own right, is neither the moon above nor the water below, but rather an ephemeral being that owes its entire existence to the accidental concurrence of certain conditions – namely, an unclouded and shining moon, a placid pool of water, and someone to look at the moon's reflection. Since the moon-in-the-water shows itself phenomenally as what it is not (water and/or moon), it is philosophically interesting: as the phenomenologist Eugen Fink put is, 'it is not easy to describe the manner of being of the reflection on water' (Heidegger and Fink 1993: 87). If this phenomenon is so beautiful and interesting, why then are Jittoku and Kanzan laughing at it?

Given its impermanence, the moon-in-the-water is a favourite Zen metaphor for the relationship between subject and object: the subject is likened to the water, the object is likened to the moon, and the moon-in-the-water is likened to the phenomenal realm of *dharmas* – transient images (Watts 1957: 118–19). Moreover, in paintings of this sort laughing is often used as a symbol for the absence of attachment. Putting all of this together, one can reasonably conclude that Jittoku and Kanzan are laughing because they are completely unattached to what they are seeing. But what exactly *are* they seeing? It is clear that they are not *just* seeing and laughing at a mundane reflection of the moon on the water, for that would hardly explain why the artist took the trouble to paint the scene. Since this genre of Zen painting is didactical, it seems reasonable to interpret the picture as a form of self-mockery. On this view, one could say that Kanzan and Jittoku are laughing at the deep metaphorical 'knowledge' that the moon-in-the-water is supposed to convey in Zen discourse. In short, they are laughing at Zen itself, and especially at the kind of pretentious Zen 'philosophy' that takes itself too seriously. In this context, it is always good to remember Fa-yen's (885–958) advice that Zen *'is not founded or sustained on the premise that there is a doctrine to be transmitted'* (Foster and Shoemaker 1996: 146). Knowing that this is so, Jittoku and Kanzan also know that only a deluded fool would ever let himself become attached to a mere *image* of the moon, whether the image is taken to be real *or* metaphorical.

14 In Japanese, *kanzan* means 'Cold Mountain', and *jittoku* means 'the founding'. The sage Jittoku and his companion Kanzan are famous figures of legend who are frequently depicted in Zen artwork.

Thusness and eternity

In a letter that he wrote in 1233 to Kōshū Yō, one of his lay students, Dōgen made the banal statement that *'firewood becomes ash, and it does not become firewood again'*. Of course: who would want to deny *that*? On the other hand, it is also the case that if firewood and ash are considered in their own right, as phenomena, each one of them is an expression that is whole and complete in itself. Of course, when a thing happens, it is just *it* that happens, and not something else – what could be more obvious? Realising that this predictable sequence of conventional 'of courses' was not enough to allow his correspondent to penetrate to the heart of the matter, Dōgen continued his observations on firewood and ash by writing the following turning phrases:

> Do not suppose that the ash is after and the firewood before. You should understand that firewood abides in the phenomenal expression of firewood, which fully includes before and after and is independent of before and after. Ash abides in the phenomenal expression of ash, which fully includes before and after. (Tanahashi 1999: 36)

To say that a thing fully includes and is independent of before and after is equivalent to saying that it has no past and future. This thesis, at last, goes *against* common sense and its tendency to say 'of course' to whatever it accepts as self-evident. Interpreting the letter from this point of view, Dōgen appears to be saying that, contrary to what everyone else thinks, time really does not pass – there is always only *now*.

The reading that I have just given to Dōgen's remarks leaves the impression that his letter conveys something like an Eastern equivalent of the traditional Western determination of eternity as the *nunc stans* (literally, 'standing now'), sometimes also called the 'eternal now'. This interpretation makes it seem that Dōgen embraced the theory that Wittgenstein referred to when he said that *'if we take eternity to mean not infinite temporal duration but timelessness, then eternal life belongs to those who live in the present'* (Wittgenstein 1974: 72). *'Live in the now'*: is there any slogan that sounds more Zen-like, or that is any riper for the kind of hilarious send-up that is given to Zen ideas in movies such as *Caddyshack*? This is the same Dōgen whom we quoted earlier to the effect that time does not 'arrive', and who declared that the time-being always abides in the moment. What is more, parts of Dōgen's letter are not at all inconsistent with the sage (if somewhat hackenyed) advice to 'live in the now'. For instance:

> Birth is an expression complete this moment. Death is an expression complete this moment. They are like winter and spring. You do not call winter the beginning of spring, nor summer the end of spring. (Tanahashi 1999: 36)

That said, however, I am afraid that I must spoil the comfortable simplicity of this interpretation. To be sure, Dōgen excelled at phenomenology long before there ever was such a discipline: there is no doubt about that. Nevertheless, it would be a grievous mistake to interpret his 'firewood and ash' letter as advocating a philosophical doctrine of the eternal present.

The eternal present is, after all, merely another kind of present. This means that one needs to be attached to the image of the latter in order to believe that the former determines the true nature of existence. A good example of this kind of attachment is afforded by the time-denying mysticism of Leo Tolstoy. In his book *The Gospel in Brief*, Tolstoy called on humanity to 'destroy the deception arising from the past and future', and he vehemently rejected 'life in time' in favour of what he took to be the *true life of the present* that is 'now present to us, common to all, and manifesting itself in love' (Tolstoy 1997: 17). Although Wittgenstein actually liked Tolstoy's book, he referred disparagingly to this kind of florid exhibition of craving attachment to the idea of the present as 'solipsism of the present moment' (1979b: 25). In any case, the Zen master Dōgen would never have counselled his correspondent to become attached to as beguiling a concept as the 'present moment' or the 'eternal now'. As he told Kōshū Yō at the very beginning of the letter, craving attachment to *anything whatsoever* is a form of delusion that leads to 'blossoms falling' and 'weeds spreading' (Tanahashi 1999: 35).

The Western conception of the *nunc stans* began with the Eleatic philosophers and reached its apogee in the Middle Ages, with Meister Eckhart's mystical thesis that 'all that belongs to the past and future is alien and remote from God', and 'God is a God of the present' (Eckhart 1994: 22, 81). As it is usually interpreted, the eternal present consists in a *state of affairs* that is full of beings that keep on presencing, either on their own or by virtue of a continual act of creation by God. This *nunc stans* is not endless duration, but rather the absolute sublation of past and future into one ever-abiding present (Heidegger 2001b: 179). The idea of thusness that Dōgen was trying to evoke in his letter is hardly this. There is a certain vehemence and inflexibility to the theory of the *nunc stans* that is completely absent from Zen's idea of thusness. These combative characteristics can be traced to the dogmatic assertions of Parmenides on the true natures of being and non-being. On the one hand, Parmenides held that what is present – being – '*is and cannot not be*'; on the other hand, he held that '*never shall this prevail, that things that are not* are' (Parmenides 1984: 56, 63). In other words, present being *is*, and what is not present *is not*: end of story. The important thing to notice about Parmenides's philosophical position is that it characterises the real in terms of a statement that firmly grasps its object within the tweezers of a verbal antithesis. The philosopher's subsequent attachment to what he has thus grasped reflects a typically Western form of obeisance to the power of language to describe (and of knowledge to inscribe) something called the 'true nature of reality', and to oppose this description to any and all deviant and untrue descriptions of reality. One might even go so far as to say that the Western philosophical tradition began, and the propositional calculus was launched, when Parmenides *decided* that being is (*p*) and everything else (not-*p*) is not.

By way of contrast, the Zen way of thinking does not count the thusness of our phenomenal illusions (*dharmas*) to be either real or unreal, and it refuses to say whether descriptions of thusness are accurate or inaccurate. To quote from Dōgen's letter again: 'Those who have great realisation of delusion are buddhas; those who are greatly deluded about realisation are sentient beings' (Tanahashi 1999: 35). As these perhaps maddening remarks suggest, Zen discourse often consists of a flagrant violation either of the law of the excluded middle,[15] the law of non-contradiction, or both. It turns out that you can almost never tie Zen *philosophy* down to a simple statement of yes or no, *p* or not-*p*, although those who practise Zen in every aspect of their lives are happy to give, and *do* give, straight answers to common questions all the time. My favourite example of this latter sort of non-philosophical ordinariness is the following story from the life of the great Chinese Zen master Lin-chi:

> The master had been invited to an army camp for a vegetarian banquet. At the gatepost he happened to meet two of the officers. Pointing at the unhewn post, the master asked: '*Is this worldly or is this sacred?*' The officers were speechless. The master struck the unhewn post and uttered: '*Whatever you can say, it is but a wooden post*', and then went within. (Schloegl 1976: 69)

So much for the metaphysics of either/or. It should be obvious from this story and from what I have said already that if thusness is taken to be a philosophical concept – a matter for serious thinking and meditation – it could never come down to a pretentious Parmenidean 'thesis' of *being-in-the-eternal-now* that would stand opposed to some equally pretentious Heraclitean thesis of *becoming-amidst-the-flux-of-time*.

I know that this last point makes my remarks about thusness sound obscure to the point of being obscurantist, so let me elaborate on them by telling you about an encounter between the Zen master Huang-po (d 850) and one of his students. The student wanted to know the difference between an ordinary mind and an enlightened mind. Huang-po began his response to this inquiry obliquely, saying '*beginningless time and the present moment are the same. There is no this and no that. To understand this*

15 The law of the excluded middle has many formulations, including '*Either A is B, or A is not B*', '*P or not-P*', and '*every proposition is either true or false*'.

truth is called complete and unexcelled enlightenment'. As any good graduate student in philosophy might have done, the student apparently understood Huang-po to be asserting a *theory* of the eternal present, and so he respectfully asked the master to give doctrinal authority for his words. Huang-po declined to do so. The text of the dialogue continues with the following exchange, in which Huang-po leaves no doubt that he chose his words not to convey a metaphysical theory, but rather to adopt expedient means for a simple encounter between a teacher and his student:

> Q [Student]: Just now you said that the beginningless past and present are the same. What do you mean by that?
>
> A [Huang-po]: It is just because of your seeking that you make a difference between them. If you were to stop seeking, how could there be any difference between them?
>
> Q: If they are not different, why did you employ separate terms for them?
>
> A: If you hadn't mentioned ordinary and enlightened, who would have bothered to say such things? (Foster and Shoemaker 1996: 93)

The words 'eternity' and 'time', like 'ordinary' and 'enlightened', have many uses. Huang-po seems to be saying that whatever these uses may be, and however many of them there are, none of them convey correct knowledge about what Zen calls thusness. Instead, insight into thusness can belong only to those who let go of attachment to all knowledge and seeking.

Emptiness as non-opposition

Philosophically speaking, therefore, the word 'thusness' is neither the name for a *state* that is full of what is, nor the name for a *non-state* that is full of what is not. This is why one of the early founders of Zen, Nāgārjuna (2nd century CE), held that *'real existence cannot be predicated of dharmas, but neither can non-existence since they clearly enjoy a mode of being of some kind'* (Keown 2003: 161–62). In other words, if you cannot rightly call thusness 'being', you also cannot rightly call it 'non-being'. Although Nāgārjuna's formal 'solution' to this enigma was to characterise thusness in terms of *emptiness* (*dharma-śūyatā*, in Sanskrit), it would be wildly misleading to understand this idea of 'emptiness' as a metaphysical thesis to the effect that the true nature of reality is that of a negation of being leading to a vacuum or lack. Although it is true that, in Zen, *'although you say "it is", there is nothing which "is" can affirm'*, this is only half the story. The *Blue Cliff Record* completes the story as follows: *'although you say "It is not", there is nothing that "is not" can negate'* (Cleary 1992: 459).

As Dōgen said, those who follow the way of Zen leap clear of both abundance *and* lack (Tanahashi 1999: 36). To switch metaphors, thusness itself always steers a middle course between being and nothingness, and this means that the Zen idea of 'emptiness' does not refer to either side of this dualism. Remember, too, what the *Blue Cliff Record* says about attachment to nothingness: *'better you should give rise to a view of existence as big as Mount Sumeru, than you produce a view of nothingness as small as a mustard seed'* (Cleary 1992: 474). The Japanese philosopher Kitarō Nishida advanced an interesting historical hypothesis when he said that the Eastern and Western forms of culture can be distinguished from one another on the basis of the dualisms 'being/nothingness' and 'form/formlessness': 'I believe we can distinguish the west as having taken being as the ground of reality and the east as taking nothingness as its ground. Or, we might say, the one looked to form, the other to the formless' (Heisig 2001: 86). But however apt Nishida's remark may be within the discipline of sociology or cultural anthropology, it has absolutely nothing to do with the *Zen* point of view that I am trying to elucidate here.

Instead of opposing thusness to being and form by describing it in terms of nothingness and formlessness, it would be far better to say that thusness is *empty of all opposition*. It would be better, that is, so long as the phrase 'empty of all opposition' is understood in two different but complementary senses of the word 'opposition'. One meaning of the word 'opposition' is logical; it refers to the stipulation that certain choices within language and thought necessarily exclude others, as in *p versus* not-*p*, or *q*. This is the kind of thing that certain postmodern thinkers mean when they object to the constraints that are imposed on them by conceptual dualisms, as in Derrida's explanation, in *Letter to a Japanese Friend*, of why deconstruction is indefinable:

> All sentences of the type 'deconstruction is X' or 'deconstruction is not X' *a priori* miss the point, which is to say that they are at least false. As you know, one of the principal things at stake in what is called in my texts 'deconstruction' is precisely the delimiting of ontology and above all of the third person present indicative: S *is* P. (Derrida 1991: 275)

In this text, Derrida left a trace of an important event-of-saying in the history of his thinking: one in which he vehemently opposed oppositions. But notice that to be opposed to oppositions is like being against being against things. This curious, if not paradoxical, state of affairs allows us to gain access to the second meaning of 'opposition'. In this *other* sense, the word 'opposition' describes a contest of wills; it refers to the event of offering resistance, as in Bush *versus* Kerry, or Derrida *versus* conceptual dualisms. If one is opposed to something in this second sense, one is attached to the idea of fighting it.

In saying that thusness is empty of all *opposition*, I mean for both of these senses of the word to work together. Thus, it is quite clear that Zen does not *cling* to conceptual oppositions, in the first sense of the word; but it is equally clear that Zen does not dogmatically *oppose* the use of these oppositions in the second sense of the word. You do not have to love justice in order to do justice, and you do not have to hate injustice in order to dismantle it. I trust that this demonstrates what I mean when I say that thusness does not 'follow' from a *theory* of non-dualism, for those who advocate such a theory stand opposed to those who advocate the contrary theory that *p* is *p*, and *q* is *q*, and never the twain shall meet. The previous discussion of the two senses of the word 'opposition' also shows why there is a third clause in the whimsical 'Zen algorithm' that makes complete nonsense out of the first two. The algorithm runs as follows: *All is one, one is none, and none is all.* Although the third clause, 'none is all', follows punctiliously from the first two – all the transformations in the algorithm are logically valid – it also deeply mocks and subverts them. 'None is all' implies that the end of thought ('none', or nothingness in all its non-dualistic profundity) is exactly the same as the beginning of thought ('all', or the world of separate beings in all of their dualistic ordinariness).

All mockery aside, non-discrimination in the Zen sense signifies not a dry axiom of logic, but rather a kind of unattached personal indifference to conceptual dualisms. Of course, this does not mean that one remains averse to using dualisms as expedient means, as in the following three sentences from a letter that was written by Ta-hui to a Song dynasty government official who had sought his advice on how to gain enlightenment: '*When a person is confused, he sees east as west. When he is enlightened, west itself is east. There is no other east*' (Foster and Shoemaker 1996: 191–92). There is no west that is not also east from another point of view: what could be simpler to understand? Why then is it so hard to grasp, *deep down*, the same sort of thing about right and wrong, and all the other word-pairs that we use to adjudicate questions of morality? To grasp non-opposition deep down is not simply to observe sociologically, as Pascal did, that there is no justice or injustice that does not change its nature with change in climate and degree of latitude (Pascal 1941: 101). This is only 'cultural relativism', which always dwells at the level of the merely theoretical. No, to grasp non-opposition deep down means to let go of attachment to moral dualisms out of *compassion for the suffering of others*. For universal compassion withers and dies when discrimination begins – a painful truth that Emanuel Levinas knew better than almost any other philosopher in the history of the West, as we shall see in Chapter 4.

The ocean and the self

The emptiness of thusness is like the kind of non-opposition that the ocean offers to objects that are thrown into it. In the sense of this metaphor, one could say that the Western idea of eternity is opposed to the idea of linear time in the way that a shield is opposed to a sword. By the same token, thusness stands unopposed to the warring ideas of eternity *and* time in the way that the ocean calmly accepts both a sword and a shield when they are cast upon its deep waters. I will even risk subverting everything about thusness that I have said up to this point by asserting that thusness is not even opposed to what would be, nonetheless, a badly misguided claim about it – namely, that it is essentially the same as what I have taken great pains to distinguish it from: the 'eternal now'. As Lin-chi put it, 'names arise from the ocean of breath in the region of the belly; their fierce drum beat rattles your teeth so that they stutter out interpretations' (Schloegl 1976: 53). So be it. What could be more natural and ordinary than to talk about things and ideas, and to interpret them? Since there really isn't anything solid for us to be attached *to*, attachment is essentially no attachment anyway. To continue with the metaphor of the ocean: one might say that thusness accepts and submerges even the attachments of those who slander and deny it.

In order to preserve the breezy tone that should leaven any serious attempt to describe thusness, I will borrow one of Wittgenstein's favourite quotes from Augustine: '*What, you swine, you want to talk nonsense! Go ahead and talk nonsense, it does not matter!*' (Waismann 1979: 69). *All* events of saying and imaging – the erroneous and the correct, the slanderous and the laudatory, the simple and the complex – are elements of thusness. For example, you will never find a Zen master arguing, as the Megarians[16] did against Aristotle, that what happens is never preceded by the possibility of its happening, because possibility is only real in its enactment, and therefore any possibility that does not actualise itself in the form of a presence cannot and does not exist (Aristotle 1984: II, 1653). If people want to keep on using words such as 'possible' and 'impossible' notwithstanding the existence of proofs against these uses by philosophers like the Megarian Diodoros,[17] that is fine as far as Zen is

---

16 From the late 5th to the early 3rd centuries B.C., philosophers who were influenced partly by the Eleatics, partly by Socrates, made up a school located at Megara, near Athens; since none of their writings survive, what we know about Megarian thought comes down to us in fragments preserved by others, primarily their opponents.

17 Diodoros's famous proof of the Megarian position is as follows: 'If something would be possible which neither is nor will be, then something impossible would proceed from something possible; but something impossible cannot proceed from something possible. Thus nothing is possible which neither is nor will be' (Heidegger 1995: 179).

concerned, at least so long as they do not make themselves miserable by making a fetish out of the binary conceptual oppositions within which they frame their discourse. When that happens, compassion is always prepared to intervene with expedient means.

I will illustrate this last point by means of another koan, this time concerning the question of whether or not there is such a thing as a 'self'. The Zen master Yangshan (d 890) once made a monk admit that the latter was an 'I' that thinks; he then asked the monk to think of this 'thinking mind' itself, rather than the outside environment about which the mind usually thinks. After reflecting on this for a while, the monk changed his mind and reversed his position. Full of what he thought was enlightenment, the monk replied: *'When I get here, I don't see any existence at all'* (Cleary 1988: 140). The technique of 'seeking the mind within' is an important tool in certain forms of Buddhist practice; the point is that you will not find any well defined mind within, only fleeting impressions and thoughts. Indeed, at one level or another, most thinking people have had experiences with this kind of intense introspection that is similar to that of Yangshan's monk: they do not find a coherent 'mind' or 'self' by looking within. Some of them, like David Hume, have even gone so far as to describe their discovery in the form of a philosophical thesis to the effect that the self does not exist (Hume 1977: 238–39).

However, Yangshan realised something about the suffering and the delusions that accompany attachment to philosophical theories about the self that Hume did not. Yangshan knew that the monk was fooling himself by trying to stake a position, as Hume did, on the 'correct' side of the opposition between selfhood and its negation. So after the monk said that he could find no self by looking within, Yangshan declared: *'This is right for the stage of faith, but not yet right for the stage of person'* (Cleary 1988: 140). What a refreshing slap in the face! A person is just a person, after all, and I am just who I am: what is the problem? By upbraiding the monk for advancing a *thesis* of no-self (*anātman*, in Sanskrit), Yangshan let it be known that although the monk was initially wrong in deciding that he was an 'I', he was equally wrong when he subsequently decided that he was *not* an 'I'. Bursting open the opposition between 'I' and 'not-I', Yangshan's criticism indicates that there is no role for faith in Zen, not even faith in emptiness. Rather than clinging desperately to an image of 'I' or 'not-I', it would be better just to leave the matter of the 'self' to the mundane sphere of the merely *grammatical*. This is what Dōgen did in one of the most perceptive and concise statements ever written about the nature of the self: *'Who says "I"? It is "I" who says "who"'* (Cleary 2001: IV, 174). Based on this remark alone, one *almost* wonders whether Wittgenstein had lived as Dōgen in some prior life, although as we shall see in Chapter 4, the most important aspect of Wittgenstein's approach to philosophy – his adamant posture of silence in the face of certain questions – is very un-Zen-like.

Ordinariness

Self *versus* no-self, strong *versus* weak, better *versus* worse, just *versus* unjust: each of these quarrelsome pairs, like the pair right *versus* wrong, is *'a narrow drum beaten on both sides'*, as the *Book of Serenity* puts it (Cleary 1998: 70). Indeed, the metaphor of a narrow drum that is beaten on both sides almost verges on being a literal truth. If you don't believe me, try *listening* to the political talking heads on radio and television, or the scholarly talking heads at academic conferences: you can almost hear the stereophonic drumbeats as one side pounds out *'p!!!'* while the other side pounds out *'not-p!!!'* As Ho-shan (d 960) said, knowing how to beat the drum (of language) is what passes for knowing 'what is the real truth' (Cleary 1992: 264). This way of putting it, which anticipated Wittgenstein's concept of 'language games' by 1,000 years, does not imply that the Zen way of being scorns truth. It indicates only the absence of a desire to worship truth. What is needed is an awareness that lies midway between scorn and adulation. On this last point, it seems to me that the Zen master Nanquan (d 834) encapsulated and surpassed even the most brilliant of Marx's insights into the baleful consequences of ruling class ideology when he said that *'knowing is false consciousness, not knowing is indifference'* (Cleary 1998: 86).

Perhaps it would be best simply to say that the word 'thusness' names a certain *attitude* or *awareness* that is essentially the same as what Zen calls enlightenment. To paraphrase Levinas, what is most essential about this interpretation of thusness does not lie in what 'it' is (or is not), but rather in the original mind's refusal to let itself be domesticated or subdued by a theme (1996: 80). However, this does not mean that there is a super-substance, super-knowledge, or super-thusness that one can acquire by being intelligent and perceptive enough, by following a sufficiently rigorous course of study or meditation, or by having the right kind of epiphany. On the contrary: as the *Blue Cliff Record* puts it, to be enlightened is to be aware that ignorance and enlightenment are essentially the same: *'The true nature of ignorance is identical to Buddhahood; the empty body of illusion is identical to the body of reality'* (Cleary 1992: 353). Among other things, this means that full realisation adds nothing to what has always been with you already, throughout all of the many stages that preceded it (Foster and Shoemaker 1996: 93). Let us just say for now that being aware of this rather boring and anticlimactic fact, *all the time*, is what Zen calls enlightenment.

Far too much popular attention has been paid to the first moment of realisation (*satori*, in Japanese) in Zen. When the bottom drops out of the black lacquer bucket, as the saying goes, this experience of *ah ha!* in no way heralds an introduction into some world-transcending mystical realm. This explains why Zen masters often say that their experiences after awakening are nothing special, nothing out of the ordinary, as in the following passage written by Yuan-wu:

> Stretch out your legs on the long-bench and lie down. An Ancient said, 'In clear illumination, there is no such thing as awakening. [The concept of] "having awakened" turns around and deludes people. When you stretch out both feet and sleep, there's no false and there's no true – thus, there isn't a single concern in one's heart. When hungry, one eats; when tired, one sleeps'. (Cleary 1992: 431)

The thrust of Lin-chi's description of enlightenment is pretty much the same: '*Just act ordinary, without trying to do anything in particular. Move your bowels, piss, get dressed, eat your rice, and if you get tired, then lie down*' (Foster and Shoemaker 1996: 108).

As these texts imply, enlightenment in the Zen sense is not a mystical state that is accessible only to those who are 'in tune with the infinite', as an old Hollywood movie might put it. To be awakened is as the name implies: no longer asleep, no longer held captive by the dream world of potent images. But what one awakens *to* is nothing special, nothing that is *essentially* different than before. One is simply aware, *deep down*, that nothing changes after one's attachment to the illusion of mastery through knowledge falls away. One day you wake up after years of struggling, despairing, elating, knowing, studying, and thinking, and … you just let go. After that, you still eat breakfast, you still go to work, you still know things, you still help others to cope with their suffering, and (if you are like me) you still read philosophy, just as before. Whatever else there may be to the Zen version of being enlightened, '*you don't eliminate delusion to find what is real*', as Hung-lien (1365–1456) put it (Pine 2001: 365). You simply act like an ordinary person.

Mountains and Rivers

In a koan that is well known to anyone who has ever seriously studied the way of Zen, Hui-neng's disciple Ch'ing-yuan (d 740) articulated the perspective that I am attempting to attain in this book – a perspective that can manifest itself *fully* only when the time comes, in the next three chapters, to reflect on the specific modes of philosophical thinking that are displayed by Heidegger, Levinas and Wittgenstein:

> When I first began to practice, the mountains and rivers were simply mountains and rivers. After I advanced in my practice, the mountains and

> rivers were no longer mountains and rivers. But when I reached the end of my practice, the mountains and rivers were simply mountains and rivers again (Pine 2001: 108).

Ch'ing-yuan describes a curious journey from the beginning to the beginning. This is not transcendence, but a sort of 'trans-descendence' (Nishida 1990: xvii), in which the simple and immediate appears to become complex and mediated, only to become utterly simple again. Freud's epigram that sometimes a cigar is just a cigar is *almost* on point, the difference being that the word 'sometimes' implies that there are occasions when a cigar is actually not a cigar; whereas Ch'ing-yuan's mountains and rivers are always just mountains and rivers, even if we do sometimes imagine that they are not. Although the idea of practise in the mountains-and-rivers koan refers to what the Japanese call *zazen*, or Zen meditation, we ought not to fixate on the details of any particular method. There are many ways to practise Zen: just sitting, sitting and meditating on a koan, walking around while meditating and, as in our own case, meditating on thinking itself. Any particular method of Zen practise becomes a fetish and an impediment to the extent that we feel we 'need' it to make progress. So let us now investigate the meaning of the journey that Ch'ing-yuan describes.

Ch'ing-yuan and Hegel

We will begin our investigation by comparing this Zen master's journey to the movements of thought depicted in Hegel's *Logic* (1975). As it turns out, it is possible to draw a productive correlation between the three stages of practice in the mountains-and-rivers koan and the three stages of thought that Hegel imputes to reason's dialectical progress towards a state of full maturity. Thus, one could say that Ch'ing-yuan's *first* view of mountains and rivers corresponds to the kind of knowing that Hegel calls one-sided and abstract: namely, knowledge produced by a mode of thinking that takes the immediate and given world as true, without paying any attention to the mediating role that the subject plays in constructing the idea of the object. As far as Hegel and Zen are concerned, we are like naïve children in the first stage of thought's journey. We are simply ignorant of how complex and mediated the world is in relation to us, the ones who perceive and know it.

This first stage ends when thought emerges from what Heidegger calls its 'dialectical adolescence' (1985: 79) into the young adulthood of a *second* view of mountains and rivers. The new stage can be taken to correspond to Hegel's dialectical triad *immediacy—mediation—unity*. Here, for the first time, thought has in view both the immediate object *and* itself as subject in a dialectical movement towards the unity of matter and method. In this, the second, stage of the journey we break through our naïveté to a *certain* kind of enlightenment. Based on what I have said already about Zen's idea of enlightenment, we must not overstress the similarity between it and the self-consciousness that belongs to Hegel's idea of the dialectic. Nevertheless, these two modes of comportment are comparable if one considers solely the distance that lies between them and the first movement. Thus, both for Hegel and for Ch'ing-yuan, the second stage of the journey consists of being attuned to reality in such a way that things no longer show themselves as the banal simplicities that they once seemed to be, before the journey began.

Thus far the comparison has worked well. Now, however, we find ourselves on the verge of the third and last stage of Ch'ing-yuan's journey. Will the comparison continue to hold? It will not, and in this failure of correspondence can be glimpsed the most essential difference between the way of Zen and Western thought. For Hegel, the third and final movement of thought is *speculative*: it overcomes the 'negative unity' of the second, or dialectical, movement to grasp the 'positive unity' of all prior movements, the abstract *and* the dialectical. In Hegel's third movement speculative thought finally recognises unity *as* unity by thinking the identity of being and thinking. Enter the Absolute Idea and the notion of the end of history, which together represent the apogee of respect for knowledge and progress in Western philosophy. The unity of all three movements in Hegel's thought is logic, defined as 'the science of the pure Idea' (Hegel 1975: 25). In contrast to all of this, the utter Zen simplicity of the third stage of Ch'ing-yuan's journey most definitely does *not* correspond to the Hegelian epiphany of the Absolute Idea or to the self-certainty of Hegel's Absolute Spirit. Unlike the 'surpassing' that occurs in the Hegelian moment of synthesis, the third view of mountains and rivers *annihilates* the prior two views without either preserving or unifying them.

Hegelian Spirit is wise, in the sense that it has transcended subject and object, as well as the abstract and the dialectical, to *know* mountains and rivers for what they truly are as reflected in their Absolute Idea. Hegel's 'Wise Man' is thus a perfectly self-conscious knower: he is capable of answering all questions put to him in such a way that his answers in their entirety form a coherent discourse (Kojève 1980: 75). Unlike the Wise Man, by the time Ch'ing-yuan reaches his third view of mountains and rivers he is altogether finished with attachment to truth and knowledge. This absence of attachment does not signify that Ch'ing-yuan has decided to scorn truth and knowledge, any more than a person's benevolent neutrality towards wine means that he has decided never to drink a glass of wine. All that Ch'ing-yuan has done is remove truth and knowledge from their shrines on the wall above him, and set them on the dusty floor below him, next to his mattress and rice bowl. If the quintessential Western philosopher[18] passionately *loves* knowledge and wisdom, Ch'ing-yuan is the kind of philosopher who calmly *accepts* knowledge and wisdom. As the words '*simply mountains and rivers again*' suggest, Ch'ing-yuan has seen that there is absolutely no difference in kind among the knowledge of mountains and rivers in their immediacy, the knowledge of mountains and rivers as the subject mediates them towards the unity of their idea, and the mature Absolute Idea of mountains and rivers. For Hegel, the highest point is reached with truth as certainty, that is, with absolute self-knowledge. For someone like Ch'ing-yuan, the highest and lowest points ultimately coincide at a place where '*there is no difference between stupidity and wisdom*' (Bancroft 2000: 110).

Although Hegel describes a vulgar first view of knowing, a sophisticated second view, and a transcendent third view, they all stand on the level of the merely *imagistic* in reference to what we have called thusness. It was Ch'ing-yuan's great and enduring breakthrough to recognise this fundamental equivalence in a way that is not at all the same as either *perceiving* it or *conceiving* of it. Given all that has been written about the faculty of perception in German idealist philosophy, 'perceiving' unhelpfully connotes the reception of objective data ('the real') originating from outside the subject, an idea that is completely foreign to what happened in the third stage of Ch'ing-yuan's journey. By the same token, 'conceiving' brings with it all the apparatus of Kant's categories of the understanding, and Ch'ing-yuan certainly would deny that his *awareness* that mountains and rivers are simply mountains and rivers again was identical to, or even accomplished by, his faculty of understanding proceeding from object to concept (reflecting judgment) or from concept to object (subsuming judgment). His kind of *awareness* is aware that his so-called 'enlightenment', as well as all the stages that preceded it, have added absolutely nothing to what has been with him all the time.

I italicised the word *awareness* in the previous paragraph to bring out a contrast between being aware (*prajñā*, in Sanskrit) in the Zen sense, and perceiving and conceiving in the Western philosophical sense. The English word 'aware' comes from the Indo-European root *wer*, meaning to turn or bend. This small etymological insight gives us a promising way of describing the third movement of Ch'ing-yuan's journey. Thus, one might say that Ch'ing-yuan's awareness consists in *turning himself to* mountains and rivers again, after having turned away from them in the second movement of his journey. This turning-to is unlike his first

18 From the Greek *phil-* (to love) and *sophia* (knowledge or wisdom).

encounter with mountains and rivers, however, for only one who has turned away from something can subsequently turn to it again. Beginning with naïve perceiving, Ch'ing-yuan turned away from the simplicity of mountains and rivers towards a deep and sophisticated understanding of them. But rather than lose himself in attachment to this understanding, he turned back to face the plainness and simplicity of mountains and rivers once again. This turning-back involves neither perceiving nor knowing, for he has forever left behind both of these ways of definitively idealising his relationship to mountains and rivers. Zen's deflationary view of language carries over to a deflationary view of knowledge: knowledge, like language, is fine *as far as it goes*, but things get dicey when we begin to attach ourselves to it and make it into an idol. The deflation accomplished by the third stage of Ch'ing-yuan's journey leaves Hegel and his ilk stranded like altitude-sick hikers upon the lofty (but hallucinatory) idea of mountains and rivers that they have laboriously constructed for themselves.

The wells of Thales and Caoshan

Hegel's distinction between the naïveté of common sense and the deep wisdom of the Absolute Idea tracks the more general distinction in Western philosophy between attachment to the sensible and conventional world of the ordinary and attachment to the supra-sensory and sophisticated 'real'. This tradition, which is with us still, began with the story of Thales (634–546 BC) and the well. Legend says that Thales, the West's first philosopher, was so struck by the wonder of the heavens above that he directed his gaze at them alone. Neglecting all vulgar and common things, he promptly fell into a well, after which a Thracian maidservant proceeded to mock him and laugh at him for his foolishness (Heidegger 2003: 38). In terms of its symbolism, the story of Thales falling into a well can be read either mockingly or philosophically. The first interpretation would make the story into a burlesque, analogous to Aristophanes's play *The Clouds* (Oates and O'Neill 1938: II, 541–608), on the self-defeating inclination of philosophers to scorn common sense. What value is philosophical speculation, the moral of *this* story would go, if it makes you fall into wells and leaves you open to derision? In the philosophical interpretation, on the other hand, the story represents the impediments that everything common and ordinary – including petty scorn coming from little brains – poses to the noble strivings of those who seek wisdom. Plato alludes to this reading in the *Theaetetus*, where Socrates compares the story of Thales and the well to the plight of any philosopher who seeks to discover the '*true nature of everything as a whole, never sinking to what lies close at hand*' (Plato 1961: 879). On the view that attending to the ordinary represents a kind of sinking or decline, the story would symbolise the old Platonic allegation that the shadows of seeming and non-being in the cave of ordinary affairs keep human beings from seeing the sunlight of truth and being outside. What value are wells, the moral of this version of the story would go, if they get in the way of philosophical inquiry?

The first interpretation of the story of Thales and the well privileges convention, while the second privileges theory. But instead of deciding which interpretation is best (according to some ponderous criterion of 'best'), I would like to tell a story about another well: Caoshan's 'Ass Looking in a Well' (Cleary 1998: 219). In this koan, the Zen master Caoshan (d 891) asks 'elder De' to explain how it is possible for reality to manifest form (is this not also Hegel's question?), and De replies *'Like an ass looking in a well'*. De's metaphor subtly implies the thesis that *we* make reality through our illusions, for the ass which wrongly thinks it is seeing itself in the well is actually looking at a mere reflection of itself. Although Caoshan admits that De has said quite a lot with this metaphor, he goes on to remark that De's answer amounts to only *'80%'*, almost as though he were grading a merely adequate answer to an examination question. This disappoints De, so he asks Caoshan to explain what the master himself thinks about the matter. The koan ends with Caoshan's devastating response to De's question: *'Like the well looking at the ass'*.

This extraordinary koan is like both interpretations of the story of Thales and the well rolled into one: philosophy is deep *and* shallow at the same time. Caoshan quite literally uses a 'turning phrase' to help De out of a rut by uttering the exact reversal of the latter's response to his question. The import of this reversal is clear. *The verbal equation* 'ass looking at the well = well looking at the ass' *means that the one is simply the mirror image of the other, and therefore that the text privileges neither of them.* The ass that thinks it sees itself in the well really sees only a reflection of itself; but the metaphor of a reflection that De so cleverly used to symbolise the illusory nature of reality bounced back at him and attached itself to his mind. That is why Caoshan reversed the relationship between the ass and the well: *he used a turning phrase to help De cure his addiction to the metaphor of illusion itself.* The ass looking in the well, together with the well looking at the ass, comprise a self-annihilating *unity* of metaphorical images that is meant to dissolve our attachment to the little distinctions we are inclined to make between such things as illusion and reality, sign and signified, self and other, and ordinary and profound.

Attachment to transcendence

It should be obvious by now that Ch'ing-yuan's phrase 'mountains and rivers' does not just refer to mountains and rivers. It symbolises the mind's reception and interpretation of *whatever* it is that shows itself to the mind in an event of showing. Humans have many names for what shows itself to the mind in this way: reality, objects, phenomena, sensations, feelings, notions, concepts, ideas – these are some of the usual suspects. Two other names are 'vulgar common sense about the ordinary' and 'the erroneous philosophising of my intellectual opponents'. Although *common opinion* and *sophistries* have been the favourite whipping boys of Western philosophy ever since Parmenides (1984: 55–91) distinguished the way of seeming from the way of truth, it is clear that Ch'ing-yuan possessed a much greater tolerance for 'lowly' and 'mistaken' forms of thought. Western philosophy has always been attached to fighting against common sense and bad theories: when it hears the bell in either case, it comes out of its corner swinging. Those who walk the path of Zen, on the other hand, feel no *automatic* impulse either to fight other people's ideas *or* to acquiesce in them. It takes a lot more than loud sounds and glittering forms to move someone like Ch'ing-yuan.

If we take common sense and the world's many philosophical theories and systems as some of the ideations that are signified by the expression *'simply mountains and rivers'*, then Ch'ing-yuan's description of his journey from start to finish implies that all of these stand on the same level – the mundane level of what is 'simply' this or that idea presenting itself to the mind. Moreover, it is clear that these ideations are exactly the same at the end of the journey as they were at the journey's beginning, at least as far as language and knowledge are concerned. That is, the difference between the beginning and the end of Ch'ing-yuan's journey does not lie in the words and ideas used to describe them, for the words and ideas are the same both before and after the journey: 'simply mountains and rivers'. Nevertheless, the modern Zen master Taizan Maezumi correctly observes that *'the "mountains are mountains, rivers are rivers" experience after enlightenment is not at all the same as before such a realisation'* (Cleary 1992: xiii–iv). As Maezumi's reference to *experience* indicates, the difference between the beginning as a beginning and the end as a beginning does not lie in the spheres of language or knowledge, but rather in the changed attitude and perspective of the one making the journey. To put that attitude and perspective in a nutshell, the one who set out on the journey has at long last *let go* of attachment to the idea of transcendence.

Attachment to the idea of transcendence is the need to imagine a world that is distinguished, in its essence, in terms of a movement or passage from this to that: from cause to caused, from ground to grounded, from origin to originated, from the one who transcends to the transcendent: in short, a world in which a decision has been made against chaos (no A, no B) and in favour of discrimination and the order it makes (A $\Rightarrow$ B). The narrow conceptual opposition between order and chaos has bedazzled (and frequently obstructed) Western thought for over 2,000 years. Those who do science, politics, law, business, and mainstream (analytical) philosophy *imagine* a well-ordered world, and because doing so rewards them with plenty of material 'results', they become attached – sometimes mildly, sometimes obsessively – to their images.

Notice that I did not say they become attached to the results themselves, although of course I could have done so. It is a regrettable truism about modern life, in prosperous countries at least, that people operating in all five spheres tend to cling to their careers and their paraphernalia as if the principle that too much is never enough were an immutable truth. While I daresay that this observation about the phenomenon of craving attachment to money, status and honour is accurate enough, what I really want to say now is that people become attached to the *idealisations* that construct the order on which the results depend. For example, it is one thing to love your position as a professor for what it allows you to do; it is another (and far more pernicious) thing to love the system of attractive images and illusions that surround the word 'professor', and that give it whatever power and allure it has in your own mind and in the minds of others. It is the latter form of attachment that I want to talk about now.

Although material results can exhibit many good qualities, they also have an ugly tendency to make us cravenly bow down to the language and knowledge that we associate with their production in more or less the same way that ancient peoples prostrated themselves before idols of the deities to whom they imputed rainstorms and earthquakes. Wittgenstein traced this worshipful tendency to believing in the illusion that the so-called laws of nature are the causes of natural phenomena, as opposed to mere norms of representation that we use to express the fact that certain phenomena tend to recur in regular sequences. In the *Tractatus*, for example, he wrote:

> People today stop at the laws of nature, treating them as something inviolable, just as God and Fate were treated in past ages. And in fact both are right and both wrong; though the view of the ancients is clearer in so far as they have a clear and acknowledged terminus, while the modern system tries to make it look as if *everything* were explained. (Wittgenstein 1974: 70) (emphasis in original).

On this view, the 'law' of gravity, for example, is not some*thing* that causes us to remain on the earth; rather, it is a way of *expressing* the fact that we just *do* remain fastened to the earth's surface. Likewise, the commutative law of addition ($a + b = b + a$) does not *cause* 1 + 2 to equal 2 + 1; to say that the latter two sums 'follow the commutative law of addition' is simply to say that they *are* equal.

To generalise the point I am trying to make: the statement '$A \Rightarrow B$' does not say that a law of nature (A) *causes* phenomenon B; rather, '$A \Rightarrow B$' *expresses* the fact that B just *is* a phenomenon of a certain type when it is looked at in relation to certain other phenomena. The popular scientific notion that evolution 'caused' organisms to be what they are is really no different in principle than the religious notion that God caused them to be what they are. Both ways of thinking inflate a mere image into an *entity*: the LAW or GOD. From a spiritual point of view, Heidegger indicated the unfortunate consequence of this transformation for *God* when he said that representational thinking has lowered God to the level of a mere *causa efficiens* (Heidegger 1977: 26). And from a secular point of view, Kafka showed the equally baleful effects of this kind of transformation on *people* when he described, in the parable *Before the Law*, a door of the law that appears so forbidding that even the one person for whom it was meant believes that he cannot enter it (Kafka 1937: 267–69).

If, with Wittgenstein, we think of the laws of nature as no more than rules of grammar that we use to express regularities of appearances that we observe in the now-time (for when else could we observe them?), then treating these laws as inviolable elements of the universe would be more or less analogous to the religious behaviour of the mutants in the film *Beneath the Planet of the Apes* (1970). These subterranean remnants of humanity from a distant post-apocalyptic future dutifully worshipped the last remaining nuclear bomb as their god. But in truth their nuclear bomb was a (horrific) tool of war that earlier humans had constructed, just as the laws of nature are tools that scientists have made for predicting events. Marx called our forgetfulness of this basic truth about 'truth' *alienation*, which he defined as '*loss of the object and bondage to it*' (1986: 37). In the phenomenon of alienation we forget our role as producers and image-mongers, and act on an illusion, whenever we worship our tools as if they were godheads. One might say that Wittgenstein and Marx arrived independently at one of Zen's most important insights: namely, if it is absurd to bite the hand of knowledge that feeds us, it is equally if not more absurd to kneel down and kiss it.

Please don't take this last series of remarks the wrong way: neither Zen thought in general nor this book in particular should be interpreted as taking a stance against order or results *per se*. After all, the very pages you are reading represent an attempt to achieve *some* kind of order and results. But it is one thing to let ways of thinking and speaking become expedient means for achieving certain results, and another thing to be absorbed in these ways so completely that one remains oblivious to any possibility of breaking free of them. Likewise, it is one thing to spend our lives relentlessly chasing after results like hungry ghosts (*preta*, in

Sanskrit),[19] and quite another to be able to calm and control our insatiable hunger for results. The point I am trying to make here is not that it is possible to escape our historical circumstances and ideological presuppositions to attain some ethereal realm where the world is immaculately conceived. The insight that knowledge depends on historical and social context, including power relations, can be very important when it comes to the project of dealing concretely and compassionately with certain problems of human suffering. That said, however, this is really a small and insignificant insight as far as our present journey is concerned. The 'social construction of knowledge' is just what its name implies: the social construction of *knowledge*. Let me say it once again: *Zen thought is not about knowledge; it is about the obsession with knowledge.*

In philosophy, the need for transcendence craves an explanation that will quell the mind's voracious appetite for solutions. Anybody who has ever spent any considerable amount of time puzzling over logical or metaphysical problems, especially the problem of the 'meaning of life', knows that the impulse to philosophise is a form of suffering. It is the suffering of a mind that is hooked like a drug addict on *explaining* and *accounting* for its being-in-the-world in terms of transcendence ($A \Rightarrow B$): the A of the *explanans* leading to the B of the *explanandum*. The craving for a well-grounded account of the world is like any other kind of craving: it consumes the one who craves it when it is absent, and even after it arrives it somehow manages to disappoint. 'Everything disappoints', wrote Kierkegaard in his diary: 'Hope, the hoped for does not come, or the hoped for comes – and disappoints' (1993: 62). Hegel was right in calling the presupposition of philosophy *'the need that has come to utterance'* (Heidegger 2003: 20). For the philosopher who writes from the need to bring something to language always expresses his or her own mental suffering in the form of what temporarily appeases it. Great philosophical texts are first and foremost traces of the writer's agony, unless they are one of those exceedingly rare cases of work that is written solely out of compassion as opposed to need.

According to *The Blue Cliff Record* (Cleary 1992: 1), there was once an encounter between Bodhidharma and China's Emperor Wu in which the emperor asked Bodhidharma to say who he was. The latter responded *'I don't know'*. An interesting answer, this. It forms part of the very first koan in *The Blue Cliff Record*, and is just the kind of simple text that Zen masters

19 These creatures from Buddhist mythology are endowed with huge stomachs but miniscule mouths, and as a consequence they are never able to eat enough to satisfy their hunger (Pine 2001: 450).

put to their students in the early stages of their training. Surely if great thinkers such as Heidegger, Levinas, and Wittgenstein had been asked to identify themselves, they would have felt no hesitation in saying what even a little child knows how to say: 'My name is Martin (or Emanuel, or Ludwig)'. Indeed, there is even a case recorded in the *Transmission of Light*, a major Zen classic attributed to the Japanese master Keizan (1268-1325), in which the fact that a person simply uttered his own name was sufficient for his enlightenment:

> When the professor Liangcui called on Mazu, Mazu shut the door when he saw him coming. Liangcui knocked on the door, and Mazu said, 'Who is it?' Liangcui replied, 'Liangcui', and as soon as he called out his name he was suddenly enlightened. (Cleary 2001: IV, 174)

It is fair to say that Liangcui realised, all of a sudden, that he had nothing to lose *or* gain by simply giving his name as the ordinary answer to an ordinary question. No one can outsmart a Zen master, but you can go beyond him by letting go of the desire to outsmart him. Emperor Wu had not yet learned this lesson, and that is why Bodhidharma said 'I don't know' when asked to say who he was. His reply brought into view one of the most important and vexing questions in Western philosophy – the nature of the self – only casually to dismiss it as irrelevant to what was going on, right then and there, between Bodhidharma and Emperor Wu. Zen's disinclination to attempt to 'solve' the traditional problems of Western philosophy – problems such as the nature of the self and the essence of justice – is relevant to the claim made in the previous paragraph that any philosophical thinking which succumbs to craving attachment is a form of suffering. We need to think about this claim more deeply, and to connect it to what will become our most important theme from this point on: *transcendence as such.*

Three Conventional Forms of Transcendence

Although philosophical craving is linked to the problem of transcendence, as yet we have not clarified, in a completely satisfactory way, the latter's meaning and structure. Let us do that now. What do Western philosophers have in mind when they talk about transcendence? The word itself comes from the Latin compound *transcendere*, meaning to climb or go across (from *trans*, across, and *scandere*, to climb). As the etymology of the word indicates, philosophy interprets transcendence as a kind of *movement* – whether physical, intellectual, or spiritual – from here to there, from A to B. To transcend is to span a gap or limit separating the one who transcends from the transcendent. The process thus involves three distinct terms: A, the one who transcends; B, the transcendent, to which transcending transcends; and ⇒, the transcending movement itself. For simplicity's sake, we will continue to represent the logical form of the whole process as A ⇒ B.

We can divide the various explicit problems of transcendence that Western philosophers have posed to themselves over the past two and a half millennia into roughly three basic categories: the *epistemological*, the *ontological*, and the *theological*. The problem of *epistemological transcendence* is how to account for the movement from knower to known: how to explain the phenomenon of an individual (or a Cartesian subject, conceived as a prisoner inside its skin) acquiring knowledge about something outside itself – something that is not the same as the individual, and thus not immediately accessible to it by means of a simple act of introspection. Next, *ontological transcendence* raises the problem of how beings in the world (including humans) are able to become what they presently are not – how the flow of existence connects an apparently stable present being to its future. Finally, *theological transcendence* is about how the contingent can make contact with the absolute; it involves the problem of finite beings like us attempting to reach the infinite in knowledge or deed, whether this infinite is thought to be God, being, another person, or anything else.

Three ancient examples will serve to elucidate the forms of transcendence just identified. I do not choose these examples because of nostalgia for the lost purity of ancient philosophy, but because they set the basic patterns for thinking about transcendence that still control our minds, whether or not we realise it. For an illustration of epistemological transcendence, consider Plato's theory of ideas. His account of knowing – most famously expressed in the allegory of the cave (1961: 747–72) – makes transcendence into a kind of intuition that 'sees' the *idea* of a being that otherwise would show nothing but a blur passing through the flux of becoming. Thus, for Plato, knowing takes the form of a passage from seeing to seen: A ('seeing' intuition) ⇒ B (the Ideas). As for ontological transcendence, I offer Aristotle's theory of movement and change. According to Aristotle, the being that can move (and therefore change, if only its position) always bears within it the origin of movement in the form of *dynamis* (*potentia*, in Latin); this origin then passes over to the actual movement, which is conceived of as *energeia* (*actus*, in Latin). Thus, Aristotle thought that movement and change are possible only because they actualise what lies already dormant and waiting to be actualised: A (potentiality) ⇒ B (actuality) (Aristotle 1984: I, 342–45). Finally, the first fragment of Greek philosophy that we know about will serve to illustrate the idea of theological transcendence. Anaximander wrote in that text of an unnamed first principle that is both the origin and the destination of all beings: a 'whence' to which they must all return of necessity as penance for their injustice (*adikia*)

(Atchity 1996: 73). Thus, for Anaximander: A (beings) ⇒ B (their absolute destination and origin).

The foregoing descriptions of Plato's theory of ideas, Aristotle's theory of movement, and Anaximander's theory of being are, of course, scandalous reductions of what another author might spend hundreds of pages interpreting. But I have reduced them to cartoons for a reason: to reveal the simple skeletal structure of transcendence, A ⇒ B, on which hangs the flesh of all three theories. This is indeed the very same skeleton that underlies the work of the three thinkers with whom we will have our primary conversations in this book. Again, at the risk of being accused of reductionism, I will briefly sketch the argument for this, while promising to complete it in later chapters. First, Heidegger's version of *ontological transcendence* holds that our being-in-the-world (A) is the 'primal transcendence' (1984: 135) that makes possible all of the intentional relations that we might (subsequently) have to the various beings (B) that concern us. Likewise, Levinas espouses a kind of *theological transcendence* when he claims that the *I* who stands face-to-face with another human being transcends itself (A) towards an encounter with an 'other' (B) who is both absolute and unknowable. Finally, Wittgenstein's life-long antipathy towards metaphysical problems such as being and ethics is a negative form of *epistemological transcendence*, because it asserts that the limits of language (A) lead to the necessity of philosophical silence (B) in response to these problems: philosophy cannot claim to 'know' what it cannot sensibly put into words. Comparing the *form* of thought in Plato, Aristotle and Anaximander with that of Heidegger, Levinas and Wittgenstein, it would appear that the old French saying is as true in philosophy as it is in so many other things: *Plus ça change, plus c'est la même chose.*

Logical Transcendence

The principle of reason: causes and grounds

All philosophical accounts of epistemological, ontological and theological transcendence take the form of a logical structure which philosophers of the Enlightenment called the *principium rationis sufficientis*: the principle of sufficient reason. Leibniz (1934: 8–9) was the first thinker to put this idea (which is also known simply as the 'principle of reason') into the explicit form of a principle: *nihil est sine ratione cur potius sit quam non sit* (nothing is without a reason why it exists rather than does not exist)(Heidegger 1984: 114). To express the principle positively: anything that is (any B) must have a sufficient reason (an A) for why it is. Since the principle of reason is itself something that exists, it would seem to be the sort of thing that must have a reason, at least if we take the view that the principle falls within its own jurisdiction. However, a truly rigorous demand for the *ultimate* reason for the principle of reason leads to a regress, since any reason one might find would have to have its own reason, as well as a reason for that reason, and so on indefinitely (Heidegger 1996b: 12). Likewise, the 'truth' of this principle cannot be proved without absurdity, for the very idea of such a proof puts one into the 'circle of demanding proof for the right to demand a proof' (Schopenhauer 1974: 33). Asking *'Why ask why?'* is a much better way of trying to get at the foundation of the principle of reason, since this question interrogates the concrete practice of *using* the principle rather than the merely abstract validity of its content. But before we can hope to comprehend the problem of craving attachment to the principle of reason, we first need to explore and clarify its essential ambiguity.

To ask a question of the form 'Why B?' is to ask for B's reason within the meaning of the principle of reason. But the question 'Why?', like the Latin word *ratio* and its English translation 'reason', is ambiguous. Sometimes when we ask 'Why?' we are seeking a *causal* reason, as in the expression *'The reason for the fire was a lit match'*. Other times we want people to say why they did this or that in terms of their *grounds* for doing it, as in the expression *'The reason I burnt my draft card was to protest against the war'*. While Leibniz himself did not attempt to clarify the ambiguity of the words 'why' and 'reason', his immediate intellectual heir Christian Wolff did. Wolff became the first Western philosopher to distinguish reason as *cause* from reason as *ground*. Wolff saw that the first kind of reason pertains to the kindred realms of cause and effect in nature (*principium fiendi*) and motive and action in human affairs (*principium cognoscendi*), whereas the second kind of reason has to do with why things are what they are in their essence (*principium essendi*) (Schopenhauer 1974: 24-27).

Reason-as-cause is closely connected to the idea of necessity, and to what Max Weber called the 'infinite causal web': cause A1 leads to effect B1, which in turn becomes new cause A2 that leads to new effect B2, and so on *ad infinitum*. *Reason-as-ground*, on the other hand, is closely connected to the idea of freedom, as in Kant's interpretation of freedom as the capacity to lay down grounds for one's future behaviour (self-legislation). We will investigate the distinction between causes and grounds more closely in Chapter 2, where it will play a prominent role in our effort to understand and critique Heidegger's interpretation of freedom as freedom-for-ground. But it is also important to get at least a brief overview of the distinction now, because the question 'Why ask why?' can lead us to an encounter with the pernicious phenomenon of attachment to logical transcendence only if we gain clarity in advance about the different spheres in which the word 'reason' operates.

In the form of Wolff's *principium fiendi*, the principle of reason eventually came to be known as the law of causality – a law that has served as a regulative principle for scientific inquiry for the past 400 years. Distilled to its essence, the law of causality says that space and time are relative: that is, that space and time are inextricably linked according to the picture of a four-dimensional manifold consisting of three spatial dimensions (x, y, z) and one temporal dimension (t). Beings and events are then seen to occupy this manifold in a theoretically determinable way, or, as in the case of quantum mechanics, in a statistically predictable way. Moreover, the science of nature is not the only science that employs the principle of causality. Think of the various 'ologies' that comprise the so-called human sciences: psychology, sociology, anthropology, and so forth. Indeed, even when it comes to explaining human behaviour philosophically, both determinists and freewill advocates alike tend to conceive the relationship between motive and action (Wolff's *principium cognoscendi*) in causal terms. Determinists such as Schopenhauer, for example, take motives to be the springs of action, but only after the motives themselves have been caused by something else – in his case a force that is exerted by the blind striving of the will (1999: 41); while idealists such as Kant, who claim that we can freely and rationally choose our motives, see a kind of causal principle at work between a motive, *once it is chosen*, and the behaviour that it aims at producing (1993: 154–229). It is as if the human being were a puppet that could will its own puppet master into being. From this point of view, the A1 of the will either *causes* (Schopenhauer) or *chooses* (Kant) the B1 of a person's motive, which in turn becomes the A2 of a cause that produces the B2 of his or her actions.

Apart from any attempt to explain the behaviour of individuals in causal terms, any analysis of existing social arrangements that attends to the 'conditions' of their present production and reproduction, or to their possible future transformation, is also beholden to the causal form of the principle of reason. In certain forms of social theory, for example, ideology is the concept of a cause that accounts for why people can be made to accept their own oppression. While in social psychology, causal mechanisms like cognitive dissonance are supposed to explain why people tend to ignore unflattering (but true) information about choices they have already made. To paraphrase von Clausewitz again, one might say that the human sciences are simply the continuation of the law of causality by other means. It is not hard to locate the source of our attachment to causal explanations: we crave them because they can give us access to what we desire. In Zen terms, the postmodern slogan

'Knowledge is power' means that the more knowledge of causal relations we possess, the more we can feed the hungry ghost of craving desire: the desire for more goods and status, more health and beauty, more justice, more happiness, and so on. However, there is one power that those who idolise the slogan 'knowledge is power' cannot realise: the power to affirm totally or deny totally without *settling down* in either affirmation or denial (Cleary 1998: 87).

The causal method of representing reality seems to force the idea on us that what Zen calls thusness is 'really' a kind of flow in which all things reciprocally and sequentially act on one another. If knowledge about causal relations leads to desirable results, we mistake the *means* of achieving results for a description of the *ends*. Gaston Bachelard gave a wonderfully succinct phenomenology of this kind of mistake when he said that the causally minded person 'explains the flower by the fertilizer' (1969: xxvi). In modern science, the repeatability of the experiment determines what is called an 'effect', and the correlation of regular sequences of events replaces the Aristotelian idea that beings affect one another because of their innate *dynamis*. Causation is conceived of as a kind of 'following upon' that is prefigured by a theory and verified by an experiment. The 'A ⇒ B' of theory merely *predicts* that B will appear if A appears first, thereby resituating the passage of transcendence from the relation between things in nature to the relation between theory and observation in the mind of the subject. According to this view, the sun does not rise each day because the earth rotates, but because the theory of rotation predicts the sun will rise and because all observations to date have confirmed the theory.

Rather than ordering beings to obey it, a scientific theory in the modern sense of the term is like a rule of law that orders humans to *employ* it as the measure of their relationships with beings. A 'reason' in the sense of a cause becomes that which is verifiably observed to appear before something else that appears in an ordered sequence of present moments. Scientific inquiry is thus conceived of as the measurement of appearances that show themselves to a subject who is armed with a method. This hypertrophy of methodological self-consciousness tends to transform truth into methodology and explanations into the explained. In throwing a 'garb of ideas' (*ein Kleid von Ideen*), as Husserl puts it, over the world of immediate intuition and experience (Derrida 2003: 112), the scientific method establishes the hegemony of calculation and explanation over speculation and interpretation. This primacy of method over matter, and of means over ends, is not a small thing. It changes the very nature of what counts as real: reality becomes the sum total of all verifiable theoretical predictions (A) about the sequence of appearances (B). This is what Heidegger meant when he said that the institutional character of modern science is 'nothing less than the making secure of the precedence of methodology over what is (nature and history)' (Heidegger 1977: 125).

The scientific commitment to explaining everything according to the principle of causality makes the idea of human freedom appear foolish and wrong, for the Western philosophical tradition has always imagined freedom as the uncaused origin of our thoughts and actions. Enter the idea of reason-as-ground. As Kant was the first to see with any degree of clarity, only the improvable possibility of an uncaused *ground* of action allows room for the idea of freedom (Kant 1998: 484-89). Even the most dogmatic determinist cannot safely ignore the distinction between a cause and a ground, for as actors, scientists of all types often succumb to the temptation to explain why (in the sense of ground, not cause) they practise, and even ought to practise, science the way they do.[20] Thus, in the form of a ground (Wolff's *principium essendi*), the 'reason' required by the principle of reason is *human freedom* in ethics, the *origin of the world* (God) in theology, and the *being of beings* in ontology. Each of these disciplines construes its subject matter in terms of what it takes to be an *ultimate* (ie uncaused) ground, broadly interpreted to include the notion of *arché*, or absolute origin. What is more, the concept of reason-as-ground is also an important component of the everyday practice of normative judgment in matters of law and morality, both of which take freedom of will and choice (Kant's practical freedom) to be primitive conditions of the possibility of legal and moral responsibility.

The discourse of grounds does not explain things by making a list of antecedents, but by conferring unique and immediate meaning on what is to be explained. That is, a ground is not merely an indifferent event or nodule of substance that was once caused and that now, in turn, causes the next event or nodule to go on its way in the endless chain of causes and effects. The image of what is right, represented as a *cause*, is a different kind of 'reason' than the image of what is right represented as a *ground*. *'I can't eat meat, it's the wrong thing to do'*: this sentence does *not* say the equivalent of *'My mother taught me to love animals, and then I saw the shocking sight of a dead animal when I was six, and then etc, etc, and* therefore *that is why I don't eat meat'*. The latter sentence gives a causal explanation of a certain gastronomic tendency, as if the speaker were observing his own eating habits in the way that a scientist might observe whether a lab rat prefers Swiss cheese or cheddar. In contrast, the former sentence indicates that the speaker is not presently concerned with the causes of

20 For example, Max Weber's famous essay *Science as a Vocation* (1958: 129–56) is an excellent example of a sociologist attempting to establish the value (as ground, not cause) of value-free inquiry in the social sciences.

his beliefs, and that his reason for not eating meat is something that he chooses to accept – right now – as the ground of his behaviour. All of this suggests that we grow attached to the practice of grounding because the discourse of grounds paints us a pretty picture of doing on the basis of something other than doing: *something else* that ratifies and approves our behaviour in the way that loving parents ratify and approve their baby's first steps. Seen from the point of view of the one who always wears his principles on his sleeve, the phenomenon of 'being principled' is not so much a virtue as it is a symptom of insecurity.

Sociology and psychology give *causal* accounts of their objects of inquiry; metaphysics, law and ethics *ground* them in determinations such as the 'law', or the 'freedom' of the universal thinking subject (Hegel 1975: 39). Causes explain action in the way sunshine explains the growth of plants. Grounds justify and give meaning to action in the way the norms of law and morality purport to justify and give meaning to their application. Sometimes we believe that we freely choose our grounds; other times we suspect that we are helpless playthings of causal forces. The first image portrays our future as an absolute origin, and our past as merely the detritus of a primal force that spends all of its energy bursting forth into the present. This picture tends to confirm our hopes that something better is coming, for it makes it seem that we control our own destinies; on the other hand, it also supports our fears that something worse may be coming, thanks to our own bad judgment. Contrariwise, the second image makes our past into the origin of all that is present, and paints our future as an heir of the third generation, destined to inherit just what the past lets the present hand down to it. This picture tends to confirm our faith in the continuity and meaning of our lives and traditions, for it makes it seem that the past coheres in the present; on the other hand, it also supports the suspicion we sometimes have that, when all is said and done, our lives will have consisted in merely plodding and deepening the rut in which history threw us at birth and sustained us in life.

We are obsessed with each of the foregoing pictures (let's call them *freedom* and *necessity*) at different times and with varying degrees of intensity. But in truth they are only pictures: *mental images drifting through the now-time*. The idea that I want to get across is roughly this: no one would say it is a serious limitation on our freedom that we are unable to step twice into a river that an artist has painted on a bit of canvas, despite the fact that Heraclitus famously said that 'it is not possible to step twice into the same river' (Heraclitus 1987: 55). Apart from stamping on the picture, it is not clear what it would look like for us even to *try* to step, even once, into a painted river. If this is so, why should we rue it as a loss that we are not free to step twice? I will therefore not attempt to 'solve' the contradiction between freedom and necessity here. In the interest of our journey, I will only point out that the question 'Why ask why?' is meant to draw attention to the possibility of going beyond the contradiction to the beginning – to the time *before* the contradiction arises in our minds.

The principle of rendering reasons

Having completed the foregoing brief survey of the principle of reason, the time has come to turn our attention to the ubiquitous human practice of demanding and rendering reasons in language. This self-conscious turn from the realm of reasons as such to the realm of language ('reasons') allows us to notice that the principle of reason has an essential corollary, namely, what Leibniz called the *principium reddendae rationis* (the principle of rendering reasons): *quod omnis veritas reddi ratio potest* (for every truth a reason can be rendered) (Heidegger 1996b: 22). If a statement holds itself out as true, then the principle of rendering reasons requires a sufficient explanation of why the statement is true. Under this conception of the way humans relate to truth, men and women become the beings who render reasons for their assertions: for every truth it claims the faculty of reason must be prepared to render a reason. Applying all of this to the various problems of transcendence that we have already identified, the *principle of reason* says that if epistemological, ontological, and theological transcendence are possible, then they must have one or more reasons; while the *principle of rendering reasons* says that no account of transcendence can be true unless it is able to put these reasons into words.

The notion that one proposition 'follows' from another proposition according to certain symbols and rules for their transformation is a special case of the principles of reason and of rendering reasons. Taking '$A \Rightarrow B$' to express an analytic or synthetic *a priori* truth, for example, the notion of 'following' makes it seem as though an eternal metaphysical arrow connected the symbols 'A' and 'B', instead of this or that *particular* human thought in the now-time. The utility and sheer reproducibility of analytic and synthetic *a priori* truths (the propositions of mathematics, for example) lead certain people to believe that such an arrow *must* be located between A and B, perhaps somewhere in the Platonic ether, or that at the very least the laws of logic correctly describe what Husserl called the 'physics of thinking' (Derrida 2003: 36). If pressed on the point, these people will argue something like a proof by negation and contradiction: if neither of these conclusions are true (they will say), then necessary truths could not be so damned *right* all the time (which they apparently are), and these truths would not appear to be the same to everyone (which they apparently do).

One of the West's most brilliant criticisms of this way of thinking about logical necessity takes the form of a thought experiment that Derrida performed against Edmund Husserl's effort to provide a secure foundation for the truths of geometry (Derrida 1989: 93–107). The example that Derrida chose is perfect, for what could be more necessary and more universal than the proofs of Euclid and Hilbert? Husserl wanted to save the internal history of geometric truth from 'all sensible aggression', as Derrida put it. He therefore could not situate its ideal truth in the various minds and tangible custodial signs that have preserved it over the many centuries since the first geometer thought of it and put it down on paper. For as Derrida famously argued, if one imagines that geometry's metaphysical truth depends on a custodian, then a worldly catastrophe of signs – a universal apocalypse of libraries and memories – would necessarily destroy geometry's ideality, and with that its claim to eternal validity. In brief, without any minds and symbols to 'contain' it, there would be no more geometry. Against this unthinkable loss of geometry's objective truth, Husserl took a step that is most unusual, to say the least, for any philosopher who aspires to stay rigorously within the phenomenal realm of 'things themselves' (to paraphrase Husserl's famous *dictum* about the task of phenomenology). He imagined geometry as a cultural ideality that is not 'bound' to any particular historical consciousness or symbolic representation – a sort of hazily pure ideality with eidetic independence that nonetheless possesses the peculiar property of historical 'reactivatability' (Derrida 1989: 166). Although Derrida did not put it this way, it is obvious that Husserl's account of geometry's truth finds its most basic motivation in obsession with Leibniz's 'principle of rendering reasons'. That is, since geometry *is* undeniably true (B), there must be some ground that *makes* it true (A), even if this ground has to be made up out of thin air. It is almost as if, for Husserl and thinkers like him, a dubious or incomprehensible ground in the air is better than no ground at all.

The kind of question that Derrida's critique of Husserl raises – 'Would two plus two equal four if no one were around to think it?' – is like the question 'Does a tree falling in the forest make a sound if no one is around to hear it?' Considered as Western pseudo-koans about the nature of truth, questions such as these are meant to move thinking *beyond* a simple yes or no answer and into the possibility of a primordial engagement with the nature of language. Heidegger gave one type of 'transcending' answer when he reformulated the idea of truth from the correctness of a proposition into the act of unconcealment. On this view, the proposition '*p*' is not true because *p* is the case; rather, it is only because we *say* '*p*' that *p* itself can be uncovered in its truth. Heidegger indicates the basic thrust of his radical rethinking of the nature of truth in the following passage from *Being and Time*:

> Newton's laws, the principle of contradiction, any truth whatever – these are true only as long as Dasein [human being-in-the-world] *is*. Before there was any Dasein there was no truth; nor will there be any after Dasein is no more. For in such a case truth as disclosedness, uncovering, and uncoveredness, *cannot* be. (Heidegger 1962: 269) (emphasis in original).

It almost goes without saying that the willingness of thinkers such as Heidegger and Derrida to question the 'obvious' truths of logic has had the profoundest sort of impact on postmodern thought. For present purposes, however, the most important thing to notice about their thinking is that it clears the way for a more radical criticism of the tendency to cling obsessively to the logical form 'A ⇒ B' in *all* of its forms. From the standpoint of Zen, one might even say that Heidegger's and Derrida's most precious legacy is to have shown that the fetish for explanation is just that: a fetish over which we have control, as opposed to an irremissible fact of human nature.

Although it may sound shocking for me to say it, as far as this book's critique of logical transcendence is concerned there is no *fundamental* difference between the passage that Derrida made from the A of deconstruction to the B of justice when he thought '*Deconstruction is justice*' (1990: 945), and the passage that the mathematician Andrew Wiles made when he went from the A of the Taniyama-Shimura conjecture to the B of his proof of Fermat's Last Theorem (Singh 1997). To be sure, it is undeniable that virtually all trained mathematicians would accept Wiles's proof of Fermat's Theorem as true, whereas many philosophers would hotly dispute Derrida's identification of deconstruction with justice. But these are merely interesting anthropological findings that have no relevance to our present journey. The only proper philosophical response to this kind of observation is to say *so what?* One cannot think about philosophy philosophically by conducting a poll.

Attachment to logical transcendence

In *Beyond Good and Evil*, Nietzsche compares Kant's account of how synthetic *a priori* judgments are possible with Molière's satire of a learned doctor who tries to explain how opium induces sleep. In Molière's play, the doctor argues that opium induces sleep 'by means of a means', namely, the *virtus dormitiva* (the power of inducing sleep). But the power of inducing sleep is not some*thing* that the doctor previously looked for and found inside the various chemical properties of opium. Rather, the *virtus dormitiva* is a question-begging appeal to a mere form of words that would fill in the space of 'A' in the formula A ⇒ B. Nietzsche's intuitive grasp of this basic point comes out in a series of rhetorical questions that he offers to show why answers like the doctor's *'belong in the realm of comedy'* rather than in philosophy: *'But what is that – an answer? An explanation? Or is it rather merely a repetition of the question?'* (1954: 392).

Nietzsche realised that Kant's answer to the question of how synthetic *a priori* judgments are possible comes down to exactly the same kind of question-begging appeal to an empty 'A' that would lead, at least on paper, to the B of these judgments being true prior to all experience. Kant's claim that synthetic *a priori* judgments happen by means of the faculty of understanding is the same as saying that they happen 'by means of a means', as Nietzsche puts it. Elsewhere in the same text, Nietzsche comes close to playing the role of a Zen master when he says: *'it is we alone who have devised cause, sequence, reciprocity, relativity, constraint, number, law, freedom, motive, and purpose; and when we interpret and intermix this symbol-world as "being in itself", with things, we act once more as we have always acted – mythologically'* (1954: 404).[21] Nietzsche realised that Kant was moved by attachment to a mere *norm of representation* to find an A to account for the B of synthetic *a priori* truths, and, if one could not be found, to invent it by hook or by crook. But one does not find something called a 'faculty' by performing a phenomenology of judgment – one finds only the concrete process of this or that particular judgment itself (more on this in Chapter 3). Unable to *find* a faculty in the brain or the mind in any normal sense of the word 'find', Kant therefore had to invent the 'faculty' and 'categories' of understanding (A) to explain how synthetic *a priori* truths (B) are possible. In other words, Kant thought that the faculty and categories of understanding simply *had to be there* in order to explain what he *was* able to observe (the expression of synthetic *a priori* truths). He failed to see that a foundation that is made entirely out of words and images supports no weight. Nietzsche did see this, and that is why he said that *'synthetic judgments a priori should not "be possible" at all; we have no right to them; in our mouths they are nothing but false judgments'* (Nietzsche 1954: 393).

Belief in the necessary truth that *every* end state or term must have a beginning state or term that leads to it belongs to an order that is at once more abstract and more corrosive than belief in the necessity of any *particular* truth, such as two plus two equalling four. Since the abstract norm $A \Rightarrow B$ precedes all particular manifestations of it, we even come to experience this empty norm *as such* in the form of a meta-truth that we also cannot get around. The felt necessity of the norm $A \Rightarrow B$ blocks our ability to think and experience a theme in any way other than in terms of

21 Compare the Buddha's comparison of the fleeting world of appearance to *'a star at dawn, a bubble in a stream, a flash of lightning in a summer cloud, a flickering lamp, a phantom, and a dream'* (Schiller 1994: 285).

a passage from one thing to another thing, however the two terms of the passage may be determined. Wittgenstein used a clever simile to uncover this phenomenon of blockage when he wrote that *'people who are constantly asking "why" are like tourists who stand in front of a building reading Baedeker and are so busy reading the history of its construction, etc, that they are prevented from seeing the building'* (Wittgenstein 1980: 40e). We will return in Chapter 4 to Wittgenstein's war on the kind of windy nonsense that philosophers like Kant produce when they ask 'Why?', and then follow norms of representation like 'A ⇒ B' into the swamps of metaphysics. The point I want to make now, however, is best illustrated by a wicked little story that Gail Machlis tells in a cartoon entitled 'Quality Time'. She depicts an outdoor scene in which a small boy and his father are looking at the moon. The boy says excitedly to his father, 'Daddy! Look how beautiful the moon is!' To this the boy's father ponderously replies: 'That's a quarter moon, son, it's waxing. That means it's getting bigger. Waning is when it gets smaller after a full moon. It's called a gibbous moon when it's almost full. The phases of the moon influence the tides, too. You see the moon orbits the earth at a speed ...' (Wolcher 1995: 1803). One might say that there are two basic morals of this story: first, it is only the boy who really *sees* the moon; and, secondly, his why-obsessed father is nonetheless trying very hard to teach him how *not* to see it.

The feeling that the norm of representation 'A ⇒ B' is *itself* a necessity – a necessity of necessities, as it were – is a great unifier. It brings together such contending intellectual positions as creationism and evolutionary theory, astronomy and astrology, conventional religion and science, globalism and anti-globalism, and Platonism and conventionalism, for every one of these ways of accounting for the world is precisely that: a way of *accounting* (in the now-time) for the world (B) in terms of an antecedent A that is felt to lead to it in the manner of a cause or a ground. I will therefore add a fourth category to our taxonomy of transcendence, and to emphasise its purely phenomenal character I will call it *logical transcendence* rather than 'the principle of reason'. As I said earlier, the question 'Why ask why?' brings the *phenomenon* (not the rule!) of logical transcendence into view. A why-obsessed subjectivity does not constitute logical transcendence so much as fall prey to it, as one of the ways the mind deals with the suffering of uncertainty. I allege that this form of transcendence, logical transcendence, is the most important of them all.

How is logical transcendence the most important form of transcendence? For one thing, the shelves of philosophy libraries are filled with many tomes about epistemological, ontological, and theological transcendence, but hardly anyone has ever noticed that without logical transcendence there would be no books explaining or criticising any other form of transcendence. This is because all *explanations* of transcendence enfold what they explain within the norm of transcendence itself. They take the form A1 ⇒ B1, where A1 is the cause, ground, or origin that leads to B1, identified as epistemological, ontological, or theological transcendence itself (A2 ⇒ B2). Or, to express the same point more simply in order to highlight the circularity (if not the vacuity) of the process of accounting for transcendence, the explanation of why there is transcendence always presupposes transcendence, presupposes precisely what it is supposed to explain. One could say with some justification that the formal structure of logical transcendence, A ⇒ B, is the very form of all explanatory structures, or, if you will, of any thinking that feels itself entitled by one idea to make the passage to another.

I am aware that to criticise attachment to logical transcendence because it 'leads to' illusions and suffering is self-contradictory: such a critique implicitly relies on A ⇒ B in order to challenge A ⇒ B. Well, so what? What a contradiction *says* (or shows) is never the same as the *saying* of it, and its usefulness as an expedient means has nothing to do with its logical content. In the *Diamond Sutra*, for example, the Buddha says that beings are not beings, and that is why they are called 'beings' (Pine 2001: 22). This statement, and many others like it in the Buddhist canon, takes the form of a contradiction ('*p* and not-*p*'). But the Zen answer to those who like their philosophy pure and without any taint of contradiction comes from Wang Jih-hsiu (d 1173), a Confucian scholar who interpreted the Buddha's self-contradictory statements in the *Diamond Sutra* as follows:

> If he didn't bring it up [*p*] up, there would be no means of understanding the truth. It would be like trying to cross a river without using a raft. And if he didn't negate it [not-*p*], people might cling to his teaching. This would be like reaching the far shore and not disembarking but staying on the raft. This is why he has to bring it up and why he has to negate it as well. (Pine 2001: 374)

I therefore confess it without apology: when I say that attachment to logical transcendence (A) leads (⇒) us astray (B), I am contradicting myself. But if the idea of logical transcendence is a sword that never stops wounding those who cling to it, then perhaps there is a way to wield this sword *without* attachment, and thereby to heal the very wounds that it has inflicted.

Attachment to the norm of logical transcendence is everywhere. Psychologism's claim that laws of logic (B) have a subjective origin in historical acts of consciousness or universal mental structures (A) occurs by means of logical transcendence, as does logicism's passage from the mind's construction of the laws of logic (A) to its claim that they have absolute objective validity (B). As one of the laws of logic, the principle of founding in general (A ⇒ B) is thus 'founded' on an act, structure, or construction that cannot itself be founded or understood without the assistance of the very principle that it founds. Logical transcendence would seem to be an effect that constitutes the sense of its own cause – a constituted that at the same time constitutes the very meaning of 'constituting'. In short, one could say that as an *idea* (as opposed to a phenomenon) logical transcendence is pre-original, and it cannot fall into the realm of the opposition between originating and originated without absurdity or aporia. But if, as Levinas said, taking the principles of method for affirmations about the foundation of things is the act of '*hasty simple minds*' (2003a: 59), then the ultimate act of hastiness and simple-mindedness would be to naturalise the principle of founding as such, A ⇒ B, by taking it for its own foundation.

That the questionability of logical transcendence should occur to a law professor is no surprise. In legal realism's early attacks on formalism – the belief that legal rules somehow determine their own applications – and in the continuation of that attack through countless deconstructions and demonstrations of legal indeterminacy by critical legal scholars over the past 30 years, one can detect the nascent possibility of a far more fundamental questioning of logical transcendence as such. For the *modus ponens*, which is widely recognised to be the form of all applications of legal rules, is but a special case of logical transcendence. That is, the expression '*If A then B. A. Therefore B*' is simply another way of saying this: 'There is this legal rule, "If A then B", and there is this fact, A, and the two of them together require me to say and do B'. If rule and fact are taken together to form a more primordial 'A', therefore, the logical form of the principle of reason and the principle of rendering reasons is also the logical form of legal formalism: A ⇒ B. In other words, legal formalism boils down to saying that given the relevant legal rules and the facts of a particular case (A) the legal conclusion (B) follows (⇒) axiomatically.

As legal realism and critical legal theory have attempted to show again and again, legal formalism not only slides over the way 'facts' get determined, it also ignores the fact that the law is no more subject to a super-law that would guarantee its own correct application than the laws of logic are subject to the laws of logic. Formalism determines the 'Rule of Law' as the door of a law that leads people to the right place by virtue of its own magical properties. If an operation is defined as the transition from one term to the next one in a series of forms, formalism is incapable of thinking the operation as such in any terms other than 'true' and 'false'. Formalism ignores the breathless tumble that takes us from term to term, and thus it cannot experience or be aware of the *transition* from A to B for what it shows itself to be phenomenally: namely, a passage that thought does not actively think so much as passively let happen or, as is sometimes the case, *cling to* with all the white-knuckled desperation of someone holding on to his seat during a roller coaster ride.

The foregoing merely deconstructive reflections on logical transcendence prompt me to make an utterly bald and (of course) unsupported assertion. This assertion can be redeemed, if at all, only in the course of the next three chapters, as we examine the particular manifestations of attachment to logical transcendence that are displayed in the thinking of Heidegger, Levinas and Wittgenstein. Here it is: *all accounts of transcendence are false idols; they are impediments, rather than solutions, to the problems of life whenever we think too highly of them.* The term 'false idols' should not be read to imply that there is a true idol of transcendence out there somewhere. Rather, it is simply a metaphor or turning phrase aimed at bringing into view the possibility of letting go of all attachment to the image of transcendence.

Let me illustrate this possibility with a short koan. A man called Lu Geng had raised a gosling to maturity inside a bottle, and now that it was too large to come out through the opening, he asked Nanquan (748–834) how to get it out without damaging the bottle or injuring the goose. Nanquan immediately replied, *'It's out'*, and upon hearing the master's exclamation, the koan says that Lu Geng was finally awakened (Cleary 1998: 90). Even if one wants to get a real goose out of a real bottle, this does not mean that it is necessary to let the *language* and *images* of causes and grounds control one's mind. The example of Lu Geng's enlightenment shows that we can let go of attachment to the image 'A ⇒ B' any time we want, without prejudice either to the goose or to the bottle. To change metaphors ever so slightly, the real task, as Wittgenstein put it, is to show the fly of the mind the way out of the fly-bottle (1953: 103e).

Plato's Paper Cave

Language, like a magician, has the power to summon up images that bewitch. This is not Plato's old point that the way things seem to be is not the way they really are, for the images that language paints continue to bewitch us even when we say sincerely and truthfully that appearances match reality. In such cases the images prevent us from seeing that a thing can be *merely* true – true, in other words, but only just as far as we are willing to let the word 'true' take us. A merely true statement is one that we are able to treat as utterly ordinary and mundane, no more and no less. Such a statement is one that is received without attachment to the conceit that there is a duality between the real and the conventional.

Plato's allegory of the cave would be just right if it said that both the cave of seeming and the external sunlit world of being were drawn by the cave-dwellers themselves on big sheets of paper, but that they had forgotten this fact. In short, the images that language makes in every domain that it touches are so powerful that they lead us to think and say with great conviction that the way things are, or the way they must be, is the same as the way they are depicted in the images. Images that are widely shared, like $A \Rightarrow B$, increase in power by virtue of their ubiquity: they come to resemble the kind of icons that are reproduced in quantity for display in the homes of the faithful. Yeats had a useful name for these, *Spiritus Mundi*, which he defined as 'a general storehouse of images which have ceased to be the property of any personality or spirit' (1983: 493).

The entire condition of postmodern thought can be traced to a conflict of images in our *Spiritus Mundi*. Postmodern, post-structuralist, and post-colonial thought all militantly reject the traditional Western claim that universal truth and values are possible, thus elevating the words 'universal truth' to the status of a potent enemy. Likewise, those who oppose contextualism and relativism say that these ways of thinking yield no grounds for progress, or for condemning historical outrages, thus conceding the power of the critics' relativistic words to subvert truth and morality. What is Satan to one is God to the other. What the one screams is impossible the other shouts back is not only possible, but real. What the one praises as scholarship the other decries as self-indulgence or apology. What the one says is philosophy the other belittles as undisciplined prattle or arid triviality. Remaining completely unexamined amidst all these salvos back-and-forth on the theme of universal truth versus universal relativism is the tendency we have to cling to the illusions that our desperate minds create because of our love affair with language.

Thus it comes to pass that many of us (myself included) have substituted the negative image of grounded truth's impossibility for what we take to be the erroneous positive image of its possibility. This substitution is not *merely* a tactic or expedient means for struggling with the arrogance of a power that makes its own point of view the standard for point-of-viewlessness.[22] Whether we are exercising power or resisting it, we actually believe our own stuff – we believe in the superior insight of our tactics. We are like silkworms, as the *Lankavatara Sutra* puts it, continually spinning the thread of discrimination, wrapping ourselves and others in it, utterly charmed by the prison we have created (Van de Weyer 2000: 8/5). We keep failing to see beyond the new image that we

22 I borrowed this last phrase from Catherine MacKinnon (1983).

have made – the image that enchants us *now*. Lao-tzu, as if presaging Hegel's theory that the history of Spirit is the ongoing dialectical sublation of all thought that went before, said in the *Tao Te Ching* that those who are attached to learning and knowing *gain* something every day (Cleary 1999: I, 31). But as good as learning and knowing are, they are not the only thing, which is why Lao-tzu said that those who seek the Way *lose* something every day. Perhaps Lao-tzu is right. Perhaps we would do better to lose something every day – indeed, to lose and to lose until there is nothing left for us to believe in or cling to, not even our own lack of belief.

Chapter 2: Heidegger's Groundless Ground

First Things First

Martin Heidegger thought more deeply about the problems of *ground* and *grounding* than just about any other thinker in the history of Western philosophy. In this chapter, we will continue our effort to understand the phenomenon of attachment to logical transcendence by investigating Heidegger's thinking on the primordial relation between a ground and what it grounds. A ground should not be confused with a cause. Today's cause is also yesterday's effect: in the endless chain of causes and effects that we call the causal nexus, causes produce effects, which then in turn become causes that produce more effects, and so on *ad infinitum*. As Hegel says, this endless progression would be meaningless were it not for the idea of reciprocity, in which the movement from causes to effects, and effects to causes, bends back on itself, transforming the infinite progression into a self-contained relationship of 'one cause and another, and their connection with one another' (Hegel 1975: 217–18). Moreover, since a cause (as substance) suspends itself in its effect, and only rises by virtue of this operation into independent existence *as* a cause, there is always just *one* cause, properly speaking, in the causes that are spoken of as two. Ground and grounded in Heidegger's sense are not at all like this. A ground never suspends its separate identity by virtue of its relation to something else. A ground not only has no ground beneath it, it also does not relate to that which it grounds through anything like the reciprocal mechanism of action and reaction. The harder you try to trap a ground by running it down to *its* supposed ground, the more it recedes from you. One might therefore say, as Heidegger does, that a ground's most essential 'predicate', as it were, is its sheer '*groundlessness*' (1985: 170).

We will have occasion soon to elaborate on the meaning of this important distinction between a ground and a cause. Right now, however, we need to focus on the simplest and most basic aspect of the phenomenon of grounding: to say that an entity is grounded is to say that it is founded, based, and set up on something other than itself, namely, its ground. The English word 'ground', like the equivalent

German term *grund*, comes from the Old High German noun *grunt*, meaning 'coarse sand, sandy soil, earth' (Inwood 1999: 82). As this etymology suggests, perhaps the most obvious metaphor for the formal relation between ground and grounded is the way the earth underlies and supports all of the many beings that dwell upon it. While it may sound as though I am belabouring the obvious, this simple metaphor indicates a fundamental truth about grounding: grounded beings must, first and foremost, have a relation of otherness to their ground. That is, they must stand in a relation to something that is not the same as they are: *something else*.

The ground as archē

The key term for understanding Heidegger's interpretation of the relation between ground and grounded is the Greek word *archē*, which is usually translated as origin, beginning, or first principle (Heidegger 1985: 181). Heidegger notes that the following fragment, attributed to Anaximander, is the first recorded Western attempt to give a distinctly *philosophical* meaning to the notion of a primal origin:

> Whence things have their origin [*archē*], there they must also pass away according to necessity; for they must pay penalty and be judged for their injustice [*adikia*], according to the ordinance of time. (Heidegger 1975a: 13)

Beyond simply quoting Anaximander, how does one even begin to describe an origin, an *archē*, in Heidegger's sense of the term? To begin with, please notice that things (beings) come *out* of Anaximander's *archē*, and go back *into* it, but that they do not appear to stand on the same level *with* the *archē* while they are in the process of producing injustice. Heidegger uses the phrase 'out of joint' to translate the Greek word *adikia*, whereas most translations, including the one shown above, use the juridical term 'injustice'. When *adikia* holds sway, Heidegger says, the world is out of joint in the sense that 'all is not right with things' (1975a: 41). Thus, the fragment appears to say that *beings* (but not the *archē* itself) are responsible for 'their' *adikia*, since they and they alone will be judged and pay penalty for it. Responsibility and judgment belong to the order of causation: beings that must pay penalty for their *adikia* presumably have caused things to be out of joint. Since the *archē* does not appear to stand *together with* these *adikia*-producing beings, it is at least plausible to say that the idea of *archē* is not the same as the idea of a cause. On this reading, an origin in Anaximander's sense would neither be subject to the law of causation, nor benefit from it, because an origin is not itself a being that functions in, or even through, the workings of the world.

The metaphysics of a highest being

This rather brief and admittedly inelegant interpretation of Anaximander's fragment is loosely based on Heidegger's, and it is consistent with what we know about pre-Socratic thought. Nevertheless, post-Hellenic philosophers managed to ignore and then forget the possibility of thinking and speaking in this manner about the concept of origin, which is one of the main reasons why it sounds so odd to modern ears. Although Heidegger claims that the historical process of forgetting the pre-Socratic meaning of *archē* actually began with Plato, a level of profound amnesia was reached only after the advent of Christianity. To be sure, Aristotle spoke of a 'first cause'. But beholden from the outset to Christian dogma, medieval metaphysicians radically transformed Anaximander's seemingly impersonal and non-causal origin into the altogether different image of 'God the Creator'. Now creation is a kind of production: it is a causal force that comes to an end once the created being has been produced. How then does one account for the ongoing temporal continuity of beings? Metaphysics could not simply postulate the existence of a historically distant single act of creation, for this would not have explained the world's continuing *persistence* in being. So Western philosophy after the Greeks transformed itself into what Heidegger calls *onto-theology*: for nearly 2,000 years philosophers attributed the past, present, and future existence of the world to God conceived as the highest being – a kind of Big Guy in the Sky who causes all of the other beings in the world to persist in being by means of an indefatigable and never-ending act of creation. The West gradually forgot the possibility that *archē* might mean or refer to an origin that gives rise to beings in a manner that is before and beyond all merely causal relations. Instead, the idea of a primal origin hardened into the rigid form of what Schelling called *creatio continua*: continuous creation by a 'highest being' (Heidegger 1985: 71).

By the end of the 19th century, the philosophical respectability of imputing everything to God-the-creator had been severely compromised by a number of developments in metaphysics. The rise of the 'subject', in the form of Descartes's *ego cogito*, had deflected attention away from God by making the subject/object relation into the centre of all serious philosophical inquiry (witness Kant and German Idealism). Likewise, the Enlightenment's strong emphasis on human reason over religious faith, and scientific inquiry over obedience to authority (including Christian doctrine), had greatly diminished the interest of philosophers in continuing to obsess about God's metaphysical status. Then Hegel's revolutionary double transformation of metaphysics put God on notice that his job was becoming redundant. Hegel brought philosophy down to earth by making it into the dialectical study of history, and he transformed the subject/object relation into the idea of Spirit. At the time, these developments seemed to have largely de-theologised metaphysical thought by dissolving all that is philosophically important about the world into the category of absolute knowledge.

Nevertheless, Hegel still retained God as a category, even if He was conceived in a rather pantheistical sort of way. God as the universal, God as unity abiding absolutely in itself: however abstract and insipid this Hegelian God seemed to be when compared to his mighty medieval Self, He was not yet dead, and He still managed to cast at least a weak shadow on philosophy. It took Nietzsche's radical announcement that God really *is* dead to finally administer the *coup de grâce* to the ancient deistic tradition in metaphysics. Having already been diminished by medieval Christianity to the level of a mere cause (*causa efficiens*), by the late 19th century God had been further reduced from the status of a self-evident truth to the status of a 'value' that individual human beings could choose to accept or reject, as they preferred. As Heidegger puts it, Nietzsche demonstrated that the 'heaviest blow against God is not that God is held to be unknowable, not that God's existence is demonstrated to be unprovable, but rather that *the god held to be real is elevated to the highest value*' (1977: 105). If God is only a value, this means His existence depends not on himself, but rather on human beings and their choices: the ground had become the grounded.

By uncovering the fact that modernity had made God-the-creator into a mere human value rather than an absolute and unquestioned truth, Nietzsche's thought set the stage for the emergence of a purely secular and impersonal interpretation of the origin of beings, which in his case became the justly famous concept of will-to-power (*der Wille zur Macht*). Will-to-power imputed the origin of beings to manifold individual centres of force, each one of which always yearns for *more*, and each one of which implements its yearning by *creating* (causing) its world through the imposition of values on the otherwise chaotic flux of becoming: '*To impose upon becoming the character of being – that is the supreme will to power*' (Nietzsche 1968: 330). In Nietzsche's philosophy, will-to-power in the form of the *Übermensch* replaced Hegelian Spirit, and art replaced knowledge as the highest value. However liberating the concept of will-to-power was, though, at its core will-to-power itself was still a kind of *being*. In other words, Nietzsche's way of thinking was still hung up, as it were, on the category of a 'highest being', even if that being did seem rather small and powerless when compared with the image of God that the medieval Christian incarnation of will-to-power had constructed for itself. Nietzsche removed God from the altar that the old metaphysics had reserved for the image of the 'highest being', but instead of smashing the altar, he fell into the metaphysical trap of simply replacing God with the image of yet another highest being: will-to-power.

This cursory sketch of Nietzsche's philosophy of will-to-power shows why Heidegger interpreted it as no less than the end or final consummation of metaphysics: after Nietzsche, metaphysics had nowhere left to turn if it wanted to persist in explaining the origin of beings by appealing to the idea of a highest being – it had already *'gone through the sphere of prefigured possibilities'* (2003a: 95). If man made God, rather than the other way around, then the human being could no longer reasonably be viewed as a mere created thing (*ens creatum*) endowed with a 'soul'. Instead, the individual human being became someone who is constantly creating himself, and the rather bleak prospect of the eternal recurrence of the same became his sole source of meaning and comfort. Picking up where Nietzsche left off, Heidegger believed that he alone was able to take the additional (and final) step of unlinking origination from the mechanism of creation-through-causation, and relinking it to the nearly forgotten resonance of the Greek idea of primal origin. It fell to Heidegger to rediscover the distinct possibility of thinking about a kind of origination that does not depend on the categories of causation and a highest being. Although Nietzsche also knew and admired pre-Socratic philosophy, Heidegger took that philosophy in a direction that was radically new precisely because he felt that he had rediscovered what was genuinely old. Radically reinterpreting pre-Socratic fragments from thinkers such as Anaximander, Heraclitus and Parmenides, Heidegger went forth to construe the concept of ground in terms of his new/old understanding of *archē*, conceived of as primal origin. On this view, a ground is no mere being, like God or will-to-power; nor does it manifest itself as a causal force 'in' the world. For Heidegger, a ground is *something else*, and it works *another way*.

The ground as 'something else'

The thought of a ground, as *archē*, standing in relation to what it grounds is an important form of what the previous chapter called *logical transcendence*. A ground is the A, and the grounded is the B, in the movement of thought symbolised as 'A ⇒ B'. In the context of this chapter, the A ⇒ B of logical transcendence is meant to signify the relation of grounding that the real historical person called Martin Heidegger thought whenever he contemplated two distinct, but interrelated, pairings of A and B: being as the ground of beings, and human freedom as the ground of grounding. As for the latter pair, Heidegger consistently conceived of freedom as no less than the ungrounded ground (A) of the event of grounding (B) itself: freedom is the originary capacity to assume its possibilities as grounds, both *as* ourselves (self-creation) and *for* ourselves (self-determination). But freedom does not just *give* ground; there is also a sense in which it *takes* ground (1998: 126). Finding itself thrown (*geworfen*) into the world from the very beginning, it is possible for freedom to recognise that it is in thrall or beholden to something 'bigger', so to speak, than itself. On this view, philosophy is the apotheosis of human freedom, for it is the event of thinking the one ground on which *everything* depends – including, paradoxically, freedom itself.

Heidegger believed that '*to philosophise is to exist from ground*' (1984: 221). He thus determined the essence of philosophy as freedom's fateful decision to exist in a certain manner – to exist in the manner of *going to ground*, as it were. To think about the grounded and only the grounded is to lose oneself in the 'giddy whirl' of beings and technology (2003a: 86). Ever disdainful of academic philosophy's tendency to wallow in the inessential by first stipulating and then following precise conceptual definitions of beings, Heidegger thought that true thinking must always let itself be determined by ... *something else*. It is easiest to see this 'something else' in Heidegger's work during the late 1920s, when he began calling the difference between being (as ground) and beings (as the grounded) the 'ontological difference' (*die ontologische Differenz*). Sometimes Heidegger coyly referred to the something else of being as '*what is to be thought*' (1991: I, 35). What is to be thought cannot be found in the officially certified canon of traditional philosophical 'problems'. Most of these problems are like last year's syllabus: fit only for framing the weekly topics of boring university seminars with titles like 'Epistemology' or 'Philosophy of Law'. Far beyond the arid survey of intellectual history that passes for philosophy in most academic settings, what is to be thought is none other than the ground of everything that is: that which, as the 'matter itself' (*die Sache selbst*), is philosophy's only authentic and proper theme.

Being as Ground

Without why

The apex of Heidegger's thinking about the relation between ground (as the 'matter itself') and grounded comes in *Der Satz vom Grund* (translated for publication as 'The Principle of Reason'), the text of an important and influential lecture course that he gave in 1955–56, at the University of Freiburg. The highest point of this already high point of thinking comes near the middle of the text, where Heidegger interprets a pair of verses written in 1657 by the German mystic Angelus Silesius.[1] These verses

---

1 The *nom de plume* of Johann Scheffler, a medical doctor who lived in Silesia from 1624 to 1677 (Heidegger 1996b: 35).

appear under the heading *Without Why* in a book of Silesius's spiritual poetry entitled *The Cherubic Wanderer: Sensual Description of the Fair Final Things* (Heidegger 1996b: 35). Here they are, in translation:

> *The rose is without why: it blooms because it blooms,*
> *It pays no attention to itself, asks not whether it is seen.*

According to Heidegger, these simple lines of poetry give thought the chance to think the innermost meaning of what formal logic calls the principle of sufficient reason. In German the principle of sufficient reason is called *der Satz vom Grund* ('the principle of ground'), and this difference in terminology is not insignificant. Although the meaning of the principle is ultimately the same in every language, thinking of it as the principle of *Grund* (ground) has the advantage of highlighting Heidegger's final argument that the principle's innermost meaning is none other than his idea of ground-as-*archē*. But I am letting us get too far ahead of ourselves. What makes Heidegger's meditations on Silesius's *Without Why* so compelling is the artful way he patiently lays the groundwork, so to speak, for the event of thinking the ultimate ground.

You will recall from Chapter 1 that Leibniz was the first Western philosopher to put the principle of reason into the explicit *form* of a principle: *Nihil est sine ratione cur potius sit quam non sit* (Nothing is without a reason why it exists rather than does not exist) (Heidegger 1984: 114). It is clear that the word 'reason' in this context does not refer to the *faculty* of reason. Rather, it seems to refer, at first blush at least, to the sort of reason that people expect to receive when they ask the question 'Why?' Hence, if we interpret the principle of reason in an everyday manner as *'nothing is without a why'*, or better still, *'everything has a why'*, then Silesius's verses appear to be saying that the principle of reason does not hold for the rose. Indeed, one could even go further and allege that these verses are irrational and obnoxious *violations* of the principle of reason: by denying the rose its proper and necessary 'why', the first verse contradicts a law of logic that Heidegger elsewhere calls even more primordial than the principle of non-contradiction (1984: 53).

Heidegger constructs the foregoing commonsensical (and hence allegedly naïve) interpretation of Angelus Silesius's *Without Why* as part of a calculated rhetorical strategy. He wants to refute this naïve interpretation decisively, and in doing so to valorise the principle of reason at a level that he thinks is much deeper than any possible conventional answer to the question 'Why?' To this end, Heidegger notices something very odd about the first verse: while it does indeed say that the 'rose is without *why*', it also says that the rose 'blooms *because* it blooms'. In ordinary speech, we normally respond to the question 'Why?' with a 'because' statement. The question 'Why does the rose bloom?', for example, might be met with the answer 'Because it was well fertilised'. This kind of response is *causal* in nature: it construes the question 'Why?' as seeking information about whether there is a relation of *production* between one being (in this case fertiliser) and another being (in this case the rose). But the first clause of the first verse of *Without Why* seems to deny any possibility of giving an answer of this sort, for it stipulates that the rose is *without* why. This leaves the word 'because' in the second clause hanging in the air, so to speak, bereft of any apparent connection or reference to the question 'Why?'

It would appear that the poet is asserting the rather puzzling thesis that the rose is *'without a why and yet not without a because'* (1996b: 36). He seems to be saying that the rose is without a why in both senses of the word 'why' that we discussed in Chapter 1: it could care less about having a *causal* reason for why it is blooming, and it could care less about having a *normative* reason (an 'ought') for why it is blooming. But if the rose itself is indifferent to why it blooms, this does not imply that the 'because' of its blooming has *no* relation to a ground. The 'Why?' *seeks* a ground; the 'because' *conveys* a ground. In this respect, at least, the two words do not completely overlap one another. Hence, Heidegger will ask his readers to consider a slyly worded and extremely radical question: *'Are the grounds that the "why" seeks and the grounds that the "because" conveys equivalent?'* (1996b: 36). This question implicitly links Heidegger's critique of the causally interpreted 'highest being' in metaphysics with his non-causal interpretation of the pre-Socratic meaning of *archē*. It opens up the possibility of thinking that the ground that seeking seeks is not always the same as the ground that conveying conveys.

The 'without why' forecloses any *seeking* of grounds on the part of the rose – a conclusion that is reinforced by the second verse, which points out that the rose *'pays no attention to itself'* and *'asks not whether it is seen'*. The meaning of 'without why' in Angelus Silesius's first verse thus becomes quite clear in light of the first part of the second verse: *'The rose is a rose without its having to pay any attention to itself'* (1996b: 37). Eerily (and probably unknowingly) echoing Gertrude Stein's famous line *'a rose is a rose is a rose'* (Bartlett 1980: 752), Heidegger notes that the rose itself is *absorbed* in blooming, which means that it has no room within it for being concerned with anything else, such as the causes and conditions of its blooming. Since the rose's attention to grounds does not insert itself between the rose's blooming and the grounds for its blooming, this implies that the rose *'does not need the ground of its blooming to be expressly rendered to it'* (1996b: 37). Of course, scientifically minded people are not like the rose in this respect, inasmuch as they are trained to ask and answer the question 'Why?' in terms of the causal nexus and its modern criterion of statistical probability. Be that as it may, however, it is doubtful that even the most dedicated scientist would assert that the rose *in itself* cares about its causes and conditions, even if it is also true that the rose needs them in order to bloom.

As my reference to the possibility of an obsessively 'why'-driven human scientific world view suggests, Heidegger reads Angelus Silesius's verses as implicitly distinguishing between the way roses and human beings relate to grounds. We humans are constantly glancing sidelong at what the world makes or requires of us. Indeed, even on those rare occasions when such an explicit sidelong glancing is absent, Heidegger says that *'we humans cannot come to be who we are without attending to the world that determines us'* (1996b: 37). In this sentence one hears an echo of *Being and Time*, written 30 years before the text of the lecture course that we are considering. In the phrase *'we humans cannot come to be who we are without attending to the world'* one can find a veiled reference to 'being-in-the-world' and 'thrownness' (*Geworfenheit*) as the most essential ontological determinations of the particular being that calls itself 'human' (*Dasein*).[2] Throughout his life, Heidegger reiterated (in one way or another) that self and world belong together in the *single* entity *Dasein*, and they should never be interpreted as *two* things, like subject and object.

It is important to understand that his emphasis on the 'founded' nature of all human comportment and discourse, including the practice of rendering of reasons for things like the blooming of a rose, is not sociological in nature. Modern sociological theory *explains* the entity called a 'human being' by appealing to the category of reciprocal causation: humans make society *and* society makes humans (Berger and Luckmann 1967). But the basic understanding of being that always lies in *Dasein*, from birth to death, expresses itself pre-ontologically and pre-theoretically, which is why Heidegger thinks that *'every science adheres only to the penultimate and must presuppose the ultimate first'* (1992a: 160). Heidegger's concept of *Dasein* is therefore an attempt to characterise the ultimate being of the human being in a way that is prior to any causal explanation.

Although Heidegger rejects the subject/object dichotomy by defining *Dasein* as the holistic unity of 'being-in-the-world', it is still the case that humans do not merely 'have' grounds in the same way that Silesius's rose has them. If, as the American Declaration of Independence says, 'all men are created equal', this does not imply that all beings are *originated* equal. From the Romans onward, the traditional Western determination of the human being has been *animal rationale* ('rational animal'). This

2 In *Being and Time*, Heidegger appropriated the German word for existence, *Dasein*, to refer to the existential determination of human beings – their 'howness'. As he said later, '*Dasein*' is simply a 'title for the Being of man' (1997c: 256).

concept is ambiguous, however, for the Latin word *'ratio'* (the root of *rationale*) can mean either the *faculty* of reason or a *rendered* reason. For this reason, among others, Heidegger always preferred to use Aristotle's definition of man, of which *animal rationale* is but a translation. According to Aristotle, the human being is *zoon logon echon*: the animal that is endowed with *logos*, the gift of speech. On this view, language is the means through which we comport ourselves towards beings in general: as *'resonant signification'*, says Heidegger, language is what *'roots us to our earth and transports and ties us to our world'* (1991: I, 145).

Heidegger observes that, as far as we know, the human being is the only kind of being that *renders reasons* for things, according to what we identified in Chapter 1 as the principle of rendering reasons. For Heidegger, this fact constitutes the most essential difference between roses and humans. Unlike human beings, he says, the rose is 'without a *reddere rationem*, a rendering of reasons, having to belong to its rose-being' (1996b: 37). The human being is 'world forming' (*weltbildend*): it has a world that it renders to itself and others in language. The rose, on the other hand, is at best 'poor in world' (*weltarm*), like an animal and, at worst, 'without world' (*weltlos*), like a rock. One might therefore say that the principle of reason holds *in the case* of the rose, as a human being glances at it and considers it, but that the principle of reason does not hold *for* the rose itself. This way of putting it also suggests the related thesis that human beings themselves cannot be fully understood if they are merely classified together with roses as a 'part of nature' (2002b: 154): for humans are the only beings that can ask and then answer the question 'Why?', just as they are the only beings that can construct systems of classification (eg, 'man *versus* nature') in the first place. Heidegger's firm distinction between roses and humans suggests the possibility that a hard kernel of 'logocentrism' (to use a much maligned word) may lie at the heart of Heidegger's desperate effort to think about being-in-the-world in a non-metaphysical way. I mean, if *Dasein* is the one being in the world that somehow has the 'why'-based norm of logical transcendence ('A $\Rightarrow$ B') hardwired into its essential nature, doesn't Heidegger's *Dasein* begin to look very much like Kant's transcendental subject?

We will return to this question later, when we confront the apparent contradiction in Heidegger's philosophy between being-as-ground and freedom-as-ground. For now, though, let us remain within the essential movement of Heidegger's thought about the principle of reason. The foregoing consideration of the main difference between roses and humans suggests that the stipulation *nothing is without reason* speaks in 'two different tonalities', as Heidegger puts it (1996b: 39). On the one hand, the principle of reason can be heard to say that *'nothing* is *without reason'*, thereby emphasising the fact that every being (including roses) necessarily has its 'why'-reason, in the sense of a cause, when considered from the standpoint of the one being who *asks* why, namely, the human being. But on the other hand, the principle of reason can also be heard to say that 'nothing *is* without *reason*', thus stressing the fact that every being (as an *existing* being) has a 'because', which is to say a kind of 'reason' that has nothing to do with causes and conditions. When heard in the first pitch, the principle of reason distinguishes roses from humans according to the criterion of whether or not they ask 'Why?' When heard in the second pitch, the principle of reason brings roses and humans together in the unity of beings-as-a-whole supported by a ground that is not itself a being: a ground conceived as an *archē*.

As for the first interpretation of the principle of reason, Heidegger articulates the most fundamental difference between roses and humans this way: 'Other earthly creatures indeed live because of reasons and causes, but never *according* to reasons' (1996b: 42) (emphasis in original). This way of putting it foreshadows what will shortly become a central concern of ours: the problem of human freedom, conceived of as the giving and the taking of grounds. As important as human freedom is, however, Heidegger thinks that even this reading does not reach the deepest level of 'what is to be thought' in Angelus Silesius's verses. There is more to *Without Why*, Heidegger says, than simply bringing the difference between roses and humans into relief. Although the second half of the first verse is apparently vacuous – 'it blooms because it blooms' – he thinks that this tautological phrase '*really says everything, namely, everything to say here, doing so in its particular manner of not-speaking*' (1996b: 43). If it were true that the only possible reasons consist of *represented* reasons, then the first verse would not have attempted to dissociate '*the rose is without why*' from '*it blooms because it blooms*'. That is because it is a matter of sound principle in the domain of represented reasons that every 'Why?' has a possible answer that takes the form '*because of X*'. But since *Without Why* does indeed sever the link between 'Why?' and 'because', this leads us to 'wonder' whether there can be '*some sort of reason which has been dissociated from every "why" and "because" and still be a reason*' (1996b: 43).

Being as such

If Silesius's rose is without a rendering of reasons, Heidegger tells us point blank that '*nevertheless, the rose is never without a ground*', for '*every being (as a being) has a reason*' in the sense of a 'because' that is not a 'why' (1996b: 37, 40). Heidegger calls this 'because' – this reason of all reasons – *being as such*, or *being as opposed to beings*. What does 'being as such' mean? Our previous interpretations of Anaximander's fragment and

Silesius's *Without Why* should have prepared us to recognise that being as such is not the same as *how* entities are: it is not merely the manner in which beings exist, which Heidegger sometimes calls their 'howness', or more often, the being of beings (*das Sein des Seiendes*). For example, Aristotle understood the being of beings as *appearance*, whereas metaphysics after Descartes has understood it as *appearance to a subject*. In neither case, however, did philosophical thought touch what Heidegger calls being as such. Nor should being as such be confused with the metaphysical categories 'essence' (*what* a being is) or 'existence' (*that* a being is), for Heidegger thinks that this distinction is itself grounded in being as such (2003a: 81). In a nutshell, Heidegger's being as such is nothing less than the *ultimate ground* that supports all of the other *mere grounds* that human freedom lays down, including the many different philosophical accounts of the being of beings that have been produced during the long history of Western metaphysics. Being as such is '*the simple, plain presence that is without why – the presence upon which everything rests, upon which everything depends*' (1996b: 127).

Always eager to distinguish his own thought from metaphysics, Heidegger remained constantly on the lookout for new ways to describe his beloved ultimate ground. Thus, he would say that being as such is the most thought-worthy – that it is the most simple – that it is always already manifesting itself (however diffidently) as the unconcealment of the ongoing presencing (*Anwesen*) of present beings – that it holds *itself* back so that all present beings can emerge as something rather than nothing – that we always already understand it, however hazily and unthematically, *before* we ever set out to encounter the world and the other beings that are in it. Heidegger thought that the decisive question of Western philosophy is '*What is this "Being" itself?*' (1991: I, 18). This question does *not* refer to the meaning, however sublime and uplifting, of this or that particular being or aggregation of beings. Rather, it refers to that which first gives (*es gibt*: 'it gives') time to space, and space to time, so that all of the world's many individual beings (including humans) can then pass their own time and occupy their own place. Beings are beings; being as such is something else. Although recognising the 'something else' of being as such in relation to beings would seem to be a simple enough accomplishment, in fact it is one of thought's most difficult tasks.

The example of earthly beings that are quite literally standing on the earth's ground provides an important clue for understanding why the problem of being as such is so difficult and elusive: although we do in fact stand on the earth, we normally do not *notice* that we stand on it. We take it for granted. Similarly, the problem of whether and how beings like pebbles, people and planets are grounded ordinarily remains invisible to us because most of the time we are unaware that there is or could be such a thing as a *ground of beings* in the first place. We tend to see only those of the world's beings that we care about – the ones that occupy and preoccupy us as we busily pursue our various projects. In *Being and Time*, Heidegger famously calls this aspect of the human situation 'care' (*Sorge*) (1962: 225). Among other things, care means that human beings spend most of their lives engrossed in the business of organising the mesmerising dance of present beings into what humans call their 'lifestyle' and 'career'. Care is like blinkers on a mule: it keeps our gaze focused on the immediate task ahead, leaving us little scope for wondering whether the beings we care about (including ourselves) are grounded in something bigger, something that is not itself a being. Care keeps our attention away from what Heidegger called 'the worthiest of all questions'. Even when we hear about this question, care leads us to scorn or belittle it as 'useless' and 'impractical'. Borrowing its particular form from Leibniz, in 1935 Heidegger puts this alleged *über*-question as follows: '*Why are there beings* [Seindes] *rather than nothing?*' (1959: 1).

Transcending representational thinking

To think this last question is to think being as ground. But in order to think being as ground, one must first get past care's most faithful and vigilant servant: what Heidegger calls *representational thinking*. According to Heidegger, this way of thinking makes people incapable of even experiencing, let alone thinking, being as such. In the act of representation, something is brought forth and contemplated – what the Greeks called a *noēton* – and this 'something' always takes the form of one or more particular beings. The mind of representational thinking firmly adheres to the belief that its symbolic representations stand for real beings, including concepts, in a manner that is analogous to the way an agent 'represents' his principal. That is, just as an agent has the legal power to bind his principal to a deal, so too representational thinking imagines that its symbols bind beings to the correctness of their idea. Interpreting truth as the certainty of a representation, representational thinking also imagines that a symbol represents in a slightly different sense: it makes the being to which it refers present again – re-*presents* it – in the form of a correct idea that is held in the mind of a self-certain subject. Merging Platonism with Cartesian subjectivism, this kind of grounding places the truth of beings on the ground of the *ego cogito*. It holds that human ideations (including the idea of 'God'), triggered or followed by utterances and splotches of ink on paper, are enough to keep the appearance of beings from falling into the abyss of non-being, and that no assistance in this task is required from anything as outlandish as Heidegger's 'being as such'.

Representational thinking only cares for and cultivates the beings that serve its needs and interests, all according to this or that theory, value, dogma or creed. To live this way is to forget the possibility that beings are grounded in something that is not itself a being. On Heidegger's view, one must renounce or let go of representational thinking – and especially what the amorphous and ubiquitous 'they' (*das Man*) think and believe – if one is ever to have a chance of penetrating the glitter of beings to the problem of the ultimate ground. 'Everyday language is a forgotten and therefore used-up poem', he once wrote, thus indicating his scepticism about the philosophical potential of categories drawn from everyday language (1975b: 215). Indeed, it would probably not be too strong to say that, at bottom, Heidegger abhorred all that is common and ordinary in everyday human discourse, despite his occasional protestations to the contrary.[3] Most of life is filled up with 'idle chatter' (*Gerede*), as he put it in *Being and Time*, which constitutes the kind of being of our everyday understanding and interpreting (1962: 211). The 'true', on the other hand, 'is not for every man but only for the strong' (1959: 133). Only the strong are capable of 'authentic discourse', whereas the average person is only fit to engage in 'mere babbling' (1959: 186). For Heidegger, the ground of what is grounded is accessible only to the kind of thinking that is not content to rest on the mere surface of things: the kind of thinking that is bold enough to risk going below everyday understanding to that which is truly primordial.

Accusing representational thinking of attempting to set up a puny and inadequate system of words and norms as a 'court of justice over being' (1959: 176, 179), Heidegger portrayed his own way of thinking as a '*step back from the thinking that merely represents – that is, explains – to the thinking that responds and recalls*' (1975b: 181). Thus, while his mature method of studying philosophy conceives of itself as taking a step *back* from the dominant academic practice of merely representing and theorising about beings, it also takes a step *into* what might be called the organic activity, or calling, of thinking *within*, *through*, and *as* being itself.

The principle of reason as an utterance of being

The activity of thinking being as such, in Heidegger's sense, is neither logical nor illogical in the conventional sense of these words. Rather, it is *pre*-logical. In *The Metaphysical Foundations of Logic*, the text of a 1928 lecture course, Heidegger attempts to refute the argument that logic, in

3 In *Being and Time*, for example, he takes pains to announce that the expression 'idle talk' (*Gerede*) 'is not to be used here in a "disparaging" signification' (1962: 211).

the sense of the rules of thought, is the foundation of all thinking. He notes that the *use* of rules in thinking, while inevitable, does not imply that the rules themselves are the *ground* of thinking, for otherwise one would be unable to think about logic itself (1984: 104). Although logical rules may be used to justify this or that decision in the ontical sphere, in the end the rules themselves need something else for *their* justification. As we have seen, Heidegger thought that this something else is being as such, conceived as *archē*. But of all the formal rules of thought – the laws of identity, non-contradiction, excluded middle, and so forth – Heidegger believed that there is one in particular that connects most intimately to the ground of being as such: the principle of reason. That is because Heidegger interpreted the principle of reason in almost military terms, as being's most important ally against the void. It is ultimately the *'principle of the primacy of something over nothing'* (1984: 114), he said, and it represents an *'insurrection against nothingness'* (2003a: 42).

How does this insurrection, this primacy of something over nothing, manifest itself? In the introduction to the fifth edition of *What is Metaphysics?*, written in 1949, Heidegger began to answer this question by thinking the relation between being and ground in terms of identity: *'Being and ground: the Same'* (1998: 278). This equation of being and ground reached its apogee at the end of *Der Satz vom Grund*, where Heidegger tied being as such explicitly to 'reason' (*'Grund'*) in the sense of the principle of reason, thus making the latter into an foundational utterance about being *as opposed* to beings: *'Nothing is without ground/reason. Being and ground/reason: the same'* (1996b: 113). In thinking about the meaning of these statements, it is important to understand Heidegger's philosophy of philosophical statements in general: he reads them as essentially utterances – deeds that were once performed in the now-time – rather than theories. Heidegger interpreted language as a way of disclosure: a 'way' in the sense of a pathway, as opposed to a mere means, or 'tool' (1992a: 67-69). Thus, he did not offer the foregoing utterances about the identity of ground and being as representational truths, that is, as signs which 'correspond' to their signified. It would be a mistake to think that Heidegger's statements identifying being with ground 'claim' that the linguistic sign 'ground' *stands for* being as such. Rather, he thought of his statements as freedom's unique way of *speaking being itself*, namely, by assuming being as such *as* the ultimate ground of all that is.

It is obvious, of course, that the principle of reason also makes a conventional statement about why, what, and how beings are. Indeed, in the form of the principle of causation it expresses the logical basis for all scientific inquiry. But that is not all that the principle of reason does, as Heidegger's reflections on *Without Why* attempt to demonstrate. He believed that 'reasons' in the sense of causes *'always refer merely to ontic [not ontological] relations'* (2001b: 109), whereas 'reason' in the sense of being as such belongs outside or beyond the sphere of beings and their relations to one another. Thus, Heidegger used the occasion of his reflections on Angelius Silesius's simple verses about the rose to show that there is a deeper level of 'reason' hidden within the principle of reason:

> The principle of reason says: *to being there belongs something like ground/reason. Being is akin to grounds, it is ground-like.* The sentence 'Being is ground-like' speaks quite differently than the statement 'beings have a reason'. 'Being is ground-like' thus in no way means 'being has a ground'; rather, it says: *being in itself essentially comes to be as grounding* [*Sein west in sich als gründendes*]. Of course the principle of reason does not say this explicitly. The content of the principle one immediately perceives leaves unsaid what the principle of reason says. What the principle of reason says does not come to language, namely, not to that language that corresponds to *that about which* the principle of reason speaks. *The principle of reason is an utterance [Sagen] of being.*(Heidegger 1996b: 49) (emphasis in original).

This passage represents a kind of spectacular *dénouement* to Heidegger's thought on the relation between being and ground. Philosophy in the form of freedom (in this case *Heidegger's* freedom) says that the statement *'Nothing is without reason'* utters being as such. But note that Heidegger did not simply stand up and say 'Nothing is without reason', and then sit down. *That* would have been a true utterance of being, by his standards. No, Heidegger said something else. He said that being as such (A) showed itself to him (B) *as* a ground (reason) within the meaning of the principle of reason. The above-quoted passage from *Der Satz vom Grund* therefore leaves a trace of something thought-worthy that is not itself being as such. The passage suggests that while Heidegger may have experienced the thought-worthy 'something' of being as such, he never experienced his *experience* of it in the form of a theme or problem. He never considered the possibility – however remote – that being as such, like the beings that it grounds, is the dangerous (and pitiable) *illusion* of an otherwise compelling and unmistakable self-showing: a mere consequence of the mind's craving attachment to the '$A \Rightarrow B$' of logical transcendence.

To be Capable of Failing

The theme of attachment to '$A \Rightarrow B$'

Despite all that I have already said about being as such and Heidegger's mode of access to it, it is important to understand that this chapter's assessment and critique of Heidegger's dependency on logical transcendence is not really directed at the contents of his conception of grounds and grounding. Far too much has been written about *what* Heidegger thought, and far too little about *how* he thought it. Moreover, quibbling about contents would leave the misleading impression that I possess a more excellent understanding of being and freedom, or that I think Heidegger's account is false. I do not. We are trying, of course, to think deeply about the substance of Heidegger's philosophy in this chapter, but this is only because we are primarily interested in uncovering something else: namely, *the event of his attachment to a mere image* – the image in which a ground, *any* ground, is depicted as an A that enduringly grounds (⇒) something else called the grounded (B).

This event of attachment is sometimes painfully visible in the way Heidegger expressed the reason why the question of being (*die Seinsfrage*) is a question in the first place. For example, since beings (B) do in fact come forth and emerge into appearance, '*something* [A] *must therefore be present letting the appearance emerge*' (1992a: 142). In this brief but extraordinary passage from one of his wartime lectures on Parmenides, Heidegger appears to let something akin to a categorical imperative gain control of his mind: pre-attachment to the stipulation that beings cannot exist unless something else allows them to exist seems to *precede* the *Seinsfrage* and make it worth asking. It is one thing simply to marvel, as Heidegger frequently and genuinely did, at the existence of something rather than nothing: one just says 'Wow!', and that's about the end of it. It is an altogether different (and more suspect) thing to go looking for an A that enables the B of present beings simply because one's norm for thinking implies that it *must* be there: B exists, *therefore* there has to be an A that enables B to exist. Yet the previous quotation from Heidegger's lectures on Parmenides not only suggests that this kind of thing was going on in his mind, at least sometimes, it is also not an isolated example. In his Nietzsche lectures, for example, Heidegger gave additional evidence that his thinking was occasionally led by just this kind of formalism: '*How could man comport himself to beings – that is, experience beings as beings – if the relationship to Being were not granted him?*', he asked rhetorically, as if he had never actually experienced being as such, but only believed, based on the norm 'A ⇒ B', that it *must* there (1991: IV, 152).

Among other things, we are speaking of no less than the possibility that a crass formalism constitutes the foundation of the entire Heidegger industry in academic thought. In a post-Heideggerian world, it is taken for granted that being-in-the-world (A) precedes the vulgar modern interpretation of truth (B) as 'a relation between things which are present-at-hand (*intellectus* and *res*) – a relation that is present-at-hand itself'

(Heidegger 1962: 267). The widespread belief in the truth of the hermeneutic situation (A) – in which we always already find ourselves understanding circumspectively that which we only subsequently interpret explicitly (B) – is another example of the taken-for-granted nature of Heidegger's insights (1962: 201). Contrary to what Heidegger would like to suppose, however, his conviction that beings could not exist without being as such suggests the possibility that the horse of logical transcendence is pulling the cart of being, instead of the other way around. Since this kind of attachment to the norm 'A $\Rightarrow$ B' is hardly unique to him, the journey of thought that we are taking in this chapter is also relevant to anyone who *continues* to think, as he did, that the A of being (or freedom) somehow enables or supports the B of beings (or grounds). Henceforth, we will try to unpack the Heideggerian relation between freedom and being in such a way that the notion of *grounding as such* is exposed for what it is: namely, the fetish of a suffering mind that refracts the images which float before it into still other images, that clings desperately to its own method for projecting these images, and that yearns, impossibly, for an account of the world that is more truthful and more genuine than everyone else's account.

It should be obvious from what I have said already that the symbols 'A $\Rightarrow$ B', as I use them here, do not merely *represent* something called Heidegger's *concept* of the relation between being and beings, or freedom and grounds. Not only would this way of putting it belie the central theme of this book, it would also amount to an unconscionable evasion of one of Heidegger's most important (and strident) philosophical positions. Most academic philosophers continue to adhere to Aristotle's doctrine that the purpose (*telos*) of thinking is that-which-is-thought. In other words, they believe that the point of philosophical research is to represent thought's conceptual *product*. Heidegger, on the other hand, follows Nietzsche in interpreting philosophical thinking as its *own telos*: a mode of being that needs no 'product' to justify itself. He refuses to interpret philosophy as a kind of joint venture amongst philosophers for producing useful new ideas to benefit a suffering humanity. On the contrary:

> Philosophy has no mission to take care of universal humanity and culture, to release coming generations once and for all from care about questioning, or to interfere with them simply through wrongheaded claims to validity. (Heidegger 1999b: 14)

True philosophy, for Heidegger, is less like collaboration and more like a lonely journey or encounter, from beginning to end. It is a task that each thinker must accomplish on his or her own, and that no amount of prior 'progress' by other thinkers can supplant or render unnecessary. Thus, the expression of even the most insightful concept is really no more than the trace of a thought, and the word-traces of such a concept are nothing at all unless they are reactivated and woven into a live event of *real thinking*.

It is clear enough what kind of event Heidegger calls 'real thinking'. He often said that there are only two basic ways of thinking still available to us: one can think by calculating with dead symbols that are handed down from past epochs (historicism and representational thinking), or one can engage in true historical (*geschichtlich*) thinking. Mere calculation dusts off old concepts and makes them compatible with the present. Real thinking, in contrast, is an event *of* history in which the thinker temporalises him- or herself *as* history (Heidegger 1985: 167). To temporalise oneself as history is to lay down one's own possibilities of being and thinking as the grounds *of* oneself and *for* one's future. Heidegger thought that genuine philosophical thinking is an event of appropriation (*Ereignis*) that responds to and recalls being as the ultimate ground. His answer to the question of philosophy's meaning was therefore quite simple and straightforward: '*philosophy means to be addressed by Being itself*' (Heidegger 1992a: 120). This way of describing the task of philosophy raises the stakes on the problem of grounding by suggesting that being-as-ground plays something like the role of a muse to any thinking that dares to call itself truly philosophical. Listening attentively to the muse, the philosopher speaks being without presuming or pretending to represent it.

It follows that Heidegger's most famous aphorism about language – '*language is the house of being*' (1998: 239) – does *not* mean that language represents and ties being down, like a Gulliver, with the Lilliputian ropes and stakes of a comprehensive theory. It means, rather, that the thinking and the speaking of genuine philosophical (and poetic) language is above all an event of appropriation in which being shows itself – right then and there – to anyone with ears to hear it and eyes to see it:

> Essential words are not artificially invented signs and marks which are pasted on things merely to identify them. Essential words are deeds which happen in those moments where the lightning flash of great enlightenment goes through the universe. (Heidegger 1985: 25)

The saying '*essential words are deeds*' is rooted in a tradition of German romanticism that goes back at least as far as Goethe, whose character Faust translates the biblical statement 'In the beginning was the *Word*' (John 1:1) as 'In the beginning was the *Deed*' (Luke 1964: 185).[4] While just

4 Goethe's actual line, in German, reads: '*Im Anfang war die* Tat'. The original biblical sentence ends with the Greek word *logos*. This term does not just refer to the word – it also means the faculty of reason, for example – although the Standard English and German translations of John 1:1 do both render *logos* as 'Word' (or '*Wort*').

about any thinking person is capable of understanding that the utterance of words is *also* a deed, it takes someone with the philosophical acuity of a Heidegger or a Goethe to recognise that in fact words amount to nothing at all unless we are able to think of them *only* as deeds.

An initial indication of Zen in relation to Heidegger's thought

Heidegger's rather poetic (some would say flamboyant) way of thinking about the relation between language and being is perfect for our purposes, for we too have said that logical transcendence is not a theory, but rather a happening. From a Zen point of view, logical transcendence does not show itself in the form of an implication or a logical inference, but rather as this or that concrete manifestation of attachment to a delusion that is born of the desire to render a binding or super-enlightened account of the world. Thus, Zen's idea of thusness, like Heidegger's *Ereignis*, focuses on what is happening right now. On the other hand, Zen's relentless deflation of philosophical pretension shows that its attitude towards grounds and grounding is just about as far from uncovering *being as such* as possible. Zen enlightenment is not knowledge or epiphany – on the contrary, it is the letting go of all attachment to knowledge and epiphany. Zen compassion is not truth – it is a wellspring of comfort and solace for those who cling to what they call 'the truth'. *'Whatever you are seeking'*, said Lin-chi, *'all becomes suffering. It is better to have nothing further to seek'* (Schloegl 1976: 38).

It is a popular misconception that a strong affinity exists between Heidegger's thought and Zen, even if it is also true that Heidegger himself sometimes touted to his visitors the 'closeness of his thinking', as Otto Pöggler puts it, to Zen Buddhism (Parkes 1987: 49). Take the important idea of 'letting', for example. In Heidegger's early thought, 'letting' (*lassen*) is primarily defined in terms of the *letting-presence* (*Anwesenlassen*) of beings by being – the bringing-into-unconcealment of that which would remain concealed without the letting. Even his later category of *Gelassenheit*, which he defines as thinking's disinterested and calm 'releasement toward things', is the kind of letting that expects something to come forward into openness (1966: 54). Letting, for Heidegger, is ultimately an unwilled waiting for that which opens itself to thinking. For Zen, however, letting is defined in terms of *letting go* of attachment to the pitiable illusion that there is something profound to be thought in the first place. Heidegger made what he thought was a passage that went far beyond the shabby sphere of mere beings; holding himself in a posture of *'openness to the mystery'* (1966: 55), he found what he interpreted as the clearing and the light of being as such. But as far as Zen is concerned, even one inch ahead is all darkness.

Nevertheless, there is at least one important point of contact between Heidegger's thinking and Zen: both realise that thinking and speaking are not at all what the Western tradition usually takes them to be. Both share an inclination to depict thinking as an *event*, and to elevate the *saying* of philosophy above any particular philosophical *said*. What for Heidegger is the only possible site for the 'lightning flash of great enlightenment' – the now-time of thinking and saying as such – is for Zen the site in which the mind reproduces its suffering and self-delusion. At a minimum, therefore, Heidegger and Zen converge in interpreting thinking as an activity that always occurs, if it occurs at all, in the now-time. This fortuitous convergence ensures that we will be able to have a conversation with Heidegger within what he takes to be his own beloved house of being. In other words, we will engage him on his own ground, as it were, for thinking about 'grounds'.

No Heidegger-bashing!

I hasten to add that none of the thinking in this chapter is meant to be 'anti-Heidegger' in any conventional sense of the term. On the contrary, our reflections on Heidegger's thought manifest the highest kind of praise that one thinker can bestow on another thinker: 'If you want to honour a philosopher', Heidegger once said, wholeheartedly adopting Schelling's words as his motto, 'you must catch him where he has not yet gone forth to the consequences, in his fundamental thought; in the thought from which he takes his point of departure' (1985: 9). The milieu for the point of departure that concerns us here is the *event of grounding as such*, during which Heidegger persistently failed (or refused) to recognise logical transcendence *as* a problem. Logical transcendence can emerge as a problem only if one is able to consider the possibility that Ch'ing-yuan's sophisticated second view of mountains and rivers, in which these features of the landscape no longer show themselves as everyday mountains and rivers, is neither the purpose nor the end of the journey. In a phrase, a thinker cannot see attachment to 'A ⇒ B' as a problem unless he or she stands ready to *let go* of the fruits of the difficult struggle to think below the vulgar surface of things. Although Heidegger changed the tone and emphasis of his thought many times during his long life, and although he possessed an admirable capacity for self-criticism, in the end he simply would not or could not let go of attachment to his hard won conviction that being *is* so that beings *can be*.

Subjective conviction, however, is not in itself the most fundamental point of departure in Heidegger's thought. Certainty about the truth of being comes from a source that precedes and enables it: attachment to the idea that the destinies of being as such and human freedom are inextricably linked. On the one hand, Heidegger thought that the truth of being as such is the ultimate ground of beings, including human beings; but, on the other hand, he also thought that human freedom is the ultimate ground of noticing and taking up being in the *form* of a 'true ground'. This would reproduce the same old contradiction between freedom and necessity that troubled Kant, were it not for the fact that Heidegger managed completely to reconfigure the terrain on which these opposing forces contend with one another. Banishing the principle of causality to the sphere of the 'ontic' (*ontisch*), in which obsession with the causal efficacy of beings eclipses all thought about being as such, he also lifted up human freedom to the different (and higher) sphere of fundamental ontology (*Fundamentalontologie*). The former sphere demarcates the 'actual' world, in which beings are merely present at hand and the human being lives as mere *bios* (the Greek term for biological life); the latter sphere inscribes human *possibilities* including, most importantly, the possibility of asking the fundamental question of being as such.

Hence, Heidegger would announce at the end of his Freiburg lectures on the essence of human freedom that freedom is not a problem of causality, as Kant thought, but rather *'causality is a problem of freedom'* (2002c: 203). How shocking this statement is, when seen from the standpoint of the Western metaphysical tradition! All previous efforts to think freedom had placed it on a direct collision course with necessity by conceiving of it as a sort of uncaused cause, as in Kant's *Third Antinomy*, which 'proves' that pure reason alone cannot resolve the contradiction between freedom and necessity (Kant 1998: 484–89). Not only does Heidegger's statement that causality is a problem of freedom effect a sort of Copernican revolution of Western thinking about the relation between freedom and necessity, it also makes the problem of being in general into a problem of freedom, rather than vice versa (2002c: 203). That is, unless freedom first notices being as such, and resolves to become its 'shepherd' (Inwood 1999: 140), then what is most thought-worthy will fall, without even a whimper of protest, into the obscurity of the utterly forgotten, and man will at long last sink, sadly and irremediably, to the level of a mere 'labouring animal' (Heidegger 2003a: 86).

It is clear, therefore, that Heidegger's thought does not purport to solve the ancient antinomy between freedom and necessity – rather, it attempts to *dissolve* it. In freely responding to that which silently addresses us beyond all merely ontic relations, we let what is hidden and withdrawn from present beings show itself as their ground. In *Was Heisst Denken?* ('What is Called Thinking?'), a lecture course that he gave in 1951–52, Heidegger described the symbiotic relation between freedom and being in terms of endowment and gratitude:

> What is most thought-provoking gives food for thought in the original sense that it gives us over, delivers us to thought. This gift, which gives to us what is most thought-provoking, is the true endowment that keeps itself concealed in our essential nature. When we ask, then, 'What is it that calls on us to think?', we are looking both to what it is that gives to us the gift of this endowment, and to ourselves, whose nature lies in being gifted with this endowment. We *are capable* of thinking only insofar as we *are* endowed with what is most thought-provoking, gifted with what ever and always wants to be thought about. (Heidegger 1968: 126) (emphasis in original).

In essence, this passage says that being as such *lets* freedom think about it, and that thinking about being as such *lets* it come forth as ground. Anointing being *as* the ultimate ground of beings was for Heidegger a self-conscious 'submission' (his word) to that which he thought had evoked the language of grounding in the first place: the call or summons of the 'essential', namely, being as such (2004a: 4). Although mortal speech is a breaking of silence, as he put it in an important 1950 lecture on language, the speaking that first listens to silence also *accepts* by responding to the 'command' of being (1975b: 209).

Heidegger's awe-struck (or is it craven?) *submission* to what he took to be the call or command of being as such is the fundamental point of departure and *sine qua non* of his thought. Thus, he continued to cling to the image of grounding, $A \Rightarrow B$, even after he demoted the ontological difference to the status of a mere transitional device in crossing from the end of metaphysics to what he called 'the other beginning' (1999a: 330). Heidegger knew that the discourse of grounds and grounding is itself metaphysical. But he also came to realise that the task of thinking being as such requires the mind to cross *from* metaphysics rather than to destroy it, as he had called for in *Being and Time* (2004a: 5). Even after his famous 'turn' (*Kehre*), therefore, Heidegger continued to imagine that something profound, however it may be named (whether being, Being, be-ing, beyng, or ~~Being~~), gives *itself* (A) to the *event of thinking* (B). The statement *'Being grounds beings'* became, after the turn, *'Being grounds thinking, and vice versa'*. The event of Heidegger's attachment to the image '$A \Rightarrow B$' had changed its venue without relinquishing its jurisdiction. Precisely because he never attempted to think about his *submission* to the call of being as a problem in its own right, he was to end up building the philosophical equivalent of an elaborate castle in the air.

Please do not take this last statement the wrong way, for to fail as gloriously as Heidegger did is a truly monumental accomplishment. He knew, perhaps better than any other Western thinker, that *every* philosophy fails, indeed fails inevitably, and that the real task of philosophy is not to succeed, but rather to be *capable* of failing. How right he was! On the other hand, if the test of a philosophy's greatness is whether it is capable of failing, this does not imply that all failed philosophies are great. Heidegger observed that *'a vigorous effort must be made to have [a philosophy] succeed'* before one can rightly say that it is capable of failing (1984: 76). I can think of no Western philosopher who made a more vigorous effort than Heidegger did at successfully understanding the problems of freedom and being in their relation to grounding. But if we take Heidegger at his word, this means that no other Western philosopher has ever failed more spectacularly. While I refuse to embrace the opposition between 'failure' and 'success' as this book's ultimate criterion for evaluating Heidegger's philosophy, I do want to give credit to his wonderful failures for making our own journey possible. For without great thinking like Heidegger's, there can be no comparably great effort to *un*-think what the merely symbolic residue of that thought would have us accept, either as our master or our muse.

Freedom as Freedom for Ground

Freedom ⇔ being as such

Given what we have said already about Heidegger's philosophy, it is not surprising to learn that his thinking as a whole displays a considerable amount of ambivalence or ambiguity about the relationship between being-as-ground and freedom-as-ground. On the one hand, he called freedom the *'ground of ground'* (1984: 214), *'the beginning that does not need grounding'* (1985: 70), and the primordial *'opening'*, *'guarantee'* and *'sheltering place'* that man must first attain if he is to be able to encounter anything at all (1992a: 143). However, on the other hand, Heidegger also said that being as such *'is that which determines what is actual in its potential for being, and determines especially the potential for human beings to be'* (1996a: 120), that *'only in be-ing does the possible hold sway'* (1999a: 330), and that humans are always released *'to the truth of Being before any human dependency on powers and forces, predestinations and tasks'* (2003a: 76). This tension or contradiction between freedom-as-ground and being-as-ground suffused Heidegger's thinking from beginning to end. For example, it is not completely clear what *kind* of ground he was referring to when he claimed, in the important 1928 essay *On the Essence of Ground,* that all striving and willing is 'grounded' in our finding ourselves (*Sichbefinden*) in the midst of beings (1998: 103). One strand of his philosophy indicates unequivocally that we find ourselves in the midst of beings because being as such puts us there, and keeps on putting us there: *'"the Dasein in man" is the essence that belongs to Being itself'* (1991: IV, 218). However, another strand indicates, equally unequivocally, that we are in the midst of 'beings' only because our freedom allows us to notice them *as* beings in the first place: *'freedom gives itself to understand; freedom is the primal understanding, i.e., the primal projection of that which freedom itself makes possible*' (1984: 192).

The first strand of Heidegger's thinking emphasises the priority of being-as-ground over all of humanity's mere thoughts and speculations about beings, as in this rather typical passage: '*Metaphysics everywhere moves in the realm of the truth of being, which truth remains its unknown and ungrounded ground*' (1998: 232, 374 n.3). The second strand of his thinking emphasises *recognition* as a kind of primal origin in its own right: in recognising something *as* this or that, we '*bring the presence of what was previously uncalled into a nearness*' by placing the recognised into its 'as'-structure (1975b: 196). The 'as' of interpretation (the '*existential-hermeneutical "as"*') belongs to freedom – *is* freedom, in fact – and it always comes first. This primordial 'as', in turn, gives rise to *discourse*, including what Heidegger calls the '*apophantical "as" of the assertion*' (1962: 201). The strong link between freedom and discourse explains why Heidegger tended to exalt language: '*Mortal speech is a calling that names*', he declaimed (1975b: 216), thereby underscoring his belief that freedom's voice is what summons everything to its proper ground in the first place. Not only does the openness of the world '*first of all burst forth*' in language (1995: 109), but also '*man utters himself and becomes present in language*' (1985: 141). What is more, freedom does not just bring beings and itself to ground in language. Freedom's discourse is also capable of speaking being as such: we have access to the *problem* of being only through freedom and its understanding of being (2002c: 86-87). Thus, if freedom is to recognise being as such at all, it must uncover it as the *ground* – it must ground the ultimate ground, so to speak – and this '*grounding must contain the nature of giving Being precedence over nothingness*' (2003a: 43).

As the previous series of remarks about language suggests, Heidegger did not interpret language as a mere agglomeration of words that humans use to designate sundry familiar things. Rather, he tended to describe language in hagiographical terms, by saying things such as '*language is ... the original resonance of the truth of a world*' (1991: II, 105). For Heidegger, the genuine word is *logos*: that which uncovers and names, in one mighty breath, both being-as-ground and beings-as-grounded (1996b: 107). Indeed, one could say that he continued to worship language even when he tried to signify what he took to be its growing impoverishment by explicitly crossing out words like 'Being' and 'man' in his texts. For the very act of crossing these words out *indicated* something: it was, for him, a free act of disclosure-through-discourse. According to Heidegger, philosophical language (like poetic language) is a supreme act of freedom that makes being as such noticeable by making it manifest (2004a: 3): both beings and being as such must be '*torn from concealment*', and it is freedom that does the tearing (1984: 217). However, on the other hand, it is also true that freedom and *logos* remain dependent throughout on being as such for the primordial gift of what they uncover. *Alētheia*, Heidegger's favourite Greek word for truth, quite literally means the 'un-concealment' (*unverborgenheit*) of that which lies concealed – an unconcealment that occurs primarily through *logos* (1977: 11–12). Since the concealed lies concealed *before* the event of its unconcealment, it follows that what is uncovered by *alētheia* also precedes *alētheia*: it would appear that the last (being) is also the first, and the first (freedom) is also the last. In light of the many puzzling cross-currents in Heidegger's thought, one can be forgiven for thinking that language conceived as being's gift to freedom sits rather uneasily, at best, alongside language conceived as freedom's gift to being.

The odd, if not scandalous, reciprocal dependence of being on freedom and freedom on being is what Heidegger meant to uncover when he said, in a 1930 lecture course called *On the Essence of Human Freedom*, that '*the question concerning the essence of human freedom is the fundamental question of philosophy, in which is rooted even the question of being*' (2002c: 203). Later in the same lecture he portrayed freedom's task in relation to being in terms of freedom's 'letting' and 'self-binding':

> Beings can only show themselves as *objects* if the appearance of beings, and that which at bottom makes this possible, i.e., the understanding of being, has the character of letting-stand-over-against. Letting something stand-over-against as something given, basically the manifestness of beings in the binding character of their so- and that-being is only possible where the comportment to beings, whether in theoretical or practical knowledge, already acknowledges this binding character. But the latter amounts to an originary self-binding, or, in Kantian terms, the giving of a law unto oneself. The letting-be-encountered of beings, comportment to beings in each and every mode of manifestness, is only possible where freedom *exists*. *Freedom is the condition of the possibility of the manifestness of the being of beings, of the understanding of being*. (Heidegger 2000c: 205) (emphasis in original).

The radical interpenetration of freedom and being suggests that even the most primordial movement of 'grounding' imaginable always remains dependent throughout on human freedom, both for its visibility and for its enactment in thought and speech. The A of being as such, for example, conceived poetically *'as a letting-lie-present that assembles'* the B of beings (1996b: 110), would amount to nothing at all were it not for freedom's decision to 'bind itself' to being as such by acknowledging and saying this. The point is not that being as such 'disappears' when no one is thinking about it, for only beings can appear and disappear, and being as such is not a being. Rather, the point is that being as such is always quite literally 'no-thing', and that all it takes for it to become *nothing at all* is for freedom to forget it. This helps explain why Heidegger so often referred to the kind of forgetfulness that holds sway in metaphysical thinking in terms of the oblivion or nothingness of being itself: *'Being has brought it to pass in history that there is nothing to Being itself'* (1991: IV, 222).

Speaking in terms of the norm of logical transcendence, it is fair to say that Heidegger thought *both* that A (being-as-ground) ⇒ B (human freedom), *and* that A (human freedom) ⇒ B (being-as-ground). In other words, he explicitly thought a contradiction: *being is first* and *freedom is first. This* contradiction cannot and should not be dissolved dialectically, for Heidegger scorned the dialectic is an 'escape' from, and hence an evasion of, the problem of freedom-as-temporality (1984: 204). The dialectic puts its thumb on the 'freedom' side of the scales by ignoring or minimising that which gives freedom the time and the warrant to *be*. As far as Heidegger was concerned, the suspension of contradiction in the dialectic does not put an end to the 'domination of the *logos*', but rather represents an extreme intensification of that domination (Heidegger 1959: 187). That is, the dialectic, if conceived as 'logic' in Hegel's sense, always takes the form of a statement about *'something handy that one handles in order to gain and secure the truth as correctness'* (1959: 188). Heidegger refused to dissolve the contradiction between being-as-ground and freedom-as-ground by casting it in the form of a thesis and an antithesis that are waiting to be surpassed by a synthesis performed in the sphere of absolute knowledge, for this solution violently *anthropomorphises* the problem by making it appear that the only real question raised by the contradiction is one of human 'knowing'. To be sure, Heidegger sometimes said that *'Being manifests itself primordially in the word'* (1992a: 76), as if being as such were merely a matter of saying and knowing. But he also said that being and the truth of being are *beyond* the traditional Western identification of being and thinking (1992a: 166), and that they perversely unfold and 'show' themselves in modernity primarily as default – as what people precisely do *not* think about (1991: IV, 214).

If, as Heidegger believed, philosophy is the highest degree of human freedom, and if, as he also believed, to philosophise means to exist from ground, then one might say that freedom's greatest gift to thought is the *chance* to think being as such. But it is important to remember always that freedom in Heidegger's sense never 'invents' this or that possibility of thinking. Freedom does not create a brand new possibility that only subsequently becomes a ground. Rather, freedom is able to 'lay down' grounds, as it were, only because it finds itself already standing on them. The first principle of all hermeneutics, Heidegger once said, is that any specific present always already understands how to be futural (1992b: 20E). Freedom is first thrown into its possibilities, and only because of this can it project itself onto its possibilities by making one of them (such as being as such) its own. In the course of this projection freedom releases itself *from* its past and *to itself*, so as to be *as* this ground. Hence, the human being does not exist before its ground, properly speaking. For Heidegger, the human being exists only *from the ground* and *as this ground* (1962: 330).

Heidegger said that the ecstatic relationship, whereby the freedom transcends itself to its ground, could not be represented, for *'as soon as I represent it, I have two objects and am outside the ecstatic relationship'* (2001b: 183). This would be a reproach to our use of the notation of logical transcendence, A ⇒ B, were it not for the fact that we are employing the symbols 'A' and 'B' as a part of a book-length koan: they are merely a rough index of craving attachment to grounds and grounding, and are not meant to inscribe a metaphysical theory. Thus, Heidegger's attempt to put the ecstatic relationship beyond all representation suggests that he clung to the belief that the language of representation (A) leads us to have a *wrong view* of the ecstatic relationship (B) – as if a few words written on a page were capable of denying us access to something really important. It also suggests the thesis that when freedom thinks being-as-ground it *is* being-as-ground – A = B – at least as far as language is concerned. To be sure, Heidegger believed that freedom exists only in the 'choice' of one possibility to the exclusion of others – that is, 'in tolerating one's not having chosen the others and one's not being able to choose them' (1962: 331). This 'decidedness' of freedom is not some revisable event from the past, but rather a decision that always already is transpiring in *'the Moment'* (1985: 156). But if freedom always decides and is deciding right now, its peculiar *manner* of deciding takes the form of an assumption rather than creation *ex nihilo*: freedom *assumes* a possibility by making it its own – by making this or that possibility a *'springboard for its subsequent trajectory'*, as Michael Inwood puts it (Inwood 1999: 83). One might therefore fairly characterise Heidegger's concept of freedom as the capacity to assume – or better still, *cling to* – possibilities as grounds. To put the matter even more succinctly, Heideggerian freedom is essentially *freedom for ground*.

Freedom for ground

If freedom is conceived in a namby-pamby sort of way as complete indeterminacy, then its indecisiveness would prevent it from ever doing anything. As the faculty of all possible faculties, *'freedom is capable only when it positions its decision beforehand as decidedness in order for all enactment to become necessary in terms of it'* (Heidegger 1985: 154). This does not mean that freedom alienates itself in its object. It means, rather, that freedom and ground coalesce as one, and that they must keep on coalescing. The following passage, taken from the text of Heidegger's 1936 lectures on Schelling, describes this essential unity of freedom and ground:

> True freedom in the sense of the most primordial self-determination is found only where a choice is not longer possible and no longer necessary. Whoever must first choose and wants to choose does not yet really know what he wants. He does not yet will primordially. Whoever is decided already knows it. The decision for decidedness and self-knowledge in the clarity of one's own knowledge are one and the same. This decidedness which no longer needs a choice because it is grounded in essential knowledge is far removed from all formalism, in fact it is its direct opposite. For formalism is sentimentality locked in prefabricated goals. (Heidegger 1985: 154)

Human beings are constitutionally inclined to fall into prefabricated grounds, including even those now-stale grounds that, once upon a time, they freely laid down for themselves. Colloquially speaking, this is called 'being stuck in a rut'. But Heidegger wants it to be known that this kind of *falling-into-grounds* is not the same as freedom's ongoing decision to *choose-and-become* its ground. The most striking idea here is that the process of genuine Heideggerian self-binding, in freedom, is both continuous and never-ending. Thus, if it is true that freedom stands 'neutral' before its possibilities, as Heidegger once said, this neutrality is not the *'voidness of an abstraction but precisely the potency of the origin'* (1984: 137). One might say that genuine Heideggerian freedom is always choosing to eclipse itself by its deeds, darkening the present with a movement from *possibilities*, in the ontological realm of grounds, to *actualities*, in the ontic realm of cause-and-effect. Since the particular ground that freedom seizes and becomes at any given moment excludes all other possibilities, it would appear that freedom's self-determination consists in freely letting its chosen ground run its course.

As I indicated briefly in Chapter 1, Heidegger made ontological transcendence into an essential determination of the being of the human being. In transcendence, the human being gives itself a world that is prior to all particular beings and projects. Heidegger called the existential movement in which the human being first surpasses itself to its world *temporality*, defined as *'the primordial "outside-of-itself" in and for itself'* (1962: 377). In the *ecstases* (Greek for 'standing outside') of temporality we transcend ourselves towards the 'for-the-sake-of'. By this Heidegger means that we transcend ourselves and other beings for the sake of our own *capacity* to be – a capacity that shows itself in possibilities that place us *'"further" than any given factical being'* (1984: 215). Since Heidegger thought that another name of our capacity to be is *freedom*, this implies that transcendence and freedom are one and the same. Indeed, this is an identity that he was quite happy to confirm: *'To put it briefly, Dasein's transcendence and freedom are identical'* (1984: 185). In transcending all merely actual beings, freedom *'gives itself to understand'* its possibilities *as* possible grounds (1984: 192).

It is therefore not at all surprising that, shortly after the publication of *Being and Time*, Heidegger declared *'the origin of "ground" lies in freedom as the freedom for ground'* (1984: 218). In identifying transcendence with freedom, freedom with its possibilities, possibilities with grounds, and grounds with their always already understood meaning-as-truth, Heidegger's thinking merged the problem of freedom with the problem of ground on the basis of a phenomenological structure that he called *freedom-for-ground*. Thus, Heidegger said that in surpassing itself *towards* its ground, the human being opens up an abyss (*Abgrund*) in which it is in each case *for itself* – that is, for its possibilities. *'Freedom is abyssal'* says exactly the same as *'freedom is freedom for ground'*. Both expressions signify that we are free from being 'besieged' by beings, as Heidegger put it, only because of *'the possibility of grounding in which man creates beyond himself'* (1999a: 334). If we did not have this possibility, he thought, we would be condemned to living like beasts, rooting around in and amongst beings according to the irresistible demands of our instinctual drives. Only the possibility of grounding ourselves saves us from a fate that Heidegger would have considered worse than death: the death of thinking itself.

To paraphrase a well-known line from the movie *Platoon*, for Heidegger hell is the impossibility of thinking. His emphasis on the absolute value or primacy of genuine thinking over sheer existing shows that there is a strong strand of the juridical in Heidegger's philosophy of freedom, despite his occasional protestations to the contrary. One simply does not *'render the quaestio juris meaningless'* by giving an ontological interpretation of subjectivity, as Heidegger believed (1997b: 272), especially if one identifies freedom with freedom-for-ground. For it is in the nature of a ground to ground *this* rather than *that*: indeed, there would be no point to freedom if grounds did not discriminate in this way – no point to freedom's choice of one ground to the exclusion of other grounds. This is what Heidegger meant when he said, in the passage quoted at the beginning of this section, that in decidedness freedom *'no longer needs a choice'* (1985: 154): one who no longer needs a choice has found at least a passable degree of lawfulness and intelligibility in the choice that he did make. All of this implies, quite correctly, that Heideggerian freedom should not be confused with libertinism. Rather, to be free in his sense is to be free and open for being *'claimed'* by something: *'This claim is then the ground of action, the motive'* (2001b: 217). Heidegger knew that it is not enough to 'have values' in freedom; one must also *'evoke powers'* in them by grounding them in deeds (1991: I, 157). Here, as elsewhere in Heidegger's thought, one can detect the strong influence of Nietzsche's philosophy, and especially Nietzsche's identification of the highest form of will-to-power with artistic creation. Thus, a free decision, Heidegger said, is the *'deepest joy'* of creating. And creation, in turn, is *'protected from degenerating into a sheer and insatiable driving around in blind urges'* by the activity of grounding (1999a: 69, 176). As a creator, the human being does not find itself adrift in an inscrutable and irrational universe. Rather, the human being understands itself *'from out of its own capacity to be'*: it temporalises itself (*sich zeitigen*) in *'freedom toward ground'* (Heidegger 1984: 214).

In a nutshell, then, Heideggerian freedom is the *ground of all grounds and grounding*, and therefore the ground of all intelligibility. Translating this into the terminology of logical transcendence, one could say that Martin Heidegger the man kept on thinking that *freedom as ground* is the A that supports the various ways that the B of *freedom as creation* establishes and differentiates grounds. Animals and rocks just *are*; their futures can be mapped and predicted according to the law of causality. But as creation, freedom is more than simple causation from out of itself. It is causation on the basis of something that lies nestled in the heart of freedom itself: namely, *the ground*. As Heidegger put it in the text of a 1928 lecture course on the foundations of logic: *'A basic problem of logic, the law-governedness of thinking, reveals itself to be a problem of human existence in its ground, the problem of freedom'* (1984: 20).

But if, as Heidegger said on the same page, *'the truth of thinking is co-governed by lawfulness'*, then what is the nature of this lawfulness, and what is its relation to the ground that freedom grounds? Is the ground itself law-like? If so, there would appear to be a sort of *legal formalism* at work in the relation between the free will and what it wills – as if a possible ground, once it is chosen by freedom, were capable of determining its own application in the process of creation, passing seamlessly into the created without any need for interpretation. Although this way of thinking about grounds would seem to be antithetical on its face to Heidegger's subtle and path-breaking philosophy of hermeneutics and interpretation in general, it turns out that just this sort of crude legal formalism is at work in Heidegger's well known effort to understand and account for what he called *'the history of being'*. For the history of being is also the history of metaphysics, and the history of metaphysics, at least as Heidegger tells it, is fraught with the kind of necessity that would please even the most hide-bound formalist.

The History of Being

To cease all overcoming of metaphysics

After his 'turn' in the late 1930s, Heidegger finally abandoned the task that he had set for himself, in *Being and Time*, of 'destroying the history of ontology' and replacing it with a 'fundamental ontology' of *Dasein*

(1962: 34, 41). It dawned on him that *'a regard for metaphysics still prevails even in the intention to overcome metaphysics'* (1972: 24). By vehemently opposing a particular way of thinking, we give our opponent permission to define us, for as Heidegger said in another context, *'everything "anti" thinks in the spirit of that against which it is "anti"'* (1992a: 52-53). Moreover, it turns out that metaphysical thinking and its immediate heir, technological thinking, *'cannot be abolished, like an opinion'*, for they are simply too deeply embedded in our world to be destroyed (2003a: 85). If people obstinately continue to *'talk past Being as such'*, even after the publication of *Being and Time*, well then, at least it is possible to say that this talking-past amounts to *some* kind relationship to being as such (1991: IV, 215). How could so many people get it so wrong, and for such a long time, unless being itself had something to do with its own oblivion? The post-'turn' Heidegger recognised that the time had come to *'cease all overcoming and leave metaphysics to itself'* (1972: 24).

Starting with his lectures on Nietzsche in 1936–1940, Heidegger began referring to the oblivion of being as such in terms of a *'self-*concealing of the origin' (2003a: 3), as if being were a naughty child that had decided to hide in the cupboard to avoid meeting the relatives. He decided to pursue a less confrontational, almost Zen-like, approach to philosophy: he began to interpret the history of metaphysics as the very history of being itself (2003a: 146). In other words, *this* Heidegger at long last realised that the many transformations of metaphysical thinking that had begun with Plato's interpretation of being as idea, and ended with Nietzsche's interpretation of being as will-to-power, were not alien grafts on an otherwise genetically pure tree of being. On the contrary, they were being's *own* productions, being's *own* self-saying, and therefore being's own peculiar manner of showing itself. Thus, Heidegger completely reformulated his relationship with metaphysics after the turn: the task was no longer to defeat it and leave it behind (*Überwunden*), but rather to surpass it and bring it along (*Verwunden*) to some kind of new beginning (2003a: 84). He resolved to boldly set out on a journey that he called *'the first attempt at a contemplation of the history of Being'* (2003a: 46).

The history of metaphysics

Metaphysical thought from Plato onward had managed to transform being as such into a being: this much was clear to Heidegger, and it became the veritable lodestone of his thinking. In *Contributions to Philosophy (From Enowning)*, a difficult but important treatise that he wrote in the period 1936–38, he briefly sketched three main stages in the history of this transformation: *'[A being] in its* emergence *into itself*

(Classical Greece); [a being] caused *by a supreme being of the same essence (Middle Ages); [and a being as] the extant as* object *(modernity)*' (1999a: 120). He traced a similar but slightly more nuanced trajectory in the last of his series of lectures on Nietzsche, in 1940:

> That every metaphysics, even the reversal of Platonism, thinks the Being of beings as the *a priori*, merely certifies that metaphysics as such leaves Being unthought. Of course, metaphysics acknowledges that beings are not without Being. But scarcely has it said so when it again transforms Being into a being, whether it be the Supreme Being in the sense of the first cause [medieval Christian philosophy], whether it be the distinctive being in the sense of the subject of subjectivity [Descartes' *ego cogito*], as the condition of the possibility of all objectivity [Kant's transcendental subject], or whether, as a consequence of the coherence of both these fundamental conditions of Being in beings, it be the determination of the supreme being as the Absolute in the sense of unconditioned subjectivity [Hegel's Spirit]. (1991: IV, 208)

As we saw earlier, Heidegger concluded this tale of metaphysics conceived as the history of being by positing Nietzsche's ontology of will-to-power as the consummation of metaphysics itself. After Nietzsche, will-to-power (as the end of the history of metaphysics) gradually released itself from all merely traditional and dogmatic (authority-based) constraints on its tendencies and spheres of operation. The being of the human being began to organise itself according to the institutional character of modern science, broadly understood as the calculation of representations according to a method. Although Heidegger *occasionally* said things such as '*the self-release of Being into machination ... is by no means a decline and something "negative" in any kind of sense*' (2003a: 103), his judgments about the current situation of being as such and *Dasein*, and where they were heading, were more often than not far more negative and mournful in tone.

According to Heidegger's well known critique of modernity, being as the history of metaphysics eventually released human beings into modern technology (*Technik*), a grim form of life in which representational thinking reduces everything – from trees to humans to oceans – to a standing reserve (*Bestand*) of merely useful things and procedures (1977: 3-35). On this view, the relentless process of 'Enframing' (*Ge-stell*) has reduced the world from the status of a God-created 'nature' to that of a vast warehouse. Technological thinking 'enframes' the world and all that is in it according to procedures for processing and control: everything (including 'human capital') becomes a fungible unit of mere matter for possible use according to the requirements of calculative reason and the techniques of scientific management. Caught in a regime of hyper-administration, beings cease to show themselves *as* the unique beings that they are. Instead, *'everything is ordered to stand by, to be immediately at hand, indeed to stand there just so that it may be on call for further ordering'* (1977: 17). In characterising this history of metaphysics, from first to last, as a *'primal refusal of an essential grounding of the truth of Being'* (2003a: 81), Heidegger drew the circle closed. He interpreted the oblivion of being as such – the 'default' of not-thinking it – as being's own peculiar manner of showing itself. Hence, he characterised *'Being itself as this very default'*, and said that *'as such default, Being itself essentially unfolds'* (1991: IV, 214). In a nutshell, Heidegger's beloved being as such conceals *itself* within and as the rise of modern technology, and it gives *itself* over to the *'extreme danger'* that it will be completely forgotten (1977: 33).

For our purposes, it is not necessary to know whether Heidegger's account of the history of metaphysics is plausible or implausible, true or false, right or wrong, correct or incorrect. Nor is it necessary to dwell on the *'saving power'* of genuine philosophical thinking that Heidegger believed might still rescue being as such from complete oblivion, if only human beings could rediscover it as a possibility (1977: 33). What are these little dualisms to us, given what is at stake in our journey? I have shortened and abstracted Heidegger's account of the rise of technological thinking here, almost to the point of a caricature, for a reason. There are times when caricatures have their uses, and this is one of those times. 'To experience the closest is the most difficult', Heidegger once said (1992a: 135), and he was right. Thus, the foregoing discussion of Heidegger's account of the history of being stealthily reveals the simplest and most essential aspect of his thinking: *namely, that it was, first and foremost, an account*. More than anything else, his account of the history of being shows itself as a *trace* of a particular outburst of thinking – an outburst during which Heidegger's brilliant mind both conformed with, *and clung to*, a series of movements organised around the Siren's song that words and ideas always sing to us as our monkey-minds make the passage from A to B. Everyone has heard the beautiful song that is sung by well-spoken words and well formed ideas – it goes like this: *'We are true – come to us – believe in us – adhere to us'*. And of course, the name that we have given to this Siren's song in this book is *logical transcendence*.

Metaphysics grounds beings in this or that highest being: *'every founding and even every appearance of foundability has inevitably degraded being into some sort of being'* (1996b: 111). But why does Heidegger use the word 'inevitably'? What is it about, say, the language of foundations that compels anything whatsoever? If Shakespeare's *The Merchant of Venice* does not predetermine exactly how it will be read or performed, if legal terms such as 'due process' and 'reasonableness' are not attached by steel wires to their absolutely correct interpretations, if 'white' can mean black, as an English court once declared,[5] then why does a statement such as *'There is nothing to Heidegger's being as such'* preclude *anyone* from subsequently experiencing *anything*, including even being as such? Putting the ontological difference aside for a moment, does not Heidegger's *history* of metaphysics take the same *form* as metaphysics itself? Granted that metaphysics grounds beings (B) in a highest being (A), does Heidegger himself not ground metaphysical *accounts* of grounding (B) in being as such conceived as the ultimate ground (A)?

With these questions in mind, permit me to present a much-simplified version of the picture that Heidegger drew for himself in the course of thinking the history of being. But first, a caveat: the chart below should not be mistaken for a metaphysical *Weltbild*. It is not *'the world conceived and grasped as picture'* (Heidegger 1977: 129), as in the morphology of world-forms that Oswald Spengler ostentatiously displays in *The Decline of the West* (Spengler 1928). It is not even offered as a *Heideggerbild*: a neat and tidy little picture that would have the effrontery to reduce Heidegger the thinker to a few well chosen images. No, this chart is the image of an extremely interesting *possible event*: the event of craving attachment *to* a picture (*bild*) – *this* very picture, in fact. The chart should be viewed as a kind of philosophical box-within-a-box: at each level in the history of metaphysics (t_2 through t_9) after the pre-Socratics (t_1), freedom in the mode of philosophy thought A ⇒ B (a highest being grounds beings) within and on the basis of *another* A ⇒ B (being as such grounds what metaphysics was doing when it offered this or that account of 'A ⇒ B'). Since the pre-Socratics also thought beings on the basis of *something else* (*archē*), I have included their movement of thought in the picture, even though they did not conceive of the *archē* as a highest being. I have done this in order to show the intimate connection between *their* non-metaphysical A ⇒ B and *Heidegger's* non-metaphysical A ⇒ B, as if the arc that began with Anaximander finally closed itself into a circle at the very same point from which it commenced, albeit some 2,500 years later.

Clinging to opposite ends of the same rope

In considering the information presented in the foregoing chart, remember that Heidegger interpreted philosophy as freedom, and freedom as grounding. For him, therefore, the history of *being as metaphysics* is the history of human *freedom as philosophy*, and the latter, in turn, is essentially

5 *Mitchell v Henry* (1880) 15 Ch D 181, 190 (*per* James J) (in a contract for the sale of wool, 'white' can mean relatively dark). The decision reversed Sir George Jessel, who stated that 'nobody could convince *him* that black was white' (Corbin 1960: III, 156 n 96).

A Picture of the History of Being as the History of Metaphysics

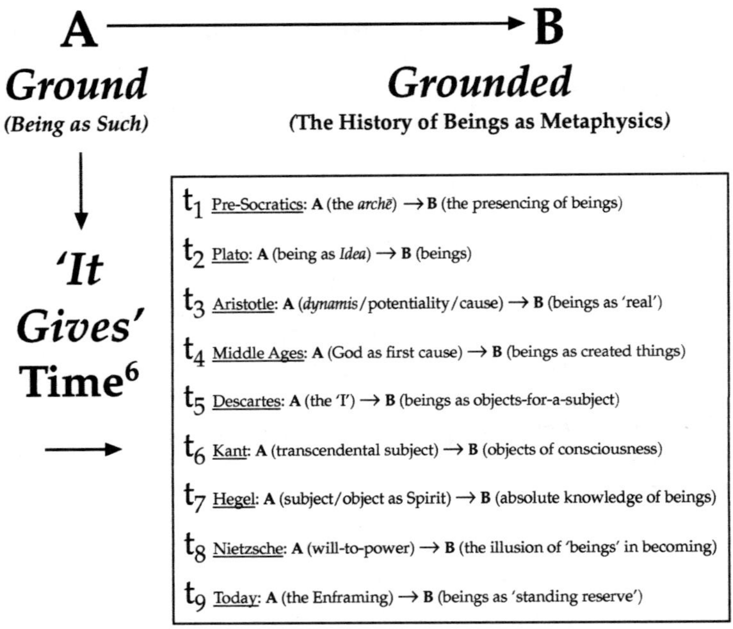

the history of *grounding*. Acting in the mode of freedom-as-philosophy, Heidegger attempted to think the history of being on the basis of the truth of being as opposed to beings – on the basis of being-as-ground, in other words. He knew that the A ⇒ B of metaphysics proceeds all too quickly *from* a highest being (A) *to* beings (B) on the basis of creation-through-causation: as fertiliser is to the flower, so too the metaphysically highest being is to its creations. In both cases the cause and its effect adhere to one another on the familiar basis of mere *production*. Metaphysics does not experience the '*difficulty of thinking the simple*' (1985: 188). It does not pause to consider the possibility that the titillating realm of present beings (B) may *lead back* to something primordial that is not another being, and that does not manifest itself through causation. Impatient to 'solve problems' with beings, metaphysics does not think slowly enough. It wallows in '*the inadequacy of common sense*' (1985: 81). It pays no attention to the

6 '"Time" is the name for the "truth" of being' (1999a: 128). 'Time *is* not. There is, It gives (*es gibt*) time' (1972: 16).

'inconspicuous' (*unscheinbare*), and quickly forgets anything that is 'intractable and inaccessible' (*unzugänglich*) from the point of view of representation (1977: 177).

While this litany of complaints against metaphysics may suggest that there is a *fundamental* difference between it and Heidegger's thought, the truth is otherwise. Heidegger's *thinking-on-the-basis-of-being-as-such* transpired by means of the very same stipulation that he claimed had caused metaphysics to forget being as such: A ⇒ B. To be sure, Heidegger did manipulate the stipulation A ⇒ B in a way that is the opposite of metaphysics, methodologically speaking. For him, '*something intelligible is already there which contains in itself the possibility of being traced back to its foundations*' (1997b: 17). This implies that the manifold of present beings we call the 'world' is not like a many-thousand-pieced jigsaw puzzle to be laboriously assembled on its cardboard backing – it is more like a tantalising clue to be followed to *something else*. In other words, Heidegger did not want to understand the B of beings – he wanted to penetrate it and leave it behind. All attempts to '*enumerate symptoms*' about the world, or to '*reckon existing reality morphologically, psychologically, in terms of decline and loss, in terms of fate, catastrophe, and destruction*', are merely technological behaviour, he said in *The Turning* (1977: 48), and most certainly he did not want to be found guilty of *that*. Heidegger's mode of thinking being as such in terms of grounding always went from B *back to* A – from the 'mystery' that there *are* beings in the first place (B) to what must be the origin (A) of the strange fact that there is something rather than nothing. Although it is first in point of importance and origin in Heidegger's philosophy, the A of being as such actually comes *after* the B of beings as far as the event of thinking it goes.

Of course, metaphysics, too, sometimes thinks back from B to A – Kant's practice of thinking back from the fact of experience to the 'condition of its possibility' is a good example of this. The main difference is that metaphysics, once it has identified its ground (A), always quickly rebounds *to* the world of present beings (B), with which it is always principally concerned, and which it is always eager to understand, whereas in Heidegger's thought there is no rebound movement, or at most an atrophied one. To put the matter crudely and perhaps even a little unfairly, Heidegger the philosopher could not have cared less about beings and their problems. What he cared about was the problem of being and *only* the problem of being. That is why you will not find among Heidegger's copious publications any volumes focusing specifically on, say, ethics and jurisprudence, whereas you will find such volumes in the philosophical output of thinkers such as Kant and Hegel. While it would be foolish for me to claim that this difference between Heidegger and the metaphysical tradition is inconsequential for the history of philosophy, I will say that it *is* inconsequential for the journey we are taking in this book. Let me be very blunt about this: as far as we are concerned, the *difference* between Heidegger's thought and metaphysical thought is not the basis for any real *distinction*. In both cases the mind clings to the stipulation A ⇒ B, even if metaphysics does hold on more tightly to the top end (beings) of this symbolic rope than Heidegger does, and Heidegger holds on more tightly than metaphysics does to the bottom end (being). Let's face it: when two people grab the opposite ends of a rope, and then tighten their grip and pull as hard as they can, the fact remains that that they are both *clinging to the rope*.

If there were a real essence of metaphysics, it would not consist in the tendency of philosophers to think beings to the exclusion of being as such, for this is a mere detail having to do with the *contents* of thought. Far more important is the *movement of thought* that we have called logical transcendence. The event of attachment to logical transcendence characterises an almost universal Western compulsion always to explain and to account for *this* on the basis of *that*, whatever the particular contents of 'this' and 'that' may be, and however the mind begins its movement, whether from A to B, or from B to A. 'All philosophy from first to last merely unfolds its *presupposition*', Heidegger once wrote (1988: 37). What he actually *meant* to say by this is made clear a few lines later: each attempt at philosophical thinking has an *'inherent content'*, he said, and this presupposed inherent content *'is the history of the manifestation of beings as a whole, which is already taking place and where we find ourselves already situated'* (1988: 36–37). Fine: we find ourselves thrown into a world. So what is next? Heidegger's statement about how philosophy unfolds its presupposition *might* have meant something that is far more radical and liberating than the 'inherent content' of the history of being. Indeed, what it might have meant is what it still *can* mean, at least if we have courage enough to read it that way.

The unfolding of philosophy's presupposition: a Zen interpretation

Our attempt in this chapter to understand the interconnected problems of freedom and ground has been informed throughout by a Zen sensibility, including the paths of thinking (and non-thinking) that I began to elucidate in the first chapter. For example, it would be very dangerous to overstress the similarity between Heidegger's view of language and Zen's, even if it is true that both views are inclined to interpret language as a kind of happening. By way of illustration, compare Heidegger's previously quoted remarks about how *'essential words'* evoke a *'lightening flash of great enlightenment'* with the following passage from the teachings of the Zen master Lin-chi:

> Followers of the Way, do not lay hold of what I am saying. Why not? My teachings have no fixed foundation; they are only designs of an instant in space, like images painted in colour, or other teaching devices. (Schloegl 1976: 60)

Like Heidegger, Lin-chi interpreted his philosophical words as merely transient deeds occurring in the now-time, rather than as labels to be learned and understood for their meaning and significance. But unlike Heidegger, Lin-chi did not valorise his words by imagining that they are 'essential'. Lin-chi compared his words to designs, images painted in colour, and teaching devices, thereby devaluing them in the minds of his listeners by placing them on a par with the mundane. Then, as now, his words do not purport to uncover anything profound, like being as such, that escapes the notice of those lesser mortals who are still tied to inferior ways of thinking.

The case is otherwise with Heidegger. In *Contributions to Philosophy (From Enowning)*, Heidegger presents the thesis that man comes *'nearer'* to being as such *'the less a being [unseiender]'* he is. The idea is that being as such does not reveal itself to mere plodders who imagine that they are 'being-like', and that it shows itself only to those who are prepared to shed the snakeskin of their selfhood, and even then, only in proportion to the amount of skin they shed. But on the very same page that he alleged the existence of this kind of inverse relationship between the perception of selfhood and the experience of being as such, Heidegger felt compelled to write, rather abruptly, that his thesis was *'No Buddhism! The opposite'* (1999a: 120). He was absolutely right – his way of thinking is indeed the opposite of Buddhism, or at least *Zen* Buddhism. Despite Schopenhauer's influential (mis)reading of Buddhism as a form of self-annihilation through denial of the will (Schopenhauer 1969: I, 383), and despite certain popular misconceptions to the contrary, Zen does not call for the effacement of the self so that something awe-inspiring can be experienced. After all, what is there to be effaced, and what is there to be in awe of? In Zen, the real enemy of great enlightenment is not the self conceived of as a being, but rather craving attachment to either selfhood *or* its negation, both of which depend on the fetish $A \Rightarrow B$ for their enactment. *'All deliberation of [mind-and-heart] misses the target. All movement of thought goes to a contrary end'*, said Lin-chi. (Schloegl 1976: 50). How amazing! Here is someone who saw that A never *really* goes to B, nor B to A: it is always only the mind that makes and clings to the illusion of this movement.

With Lin-chi's words in mind, permit me to give my own interpretation of Heidegger's statement about the way that all philosophy merely 'unfolds its presupposition': *Unless it is undertaken as a journey* through (not 'to') *the truth of being, all philosophy, from first to last, merely unfolds the mind's craving attachment to the norm of logical transcendence – it unfolds our ceaseless attempt to explain and account for one image by appealing to another image – and it fails to recognise that even great knowledge, great thinking, and great enlightenment are like pieces of dung in our mouth: we must spit them out before they choke us.*

A Billion Glittering Images: the Disunity of the Ground

Freedom versus necessity in the movement from A to B

And how they do choke us! On the one hand, Heidegger conceived of his *own* philosophising as a free happening – a recollection and response to being as such, rather than a mere calculation proceeding along lines established by pre-given conceptual grounds. However, on the other hand, he conceived of the possibilities for thinking that were made available during the various stages in the history of Western metaphysics as mechanically constrained, if not utterly determined, by the particular accounts of grounding that his predecessors laid down for themselves. Thus, Heidegger believed that the Cartesian and Kantian accounts of being – wherein the A of subjectivity grounds the B of objectivity – somehow prevented their proponents from experiencing anything other than beings. Kant, for example, was allegedly unable to carry through a '*more original interpretation*' of the '*essential constitution of humankind*' by tracing it back to its ground in temporality. And why was it that '*Kant shrank back from this unknown root*'? (1997b: 112). Heidegger's answer was that Kant needed a '*fixed and abiding self*' to ground the objectivity of objects, and since anything historical would have threatened that objectivity, time had to be banished from the constitution of the categories of understanding (1997b: 256).

But this account of Kant's blindness to temporality tells us *why* he was blind – it does not yet tell us *how* the event of making-blind occurred. Let us therefore ask how, *exactly*, does any particular 'A ⇒ B' enslave those who announce and believe in it? More generally, what is it about believing in idea '*X*' (or 'having' it in Heidegger's sense of a fore-having) that *entails* anything whatsoever? These questions suggest the hypothesis that Heidegger may have unreasonably denied his predecessors the very gift of freedom that he acknowledged in himself and, moreover, that in doing so he relied on a sort of crude formalism, according to which the A of a philosopher's belief in 'A ⇒ B' *necessarily leads to* (⇒) the B of his or her thinking, writing and other comportment. By way of evidence for this hypothesis, consider the following passage, in which Heidegger explains why metaphysics thinks in terms of a 'highest being', rather than experiencing being as such:

> Metaphysics has this character because it is what it is: the representation of beings as beings. *Metaphysics has no choice. As metaphysics, it is by its very*

> *essence excluded from the experience of Being;* for it always represents beings only with an eye to that aspect of them that has already manifested itself as beings. (1998: 288)

On its face, this text seems to claim that when metaphysics asserts *'A (the highest being) ⇒ B (other beings)'*, this very way of thinking and talking *compels* people to ignore being as such, and *compels* them to slide down a slippery slope towards the vacuity of technological thinking and its construction of a soulless world in the form of a standing reserve of useful matter. The best analogy to this thesis of necessity comes from the sphere of legal theory. The statement *'metaphysics has no choice'* is akin to the formalist assertion that words like 'due process' *automatically* produce their correct interpretation (and proscribe all incorrect interpretations), or that the word 'white' in a contract could *never*, under any circumstances, be rightly interpreted to mean black. It is important to understand that neither legal formalism nor Heidegger place that which they think determines human behaviour into the category of psychology: for legal formalism, legal texts are *metaphysically* related to their correct interpretations; and for Heidegger, our fore-havings and fore-conceptions are *ontological* determinations of our being-in-the-world, and therefore prior to all merely 'founded' modes of explanation, such as psychology. Science explains why and how A leads to B in terms of causal mechanisms and statistical probabilities: not so legal formalism and Heidegger. This makes Heidegger's assertion that *'metaphysics has no choice'* all the more puzzling: if believing in or having this or that version of 'A ⇒ B' leaves metaphysics no choice, and if this phenomenon of being-left-no-choice is not to be explained causally, then how *does* 'A ⇒ B' perform its dark magic? How *does* it manage to eclipse human freedom?

If the above-quoted passage on metaphysics and necessity were an outlier – an isolated instance of hyperbole on Heidegger's part – then it would be both possible and appropriate to overlook it. But the passage does not stand alone. Countless other similarly worded passages, of like import, are scattered like autumn leaves throughout his *oeuvre*. Here are just a few of them, by way of illustration:

- 'Calculative thinking *compels itself* into a compulsion to master everything on the basis of the consequential correctness of its procedure' (1998: 235)
- 'Every science adheres only to the penultimate and *must presuppose* the ultimate as first' (1992a: 160)
- 'Everywhere we remain *unfree and chained* to technology, whether we passionately affirm or deny it' (1977: 6)
- 'Enframing (*Ge-stell*) challenges itself forth into the frenziedness of ordering that *blocks every view* into the coming-to-pass of revealing and so radically endangers the essence of truth' (1977: 33)

- 'The still hidden truth of Being *is withheld* from metaphysical humanity. The labouring animal *is left* to the giddy whirl of its products so that it may tear itself to pieces and annihilate itself in empty nothingness' (2003a: 87)
- 'The tradition of the truth about beings, which goes under the title "metaphysics", develops into a pile of distortions, no longer recognising itself, *covering up* the primordial essence of Being' (2003a: 19)
- 'Being as presencing in the sense of calculable material ... *claims all the inhabitants of the earth in a uniform manner* without the inhabitants of the non-European continents explicitly knowing this *or even being able* or wanting to know of the origin of this determination of Being' (1972: 7)
- 'Metaphysics, insofar as it always represents beings as beings, does not recall Being itself' (Kaufmann 1956: 208)
- 'Being has brought it to pass in history that there is nothing to Being itself' (1991: IV, 222)
- 'The primordial problem of ground *cannot be conceived* on the basis of propositional truth' (1984: 128)
- 'In the history of metaphysics "being" *is always grasped* as beingness of beings and thus as these beings themselves' (1999a: 177)
- Representational thought '*cannot overcome* Descartes, nor even rise up against him, *for how shall the consequence ever attack the ground on which it stands?*' (1977: 148)

After reading these and other similar passages, one almost wishes one could bring Heidegger back to life and ask him to recall his conception of freedom as the taking *and the giving* of grounds. Whatever happened to this glorious freedom, and where did its 'giving' part go during the dismal history of being conceived as the history of metaphysics? Was freedom during the age of metaphysics like a Xerox machine, exactly reproducing the thought '$A \Rightarrow B$' indefinitely, until some 'great thinker' came along who somehow managed to create a new image of $A \Rightarrow B$, which freedom then chose to copy for a long while until *it* was replaced, and so on and so on, down to the present day?

These questions bring to mind Derrida's influential critique of structuralism in social theory and philosophy: the thought that structure *necessitates* social life seems to deny all possibility of change through 'play' (Kamuf 1991: vii–viii). Could it be that Heidegger was a closet or unconscious structuralist, despite the fact that he derided any philosophy which stops short of being as such as but '*an unattached shifting around in concepts as mere signs*'? (1985: 65). Could it really be the case that Heidegger thought that the '$A \Rightarrow B$' which characterised any particular era during the long history of metaphysics necessarily *entailed* the behaviours of those who internalised it as the self-evident truth, *entailed* that this particular ground led to its world in the way that '1 + 1' leads to '2'?

I am using the word 'entailed' quite carefully here, for despite his obvious sensitivity to historicity and the indeterminacy of language, Heidegger's critique of metaphysics betrays the belief, at least at some level, that something important *depends and must depend* on the way people talk and think. I say this not just because of the material quoted earlier, but because of a thought experiment that I have performed many times, and that I invite you to perform. I imagine taking Heidegger to a world that cannot help but gratify and please in every respect – a world without pain or suffering, for example, full of genuine joy and satisfaction, where people always treat both nature and one another with enormous respect, compassion and love, and where no one has ever heard of war, genocide, cruelty and environmental degradation. In this world, rivers such as Hölderlin's *Der Ister* sparkle and shine in people's lives in a way that would please Heidegger even during his most pernickety and poetic moods (1996a). The main problem is that all of the people in this world (except Heidegger, of course) talk and have always talked like vulgar yokels, in terms of representation, either/or, and the metaphysics of presence. Phrases such as '*the worldhood of the world*' (1962: 582), '*the thing things*' (1975b: 174), and '*appropriation appropriates*' (1972: 24) mean nothing to these people: for them, the world is the earth, a thing is just a thing, and an appropriation is what their legislature does when it votes to allocate funds. Every now and then, however, these people *do* ask themselves '*Why is there something rather than nothing?*', after which they always have a faraway look on their faces and exclaim 'Wow!', without further comment. In other words, the people in this world *experience* the wonder of being as such without ever feeling the need to *think* it.

I have to admit it: when I run this thought experiment, I almost always see Heidegger having a massive nervous breakdown from irresolvable cognitive dissonance. I am referring to the kind of dissonance that I imagine would spring up in him after he observed the utter absence of any apparent relation of 'leading to' (⇒) between these people's manner of speaking and thinking (A) and the shape of the world in which they live (B). Unless he believed in the order-giving comfort of something *like* a causal nexus between language and world, why did the early Heidegger, for example, think that traditional ontology had 'covered up' the question of Being, and why did he think that the destruction (*Destruktion*) of the history of ontology was worth doing at all? (1962: 44). And why did the later Heidegger think that calculative thinking 'compels itself' to mastery of the world? (1998: 235). Nietzsche's trenchant remark on the absence of a provable link between our opinions and our actions has always struck me as drawing a useful antithesis to our deeply ingrained prejudice that ways of talking and thinking really *do and must* matter: *'certainly our opinions, valuations, and tables of goods are among the most powerful gears in the clockwork of our actions'*, he wrote, *'but in every particular case the law of their mechanism is unprovable'* (Nietzsche 1995: 335). Although Heidegger knew this too, I am not speaking of merely 'knowing' something here, but rather of a tendency that lies buried deep in all of the ways of Western thought: the tendency to think that if the abstraction A is counted as 'true', then belief in the abstraction *must* lead to concrete outcome B.

Although he probably did not recognise this tendency in himself, Heidegger would undoubtedly have agreed that as a general matter the tendency to find a 'hardwired' connection between beings remains stuck at a level of thinking that is not yet mature. 'Mature' (ie Heideggerian) thought recognises that all necessity is grounded in unity – A cannot 'compel' B unless A is stable enough to be described as a unity resting in itself. The problem of unity is therefore absolutely central to a thinking engagement with metaphysics. Genuine thinking needs to ask: how can the stability of the ground emerge and sustain itself? Indeed, Heidegger himself knew that in metaphysics *'unity constitutes the beingness of beings'*, and that metaphysics always conceives of this unity, however casually and unthematically, on the model of a *'constancy that persists'* (2003a: 33, 87). He also knew that thinking had to deconstruct the absolute unity of metaphysical beings and their relations *before* penetrating to the ground. 'Temporality' and 'historicity' are, of course, the names of his main lines of attack on the unity of the metaphysical being. For Heidegger, metaphysical thinking blocks access to being as such in the way that an opaque curtain blocks access to what lies behind it. Extending the curtain metaphor a bit further, one could say that Heidegger knew that the curtain of metaphysical unity had to be ripped open before being as such could be seen. What he did not fully recognise, however, is that the deconstruction of unity is also the deconstruction of necessity: to show that there is such a thing as being as such requires deconstruction of the unity of the metaphysical being, but the deconstruction of this unity also proves that metaphysical thought cannot 'lead' to anything at all, let alone the oblivion of being as such.

The problem of unity

Heidegger's interpretation of philosophy as freedom, and freedom as freedom for ground, ultimately raises the problem of the *unity of the ground* that freedom supposedly takes and gives. In approaching this problem it is useful to ask how (by what means) the thought of 'A' *now* is the same as (or different than) the thought of 'A' at some *other* time. Even if Heidegger is right that language in general means *'signifying'* and *'letting notice'* (2004a: 17), the sameness-through-time of a mere sign (*'X'*) is not the same as the sameness of the sign's *interpretation*: it does not take a degree in law, literary theory or the philosophy of language to know that the sign *'X'* can mean (let-notice) one thing one day and something else the next. We know how Heidegger described the 'as-structure' of this or that being: he described it in terms of our fore-havings and fore-conceptions, both of which he conceived of as freedom's grounds for being-in-the-world *before* it approaches any particular being (2002b: 12). He formally defined the hermeneutic situation by the *initial position* of looking, the *direction of looking* (the 'as'-what), and the *scope of looking* (claims about the objectivity of an interpretation that happen to prevail at any given time), all of which *precede* the acts of looking and interpreting (2002b: 112). Since Heidegger made the initial position, direction and scope of looking into the *sine qua non* of the hermeneutic situation, let us call them the *a priori grounds* of looking and interpreting. That said, we are still entitled to ask how things stand with these grounding entities themselves. In particular: in what way is a fore-conceived ground for understanding and addressing beings the very 'ground' that *it* is, and how does it maintain the unity required of something that is allegedly so basic that it launches everything we think and do?

'If man did not already have Being in view', Heidegger once said, 'then he could not even think the nothing, let alone experience beings' (1992a: 146). Fine: from Heidegger's point of view the A of having-being-in-view grounds the B of all thinking and experiencing – this much we already know. *But now the time has come to ask what exactly it is that man has-in-view already before he experiences beings, such that precisely 'it' keeps on grounding his experiences right now, and then later, and then later still.* I mean, what *is* the ground that freedom takes and gives, such that we can say that it *is* its grounding self, as opposed to, say, an illusion – a mere trifle of beguiling images that we have thrown together to feed our desire for explanations?

Now it happens to be the case that the theme of the unity and disunity of *representations* is one that Heidegger extensively analysed and deconstructed in his exhaustive meditations on Kant's philosophy during the late 1920s. These texts, including especially the so-called *Kantbuch*, contain some of the most enlightening and significant thoughts ever written about the alleged self-identity of grounding ideas. In Kantian philosophy, the linguistic or pictorial 'representation' (*Darstellung*) of an image of ground presents itself to the consciousness of each subject that perceives it as the concrete-here-and-now of a stream of sense impressions that (as yet) lack the unity of form. The manifold of the sensible image of the ground still waits for the moment in which the pluralities that it loosely contains are transformed by abstraction from what the senses perceive into what the understanding knows *as* the unified image (*Vorstellung*) that it is. But *how* does this *Vorstellung* achieve its unity? This is the question Heidegger wanted to pursue. Logically speaking, Heidegger began his critique of Kantian idealism with the insight that the latter's project of grounding all objectivity in the transcendental subject requires that the categories and concepts of pure reason be immunised from all becoming-in-time, for Kant knew that their unity and universality would be compromised if they were exposed to the corrosive effects of history. It did not escape Heidegger's notice that Kant used *juridical* concepts to do metaphysics (as if he were a crusty legal formalist), since such terms tend to *'demonstrate ... [the] legitimacy, the justification of the ob-jective reality of empirical concepts'* (Heidegger 1997b: 208). The main consequence of Kant's need for lawfulness and stability was that he *'conceived the concepts, so to speak, as cut off from any relation to time'* (1997b: 212).

After exposing Kant's attempt to legislate a rigid separation between time and the concepts of pure reason, Heidegger proceeded to reveal a fatal gap, or circularity, in Kant's theory of how these allegedly timeless concepts achieve their unity: he showed that the concepts of pure reason, which are supposed to be *prior* to all experience and all understanding, cannot themselves achieve their own unity except *in* time, which is to say, *in* experience and history. Kant had stipulated that each representation, insofar as it is contained in a *single* moment, *'can never be anything but absolute unity'* (Heidegger 1997b: 234). The problem, however, is to understand *how* a representation can acquire even this modest level of unity, not to mention the more complex unity of its persistence throughout multiple moments. Heidegger's solution to this problem was simple and forthright. Since *'understanding of being in general is constituted on the basis of the temporality of Dasein'*, he wrote, Kant's schemata of the pure concepts of understanding (the categories) are *'a priori time determinations, and as such they are a transcendental project of the pure power of imagination'* (1997b: 289, 292). Only Kant's 'crudeness' and 'violence' with respect to the power of imagination prevented him from recognising it as the indispensable engine of all unity and disunity (1997b: 236).

As the foregoing discussion suggests, the most important concept for Heidegger's critique of Kant's philosophy is the 'faculty of the imagination', which Kant defined as 'a faculty of intuitions without the presence of the object', and therefore as a kind of 'productive power' in its own right (1997b: 280). In the first edition of the *Critique of Pure Reason*, Kant had characterised the imagination somewhat vaguely and mystically as *'a blind though indispensable function of the soul'*. However, after a while Kant grew 'afraid', as Heidegger put it, of sacrificing the transcendental apperception, which is the basis for the deduction of the categories, to the transcendental power of imagination (1997b: 279). Kant therefore deleted the phrase 'a blind though indispensable function of the soul' in the second edition of the *Critique*, and substituted a description of the imagination that demoted it to the undetermined status of a '*function of the understanding*' (Heidegger 1984: 211). This change shows, Heidegger said, '*how fundamentally uncertain Kant was, not only with regard to the power of imagination but also with respect to the basic relation between intuition and thinking*' (1997: 191). For how could the faculty of imagination be a mere 'function of the understanding' if all unity (including that of the understanding itself) is a function of the imagination? Heidegger noted that Kant never managed to resolve his uncertainty about the relation between the faculties of understanding and imagination – he never resolved whether the pure synthesis of imagination comes before the transcendental apperception, or after it (1997b: 279). Moreover, this unresolved uncertainty had disastrous consequences for Kant's philosophy as a whole: in leaving the unity of the ideas of pure reason without a determinate origin, he had also left his entire system hanging in the air, without any ground (1985: 141).

To recapitulate: if the Kantian synthesis that pushes the manifold of empirical intuitions into conceptual unities *takes time to accomplish*, as Kant acknowledged, then what about the intuitions that comprise the pure concepts of understanding? The suspicion arises that the impressions which Kant organised when he gazed within and saw what he took to be the categories of unity, plurality, totality, etc, acquire their unity in the same way that the empirical concepts do: that is, through the work of the faculty of imagination in time. Heidegger saw that if the categories are assembled *in* time, then Kant's 'reflecting judgment' (which passes from the objects of perception to the concept), and 'subsuming judgment' (which passes the other way), are no longer secured by a power of judgment that has been enabled by the categories *before* it enters time. This implies that reason is not a pure, isolated, and 'logical' faculty after all. Reason does not consist of timeless truths that only *then* get applied in time. On the contrary, the time-relatedness of the categories and concepts, which are pushed together as unities by an imagination that requires time to act, always precedes them as the condition of their possibility (1997: 193). Hence, Heidegger would say that '*the transcendental power of imagination is ...the ground upon which the inner possibility of ontological knowledge is built*' (1997a: 90). Although Kant had placed the cart of subjectivity before the horse of history, Heidegger put matters right by demonstrating that Kant's alleged transcendental subject is always already an immanent historical subject. The fog lifted, and it could be seen that the horse of being-in-the-world, ridden by freedom, had been pulling the cart of so-called 'subjectivity' and 'objectivity' all along.

These days the name that is given to the historical transformation of plurality into unity is *interpretation*. Heidegger once said that *'the utterance of the word is the speaking of the word into the ground, into the unruly in order for it to elevate itself into unity'* (1985: 128). Now recall his idea that freedom is the giving *and* the taking of ground. Although freedom simultaneously *takes* the unruly as its ground and *gives* back unity as ground, it is important to understand that Heidegger did not conceive of speaking unity into the unruly as something people do only once and a while. On the contrary, he called the becoming of freedom a *'standing in creation'* (1985: 131), and this means that freedom is always already ahead of any *particular* idea or past interpretation of its ground. One might say that freedom's utterance of the grounding word is an unceasing task with ontologically insecure results – a kind of endless singsong of interpretation, from birth to death.

The idea of freedom conceived as the ceaseless becoming of an interpretation leads to the question of *what*, exactly, interpretation interprets. If interpretation (as freedom) interprets the ground it takes and gives, and if this interpretation is a constant process of 'standing in creation', then what is it that creation creates, and interpretation interprets? The soundless dialogue between me and myself (*eme emautō*) that Plato calls 'thinking' will serve as a useful metaphor for understanding what this question asks. What do 'I' say to 'me', such that the unity of 'my' message to myself is preserved in its transmission and reception? Even Wittgenstein recognised that this kind of question raises a serious problem, and he attempted to solve it in his famous 'private language argument', which denies the possibility that we can sensibly employ a personal code to speak about the identity of our mental states over time (Wittgenstein 1953: 94e–95e). Although Wittgenstein would undoubtedly have been appalled by the mention of his argument in this context,[7] the alleged slipperiness or impossibility of 'I' saying something determinate to 'me' – something that holds up as an absolute unity

---

7 The point of Wittgenstein's private language argument is to disabuse philosophers of the belief that words such as 'thought' and 'pain' designate inner states. Thinking that they do leads to puzzlement about how one can ever *know* if another person is thinking, or in pain, since no one has any direct means of access to other people's inner worlds. The 'therapy' performed by the argument is supposed to *'shew the fly the way out of the fly-bottle'* of puzzlement by demonstrating that public words such as 'thought' and 'pain' have public criteria of use and verification that have nothing whatsoever to do with the 'inner' world of consciousness (Wittgenstein 1953: 103e). We will have much more to say about Zen-master Wittgenstein in Chapter 4.

through time – brings out the most important sense of Derrida's idea that there is always something *going on*, so to speak, that is *beyond* language, duty, law, and ground. As Derrida might have put it, this 'something' is an excess that haunts every event of certainty with the ghost of uncertainty, and that says to any claim that a ground is precisely itself and only itself, without remainder and without dispute, *'But of course, you know it might have been interpreted another way'*.

From the standpoint of the ground itself – *any* ground – having to undergo just *this* particular time-bound act of interpretation is its first historical moment. This moment, like all moments, does not last very long. The ground undergoes its second historical moment as its first interpretation slips into the past. Heidegger had the extreme acuity to see that the giving of ground (as a Kantian 'law' that the self gives unto itself) is a project that must *constantly* occur, if it is to occur at all:

> The pure will is not a mental occurrence that perceives the value of an independently existing law and directs our behaviour accordingly, *but itself constitutes* the factuality of the law of pure practical reason [in Kant's sense]. *Only because and insofar as the pure will wills, does the law exist.* (Heidegger 2002c: 200)

By way of connecting this passage explicitly to Heidegger's interpretation of freedom, one could say that freedom *takes* its ground from being and *gives* its ground back by willing it into being, but that the latter ground *as such* exists only in willing, and it is only as stable as willing is able to make it. This is because the 'second moment' of willing the ground as law is followed by a third, then a fourth, and so on. During these multiple time-bound acts of interpretation the image of the ground/law is exposed to still more contingency, as the will wills the ground *X* now as X_1, now as X_2, now as X_3, and so on. Always on the verge of breaking up into a multiplicity of possible or actual interpretations, the ground loses any *a priori* claim to *absolute* self-identity. The LAW becomes laws; the GROUND becomes grounds.

If human work is prior to the identity of the ground, it follows that different works can and do yield different identities. The 'same' ground is also always a 'different ground', because *this* work of interpretation is not *that* work of interpretation. At best the law of identity permits the two works of interpretation to by judged 'alike' by means of still another time-bound act of interpretation. The event of having the image of a ground to begin with (at t_1), and thereafter attempting to think and accomplish it (at t_2, t_3, and so on), comprises a historical *passage* that ruptures the ground's claim to any *a priori* self-identity. If unity is always the work of time, then each now-time of interpretation lacks any sort of *necessary* connection to another now-time of interpretation that would make 'the' abstract image of a ground into 'the' criterion of its accomplishment through willing. 'To think X and to will X': this way of putting people's relations to their grounds represents X as an abstract and unmediated unity. It fails to account for the passage between thinking then and thinking now: a passage that sunders X_1 as idea from X_n as accomplishment. In his work on Kant, Heidegger demonstrates that history is always intruding, as it were, on the way the operations of reason and understanding either hold concepts together, or let them fly apart. In a word, he *exploded* the presupposition of a ground's necessary unity, leaving it exposed to the corrosive drip-drip-drip of time. Although as far as I know Heidegger never explicitly made the connection between his deconstruction of unity and Buddhism, Buddhists have a name for the phenomenon that he uncovered: *impermanence.*

The neglected connection

It is a central tenet of Heidegger's thought that the meaning of truth and knowledge was radically transformed during the history of metaphysics. Truth as the un-concealment of what-is-present (*alētheia*) became truth as the certainty of a representation (1972: 79); and knowledge as a *journey* towards the event of pure seeing (Plato) became knowledge as a *destination* predetermined by submission to the authoritative word (1977: 122, 127). In *Being and Time*, Heidegger launched a direct attack on the modern precedence of certainty and authority over *alētheia* and freedom: although 'they' (*das Man*) apparently give freedom a comfortable and secure basis for generating and interpreting its grounds, he said that to submit *constantly* to what 'they' say is an inauthentic mode of being (1962: 167). The early Heidegger's opposition between the *'they-self'* and *authenticity* was the beginning of what became, in the *Kantbuch*, the even more radical deconstruction of the idea of representational unity as such. Heidegger very much wanted to upset truth-as-certainty and knowledge-as-authority by revealing that they are grounded in the history of being and the phenomenon of interpretation. Contemptuous of the kind of thinking that relies on *'a guiding image rendered secure in advance, as well as a standing ground fortified on all sides'*, he was always trying to disrupt the smugness of metaphysics by deconstructing the self-contained and self-sufficient unity of all merely conventional grounds (1977: 180).

Indeed, Heidegger's radical *doubt* about the unity of representations, and his almost violent subordination of the idea of conceptual unity to historicity, were to exert the profoundest sort of influence on the development of postmodern thought. *'Cultural significations posed as ultimate are the explosion of a unity'*, wrote Levinas, drawing attention to what he called the *'crisis of sense'* that Heidegger helped spark in the contemporary world (Levinas 2003a: 24). This crisis of sense is not *just* experienced as a loss of faith in monotheism (the death of God), but also includes the loss of 'rational faith' (my hopefully apt oxymoron) in the unifying power of the *logos*. One recalls immediately the 'deconstructive' thought of one of the West's most important post-Heideggerian thinkers, Jacques Derrida. For what is the practice of deconstruction, if it is not the demonstration that a ground purporting to be the *basis* of something else always carries within itself the seeds of its own dispersal and disunity? If ground X is always already on the verge of being deconstructed (or rather, deconstructing itself) into interpretations X_1, X_2, X_3, and so on indefinitely, then the problem of the ground in general becomes the problem of the ground's indeterminacy. But from the standpoint of Heidegger's thinking as a whole, all sufficiently radical demonstrations of a ground's indeterminacy create the risk of a dangerous kind of 'blow-back', so to speak. In opening the Pandora's box of indeterminacy in the *Kantbuch*, Heidegger exposed his concept of freedom (the power to give and take grounds) to the gravest risk of unintelligibly, or, what is worse, irrelevance. For what good is there in thinking in terms of grounds and grounding if a ground is never *itself* long enough to support anything?

After the publication of Heidegger's meditations on Kant, no serious thinker could ever again rightly take the unity of a concept for granted. In a world where the image of *a* ground immediately begins to break up into a plurality of different images of grounds, there can be no such thing as a stable 'ground' as such: there can only be the *illusion* of a stable ground. As Nietzsche put it, words that seem true to us are always only '*rainbows and sham bridges connecting what is eternally distinct*' (Heidegger 1991: II, 53). Freedom confronts each moment as '*lack*', Heidegger said, in the sense that it '*lets things matter in each case according to circumstances*' (1984: 196). But circumstances are constantly changing, and this means that the unifying power of the imagination is no mere 'conceptual' determination, as Kant said, but rather a contingent *seizing* (*Auf-greifen*) of this now in relation to other nows. If Kant defined the image as the unity of a *concept*, one could say that Heidegger defined it in a Greek manner, as *phantasia* (1991: IV, 228). This ancient word for 'image' signifies not the stability of an abiding unity, but rather the '*coming to presence*' of what comes to the fore in time: now this, now that, now something else – a moving kaleidoscope rather than a still photograph. Hence, unlike the Kantian movement from freedom to self-legislation, according to which everything follows clearly once the initial decision has been made, the Heideggerian movement from freedom-for-ground to ground represents a passage into uncertainty – the uncertainty of the ground's subsequent interpretation. Instead of $A \Rightarrow B$, we get $A \Rightarrow ?$.

If the unity of this or that ground that freedom chooses from its possibilities is always at risk, it would seem that the unity of *all* of

Dasein's possibilities are equally at risk, *including even the possibility of thinking being as such*. In other words, freedom as philosophy in Heidegger's sense undoubtedly seizes a starting point, an ending point, and all points in between, but there is no single 'where' and no single 'when' for this manifold of ground-points to *cohere* as an authentic saying of being as such. There is always only *now* and the images that transpire *now*. Under these circumstances, the real question is not whether being *is* or *is not*. The real question is much less grandiose, and goes to the *attitude* that one takes towards images: should one submit to the image that one has now by seizing it and trying to hold on to it for dear life, or should one just *let it come and go*? Heidegger had used the categories of temporality to deconstruct the difference between ground and grounded in Kant's philosophy. This led him to notice the phenomenon (and problem) of the ground's disunity, or impermanence. Would he now take the next and most important step? Lincoln once described wisdom in terms of a simple motto that the wise say to themselves: *'And this, too, shall pass away'* (Bartlett 1980: 520). Would Heidegger follow Lincoln's advice and use the category of impermanence to deconstruct the difference between being-as-ground and beings-as-grounded in his *own* philosophy? Would Heidegger finally let go of his attachment to the problem of being?

He would not. Despite the brilliance of Heidegger's early insights into the relation between unity and temporality, he did not thereafter make a connection between the *general* problem of the unity of representations, which he had uncovered in the *Kantbuch*, and the *specific* problem of freedom conceived of as freedom for the ultimate ground, being as such. In part, this neglect can be explained by his 'turn', after which he began to devote far less attention to the theme of human being-in-the-world (*Dasein*), and far more attention to the non-anthropocentric task of uncovering the truth of being as such. But in his post-'turn' attempt to let the dog of being wag the tail of *Dasein*, Heidegger almost forgot that he, too, was a human being, and that his access to being as such depended on freedom-for-ground – the *unity* of freedom in the form of thinking-being-as-ground. He did not recognise that the unity of the ultimate ground that freedom gives and takes in the mode of doing philosophy – the 'opening' or 'clearing' that is the gift of being as such – is also a *problem* that simply cannot be taken for granted without great danger of the worst kind of confusion. I am referring to the danger of mistaking a merely contingent image labelled *'being as such'* for the light of being itself. The point is not that Heidegger may have slandered being by confusing it with this or that image floating through his head. No, no, no! *'Though you say "It is", there is nothing which "is" can affirm; though you say "It is not", there is nothing that "is not" can negate'*: this is how the *Blue*

Cliff Record puts the point I am trying to make (Cleary 1992: 459). It seems to me that Heidegger missed the greatest of all chances: the chance to recognise that his cry *'Being is!'* is no more a response to being as such than the vulgar and thoughtless cry *'Being is not!'* is an evasion of it.

Had Heidegger connected his critique of the unity of the ground in Kant's philosophy with the problem of the ultimate ground (being as such), something extraordinary might have dawned on him. He might have realised that unless the mind stipulates uncritically in advance to the unity of the ground that freedom takes and gives as one of its possibilities, freedom, and with it being as such, would shatter into a billion pieces – *a billion glittering images*. He might have realised that submitting to the call or summons of being as such is like Caoshan's ass looking in a well, seeing its own reflection and assuming that it is looking at another ass (Cleary 1998: 219). And he might have been able, at long last, to escape from his self-imposed indenture to being as such by entering into what I can only call *the compassionate pursuit of the ordinary*.

'A Rough Idea'

We will end our meditations on Heidegger's thinking with a little story. In 1938, while he was teaching at Freiburg, Heidegger received a birthday gift from Keiji Nishitani, a young Japanese philosopher who was then doing research at Freiburg: it was a book of DT Suzuki's essays about Zen. According to Nishitani, shortly thereafter Heidegger sent him a card asking him to make a visit to Heidegger's home. When the two men at last sat down together, Nishitani discovered (perhaps much to his surprise) that Heidegger had already read the book, and that he was particularly interested in discussing a Zen koan mentioned in one of the essays. The koan itself is quite ancient, and is well known in Zen circles. It concerns three famous personages in the history of Zen: Rinzai, then a student of the Zen master Ōbaku, Ōbaku himself, and Daigu, another Zen master.[8]

The koan takes the form of a story, and within the present context this means that it is a story within a story. The tale begins with the young Rinzai having become dissatisfied with his progress under Ōbaku's teaching – it seems that the latter physically beat him every time he asked a question about the essence of Buddhism. Imagining that he could make more progress towards enlightenment by going to study with Daigu, Rinzai undertook the difficult journey to the latter's monastery. During

8 'Rinzai' and 'Ōbaku' are Japanese translations of the names of the 9th century Chinese Zen masters Lin-chi and Huang-po.

his first audience with Daigu, the master asked Rinzai to tell him what Rinzai's former master, Ōbaku, had to say about Zen. Rinzai answered: 'I asked him three times what was the essence of Buddhism, and three times he beat me'. Daigu replied: 'When Ōbaku, like a good old grandmother, has taken all this trouble over you, you still come here asking me whether you were at fault or not', and it was during these words, the story says, that Rinzai 'had the great awakening'. After a while, Rinzai returned to Ōbaku's monastery, whereupon Ōbaku asked him to relate what Daigu had said to him about Zen. After Rinzai told Ōbaku what had happened at Daigu's monastery, Ōbaku exclaimed, 'Just wait, I'll beat you up!' To this Rinzai immediately rejoined, *'What do you mean about waiting? Get it right now!'*, and then proceeded to punch his former master. Ōbaku then said, 'This madman who comes here to stroke the tiger's whiskers', and gave a *katsu*.[9] Thus ends the koan (Schloegl 1976: 77–79).

Now back to 1938. Nishitani took the occasion of his first meeting with Heidegger to give a philosophical explanation of this koan. Nishitani began by telling Heidegger about what he called the *'living logic of the oneness of Rinzai's affirmation and negation of Ōbaku'*. He then got to the bottom line, as it were, by explaining to Heidegger about the *'complex transformation between self and other'* that is shown by *'Rinzai's identifying Ōbaku with Daigu, and himself with Ōbaku'*. In other words, Nishitani interpreted the koan as a thesis about the illusory nature of our ontic distinctions between self and other, enlightened and unenlightened, and the essential and the non-essential. Distilled to its essence, he gave the sort of explanation that says *'What you call Being and we Japanese call Nothingness makes all human distinctions between beings look puny and artificial'*. After listening to Nishitani's subtle philosophical interpretation of the koan, Heidegger said, with a smile, that he had *'a rough idea'* of what Zen was about. Nishitani recalls that evidently Heidegger's interest in Zen was sufficiently piqued by this encounter for him to search out and read the only other book on Zen he could find in the university library, an obscure German text.[10] Heidegger later told Nishitani that he had found it *'also very interesting'*. And that's it: so ends the story of Heidegger and the koan.[11]

---

9 In Japanese Zen, a *katsu* is an expletive or shout uttered in the context of someone realising enlightenment.

10 The book is *Zen: der lebendige Buddhismus in Japan*, by Ohazama and Faust (Parkes 1987: 10).

11 The substance of this information about Nishitani's interactions with Heidegger comes from Graham Parkes's excellent introduction to a book of essays entitled *Heidegger and Asian Thought* (Parkes 1987: 910).

It is of course possible that Heidegger's 'rough idea' remark was simply a polite way of getting rid of a difficult guest, although his subsequent behaviour suggests otherwise. But to be honest, I don't really care about Heidegger's true motivation. I would like to view this story *as if* it portrays what Heidegger would have called a 'genuine encounter of thinking'. This is not because such a reading would show that there can be something like a *'mutual understanding'* between Heidegger's thought and Zen, as Nishitani himself would like to have it (Parkes 1987: 145), but because viewing Heidegger's reactions to the koan as 'thoughtful' may just allow *us* to achieve a breakthrough. Here's the thing: contrary to what Heidegger said, Zen is *not* 'interesting' – it is about as ordinary and uninteresting as this morning's bowl of cereal. What is more, a 'rough idea' of Zen, like a fully developed and correct one, is far, far worse than no idea at all: as Yun Men put it, in Zen *'a good thing isn't as good as nothing'* (Cleary 1992: 472). It would have been better for Heidegger if Nishitani had told him about the boring and unsophisticated interpretation of philosophy that Rinzai gave to his students in one of his lectures, after he had become a master: *'As I see it, there are not really so many principles. If you want to act, just act; and if you do not want to act, then rest'* (Schloegl 1976: 56).

Better still, Nishitani could have related a brief exchange to the same effect[12] between the Indian master Vashashita and Prince Punyamitra, the man who would eventually become his successor. At the time of the exchange, Punyamitra was trying to decide whether to become a Buddhist mendicant priest, a job for which he needed the master's approval. According to the story as it is told in *Transmission of Light*, Vashashita interviewed the prince to discover whether he was fit to become a mendicant. Here is what happened between them:

> When Punyamitra was a prince, the Buddhist master Vashashita asked him, 'Why do you want to leave home?' Punyamitra said, *'If I do leave home it is not for anything else'*. Vashashita said, 'Not for what?' Punyamitra said, 'Not for anything mundane'. Vashashita said, 'Then for what?' Punyamitra said, 'To do buddha work'. Vashashita said, 'Your wisdom is natural; you must be an incarnation of one of the sages'. Then the Buddhist master permitted the prince Punyamitra to leave home and become a mendicant. (Cleary 2001: IV, 115)

Why was Vashashita so impressed with Punyamitra's answers to his questions? The commentary points out that in Zen, so-called *'buddha work is not for oneself, not for others'*. Why do it then? From the standpoint of the

12 Actually, there is no Zen story that is not to the 'same effect'.

original (Zen) mind, the text says, there is no such thing as buddha work, and to understand that this is so is merely called 'buddha work' (Cleary 2001: IV, 116). Keeping in mind that Heidegger interpreted the principle of reason as human freedom's sublime way of uttering being as such, it is as if Punyamitra preferred to identify himself with the rose in Angelus Silesius's poem *Without Why*: if Punyamitra leaves home, it will be because he leaves home. Period. All of this suggests that Vashashita was not impressed with Punyamitra's answers because he thought that they had furnished some sort of *explanation* or *ground* for why the latter wanted to leave home. Indeed, Punyamitra's first answer denies that his hypothetical decision to leave home would be based on anything other than *just leaving home.* In this remarkable (one might say breathtaking) answer to the question 'Why?', one sees Punyamitra turning the form of a grounding statement ('A ⇒ B') back on itself: '*If I do leave home* [let us call this leaving B]', he says, '*it is not for anything else* [than B]'. Or, to put his answer in a more rigorous and precise form: 'B ⇒ B' – a thing like leaving home just is what it is, neither grounded nor ungrounded, neither exalted nor ordinary – in short, neither this nor that in any of its forms. A thing like Punyamitra's leaving home calmly and quietly repels all explanation – unless and until, of course, someone else's restless mind forces it into the Procrustean bed of a firmly held grounding-statement, 'A ⇒ B'.

It seems to me that recognising one can let go of craving attachment to the taking and giving of grounds is the final and most precious form of freedom. It is also the most difficult to achieve, largely because it is such a ridiculously simple thing to do. Letting go is not freedom *for* grounds, as Heidegger would have it. It is not even freedom *from* grounds, as a libertine or philosophical nihilist might say. Unlike Heidegger's thinking-being-as-such, which is always *something else* in relation to representational thinking, one might say that the recognition to which I am referring is the kind of awareness that enfolds all modes of thinking within the compassionate embrace of ... *nothing else.*

Chapter 3: Levinas's Problem of the Passage

Introducing the Problem

Very few thinkers in the Western philosophical tradition have ventured further into the problem of suffering than Emmanuel Levinas, and the originality and fecundity of his analysis of the relations among suffering, ethics and justice are undeniable. However, the surest criterion of a thinker's greatness is not the height of his achievement. Rather, it is the extent to which his thinking enacts a kind of spectacular failure: whether it brings into view *un*explored territory that is worthy of thought, and that can belong only to those who follow the thinker's journey to the outer boundary of the territory that he did explore. Precisely because Levinas took the problem of suffering to such depths, his work unveils a profound difficulty, if not an enigma, in these relations that the analyses of philosophers before him always overlooked or masked. This difficulty or enigma, which I will call the *problem of the passage*, can emerge only if thinking achieves a perspective that is capable of envisaging suffering *as such* – suffering without regard for its causes and justifications. Throughout his life, Levinas was transfixed by the phenomenon of universal suffering, and the *problem of the passage* names his own peculiar and very subtle manner of dealing with it: namely, by clinging to the fervent hope that the A of ethics could somehow be made to lead to the B of justice.

Ethics as first philosophy

Contrary to most Western philosophers, Levinas thought that the philosophical conventions associated with the terms 'origin' and 'ground' have constructed a kind of prison. They imprison thought in the language of being and knowledge: a discourse of beings that show themselves as present, and a discourse of what is or can become known about them. He did not despise that discourse, to be sure – indeed, he found it indispensable to justice – but he did find it inadequate to the task of uncovering the moment of ethics. 'The ethical moment', he writes, 'is not founded on any preliminary structure of theoretical thought, on language or on any particular language' (Levinas 1996: 148).

By his own admission, Levinas owes much to Heidegger's early thought, especially *Being and Time*, which Levinas calls 'one of the greatest books in the history of philosophy' (1998: 225). However, as we saw in the previous chapter, in one way or another Heidegger, like all philosophers of being before him, privileges the thought of a unifying ground over the thought of differences that not only persist without synthesis, but also repel reduction to a common origin. What is more, Heidegger characterises the being of the human being in terms of a care (*Sorge*) that is *for* itself and that always returns to itself. This way of describing the human being privileges the Same over the Other, and hence Heideggerian *Dasein* leaves little room for ethics as Levinas conceives it. Even Heidegger's interpretation of sociality as being-with-the-other-person (*Miteinandersein*) also rests ultimately on *Dasein*'s care for *itself*. '*Only because Dasein is primarily determined by egoicity [Egoität]*', says Heidegger, '*can it factically exist as a thou for and with another Dasein*' (1984: 187). While 'egoicity' is not the same as egoism – Heidegger claims that it is the ontological basis of both egoism *and* altruism – his interpretation of the human being seems to adopt a shocking indifference to the ethical implications of the various ways that *Dasein* can comport itself towards others. To be blunt about it: one gets the impression that the possibility of savagery and the possibility of kindness stand on an equal footing for Heidegger. Levinas alludes succinctly to his main difference of opinion with Heidegger on this score in one of his many interviews: 'I don't think he thinks that giving, feeding the hungry and clothing the naked is the meaning of being or that it is above the task of being' (1998: 116).

Levinas wants to exhibit, as ethics, a phenomenon of care for the other person that surpasses being and the ecstatic unity of Dasein's for-itself – that is 'otherwise than being' in a manner that is even more radical than Plato's *epekeina tēs ousias* (Levinas 1996: 114–15). The latter, in Book VI of the *Republic*, determines the good as that which 'transcends [*ousias* (being)] in dignity and surpassing power' (Plato 1961: 744). As Heidegger correctly notes, '[t]he expression "the idea of the good" [in Plato] – which is all too misleading for modern thinking – is the name for that distinctive idea which, as the idea of ideas, is what enables everything else' (1998: 175). The metaphor of the shining sun in Plato's elucidation of the meaning of the good indicates a kind of enabling that grants humans the ability to see and know what *is*, which Plato interprets as the stable presencing of what shows itself to reason in its idea amidst the flux of non-being that continually bombards the senses.

Levinas, however, finds in the face of the other person a haunting opacity that at once excludes the light of knowledge and kindles the heat of a radically *asymmetrical* responsibility – a debt that is due without any prior loan or trespass, a kind of 'guilt without fault' (Levinas 2001b: 52). He is determined to resist any attempt to place ethical responsibility in the category of an unveiled and understood idea, and he will not let the symbol 'ethics' drag its signified down to a world that would be accessible to reason. His stated point of departure is not the mystical, which he once said was 'always suspect to me' (2001b: 58), but rather the evidence furnished by phenomenology and by certain literary and biblical texts. Speaking in the idiom of phenomenology, Levinas is unequivocal. He discovers, beyond all doubt, the appearance of the 'for-the-other' in the phenomenon of the Other's '*face*' (2001a: 54), in which he catches sight of 'all the enormity, all the immensity, all the Infinity of the absolutely Other, escaping ontology' (2003a: 41). In the literary realm he is moved in the same direction by such works as Vasily Grossman's novel about the death of the socialist dream, *Life and Fate* (1986), which depicts numerous inexplicable acts of goodness 'from man to man', as Levinas puts it, in the midst of the Second World War and Stalinist repression (Levinas 2001b: 80–81). He also locates an important point of departure for his thesis that the I/Thou relation is asymmetrical in the following sentence from Dostoevsky's *The Brothers Karamazov*: '*Each of us is guilty before everyone and for everything, and I more than the others*' (2001b: 72). Finally, the fact that the command 'Thou shalt love the stranger' appears 36 times in the Pentateuch gives Levinas a certain kind of evidence (albeit admittedly not philosophical 'proof') that his phenomenological and literary findings are on the right track, at least as far as philosophy is concerned (2001b: 61–64).

Feeling abundantly supported by phenomenology, literature, and scripture, Levinas describes a responsibility for the Other that is 'prior to deliberation and to which I was exposed and dedicated before being dedicated to myself' (Levinas 1998: 230). In this respect, Levinas will consider the single and uniterated biblical injunction to '*love thy neighbour as thyself*' (Leviticus 19: 18) to be palpably inadequate when compared to the oft-repeated scriptural command to '*love the stranger*', for the former implicitly makes the ego's self-regard into the proper measure of its regard for others, while the latter puts the Other first in a regard that on its face appears to have no measure or limit (2001b: 64). The desire for the Other that is signified by the latter kind of love does not stem from egoistic need, but rather from a radicalised kind of compassionate concern for others. Quoting Dostoevsky again, Levinas calls this kind of compassion '*insatiable*', indicating that its intensity does not diminish with each new instance of its expression, as if it were a hunger that remains hungry no matter how much it is fed (Levinas 2003a: 31).

Levinas's 'other person' is not a knowable something, but neither is it an unknowable nothing: this Other (*L'Autrui*) transcends the categories 'being/non-being' and 'known/unknown', and its face marks the site of the *I*'s encounter with an otherness that is absolute. Ethics, Levinas says, is 'a comportment in which the other, who is strange and indifferent to you, who belongs neither to the order of your interest nor to your affections, at the same time matters to you' (2001b: 48). His notion of responsibility is not reducible to a scientific claim about some universal animal instinct of man, an argument that in any event would have to be judged unconvincing in the court of knowledge: our documents and memories contain a historical record of interhuman brutality that is too big and too depressing for this sort of claim to be believed. Rather, as Jill Robbins has put it, Levinas thinks that the evidence for his idea of ethics is 'more originary than the empirical' (Levinas 2001b: 1). His notion of responsibility comes into view somewhere between observation and aspiration, and finds its confirmation and its hope in the countless small acts of kindness that we perform daily for our neighbours and that they perform for us – each one *'a "small goodness" from one person to his fellowman that is lost and deformed as soon as it seeks organization and universality and system'* (Levinas 1998: 230). Without arrogantly claiming the right to institute charity in the guise of a political regime, Levinas appeals to the witness of 'goodness without regime' and to the ubiquitous acts of goodness that pass from person to person in a way that is 'exterior to all system' (2001b: 81). Ethical responsibility born of the everyday sociality of the face-to-face encounter is *the* primordial *datum* in Levinas's thought: it precedes all egoism, all rational calculation, all thought and all affective states. Breaking with any so-called 'cultural relativism', Levinas insists that ethics is prior to culture, in that it indicates a compassionate point of view that 'allows us to judge culture, to evaluate the dimension of its elevation' (2003a: 36).

Levinas will therefore construe the ethical relation – thought in terms of the intimate sociality of the '*I* and *you*' – as pre-reflexive, pre-gnostic, and pre-original. Reflection, knowledge, and origin have always belonged, in Western thought from Parmenides to Hegel (and beyond), to this or that totality conceived as the being of beings. They characterise a kind of thinking that denies the ultimate strangeness of the other person, and insists on an ethics of universal rules that are predicated on a thoroughgoing knowledge of being. Reflection, knowledge and origin belong, that is, to ontology and not to ethics, as Levinas interprets it. That is why I use the term 'passage' in this chapter, for it connotes a vague connection to, but also a certain unspecified distance from, the metaphysics of origins and grounds. The pre-original in Levinas remains the site for the commencement of a passage because his 'ethics as first philosophy' (1989: 75–87), while overthrowing ontology as the proper and only beginning point for philosophical thought, still leads *from* here (ethics) *to* there (ontology, including politics, law and justice). Although he reverses Heidegger's philosophy by making ethics the site from which ontology emerges, his thinking and Heidegger's both *move* identically: they move, that is, according to the structure of logical transcendence, whereby a thing is always a 'to' (B) that must be accounted for by a 'from' (A) that leads (⇒) to it.

From ethics to justice

Levinas's interpretation of the passage from ethics to justice slips profoundly into the difficulty or enigma of *how* A is supposed to move to B. *This* slippage is not the consequence of sloppy or 'illogical' thinking. Nor does it come from a conflation of metaphor and being (or otherwise than being), as Derrida claims, for that claim too is a problematic passage. It slips mysteriously 'from' a metaphor in the medium of language (or one text), 'to' a confusion or arrogance in the medium of thought (or another text), without making a problem of the assertion that the one 'leads', presumably in the manner of a cause or ground, to the other. Such a claim makes sense of the slippage from A to B, while also covering it over by appealing to authority drawn from the same metaphysical order that the claim was intended to deconstruct. There is nothing wrong or lamentable in this procedure – indeed, it may be an inescapable feature of any deconstruction whose intelligibility depends on the tools of the very discourse that it deconstructs. But such a method cannot aspire to uncover the very problem (of the passage) of which it is an unthinking manifestation. Derrida's slippage and Levinas's are profounder by far than any opposition between deconstruction and empiricism. They are the inheritance of all thinking in the Western tradition, and in particular of what Chapter 1 identified as *the* guiding principle of that thinking: *logical transcendence*. Craving attachment to this principle attempts to inscribe the 'from/to' movement in the innermost essence of being and thought. According to the norm of logical transcendence, if suffering (B) exists then it must have an addressable cause or ground (A): enter the justice that seeks to ameliorate at least some kinds of suffering by employing techniques to overcome the conditions that lead to it.

Amanda Loumansky has written that Levinas 'rarely speaks of justice *per se* because he is not content to be held within its boundaries' (2000: 389). While this accurately describes Levinas's stance on justice conceived as an *end*, it ignores the fact that Levinas has written much about the violent *means* that necessarily attend the movement towards any imaginable justice. For Levinas, the hour of justice necessarily 'offends the alterity of the face' by reducing the singularities that are both the unjust and those who seek justice to knowable and manipulable categories (1998: 167). Yet this hour is preceded by a moment of ethics when the face signifies without being either known or offended. Opposed to an ethics of norms and reciprocal obligations, but also opposed to the passive acceptance of evil, Levinas will both have his cake and eat it by making ethics the basis of justice: '*Ultimately it is a question of founding the justice that offends the face on the obligation with respect to the face*' (1999: 34). By using the phrase 'a question of founding' in this sentence Levinas did not mean to put the problem of the passage *into* question – indeed, the problem of logical transcendence as such always remained hidden from him. Rather, in aphorisms such as 'justice is warped without charity' (2001b: 181) and in countless other texts, Levinas makes it clear that he interprets the 'question of founding' as the irremissible *task* of founding justice on ethics. An odd kind of founding this is, however, in which the absence of a unifying milieu for the passage (or leap) from ethics to justice threatens the very intelligibility of the project.

The site of ethical responsibility

In traditional accounts of ethics the site of ethical responsibility is the *subject*. Secure in its identity with itself in being, the subject bears its responsibility the way that a dump truck carries a load of gravel: that is, in such a way that it is capable of carrying the responsibility and eventually discharging it. This subject is not the body, but the *I* of the 'I think'. It finds in *what* it thinks adequate representations of its various relations with others and the ethical norms that regulate those relations. On this view, ethics is a matter of knowing: the traditional ethical subject is an *intentional* being who gathers representations within itself and then uses them to take aim at its future behaviour.

Levinas plainly cannot find the milieu for the passage from ethics to justice in one such as this, for the immanence of knowing that belongs to the traditional ethical subject completely obliterates the otherness of the Other. Levinas will therefore find a milieu for the passage in a subject who is enmeshed from the outset in a relation with the Other – a subject construed as pre-theoretical, in the phenomenological tradition, but also as pre-reflexive and non-intentional, contrary to that tradition (Levinas 1998: 26). Levinas's ethical subject does not *comprehend* the ethical encounter, but rather is *put into question* by it. Consequently, against Husserl's claims about the constituting and knowable essence of transcendental apperception, Levinas interprets the *I* as essentially *ineffable*: the 'oneself', although '"in itself" as one is in one's skin', is nonetheless a kind of identity that is 'unutterable'; hence, it lies on 'this side of the distinction between the particular and the universal' (1996: 84–86). Levinas writes that 'the wonder of the *I* relieved of self and fearing for the other is also something like the suspension – the *epoché* – of the eternal and irreversible return of the identical to itself, and of the inviolability of its logical and ontological priority' (1998: 147). This would come close to being Buddhism's thesis of compassionate no-mind (*anátman*, in Sanskrit) – the mirror that both reflects without attachment and seeks to liberate others from suffering – were it not for what is supposed to 'follow' from Levinas's conceptual effacement of the other-regarding self.

If, as Spinoza said, *conatus essendi* is the metaphysical determination of a being's striving to persevere as a unity through time (Spinoza 1955: 135), then it was Levinas who first uncovered the 'hidden violence' of this perseverance (1998: 194). Levinas is fond of quoting Pascal's aphorism that the statement 'this is my place in the sun' is the 'beginning and the image of the usurpation of all the earth' (Pascal 1941: 102). However, he radicalises Pascal's words by transforming them from an ironic comment on the proud and belligerent cry of the possessor into the genuine expression of a kind of *anxiousness*. This anxiousness worries whether the 'innocent' *I* is not so innocent after all – whether it may be ethically responsible merely for taking up a place in the world that might have been, and might still be, the salvation of others, in the third world and elsewhere. '*My "being in the world" or my "place in the sun", my home – are they not a usurpation of places that belong to the other man who has already been oppressed or starved by me?*' (Levinas 1998: 130). Hence, Levinas will construe the suffering of compassion as meaningful in this anxious *I*, but the suffering of the Other as useless.

Levinas's anxiety-ridden *I* transcends itself in the moment of ethics, but not so that responsibility can be borne by some diaphanous transmutation of a previous solidity. The ethical self is not a modification of a prior self that may or may not subsequently choose to become ethical. For Levinas, we are all ethical beings from the outset, and he construes the possibility of behaving unethically as merely a modification of an always-prior and pre-original sense of ethical responsibility. Thus, Levinasian self-transcendence lets responsibility become the determination of *both* the transcending and the transcendent self, which means that prior to the moment of ethics there is no comprehensible *I*, strictly speaking. His ethical *I* is *a priori*, and it is none other than ethical responsibility itself. An originary responsibility to use the body that lacks a 'user' or a stable site in (or as) a thematised consciousness, Levinas's concept of the ethical *I* relegates the transcendental ego, which Husserlian phenomenology alleges is the source of all meaning and intentionality in empirical history, to the status of a superstructural and *a posteriori* construction.

Nevertheless, if this anxious, pre-theoretical and ineffable subject is an ethical responsibility *before knowledge*, and if the work of justice is pursued *by means of knowledge*, where or how is the traction (or transition) that accommodates the passage from the one to the other? This question begins to indicate a slippage that is not so much a category mistake as it is a manifestation of the mind's intense desire to achieve a solution to the problems that it poses to itself. Of course, thinking's intense desire for a solution to the problem of suffering is itself a form of suffering – does not Wittgenstein compare philosophy to a disease? (1953: 155) – and it is understandable that thinking would want to put an end to its torment in this way. But could it be that the momentary cessation of thinking's torment through attachment to a solution or the possibility of one is merely one mode – perhaps even a deficient mode – of thinking's persistence in being? In that case, the thesis that ethics leads or can lead to justice would be a kind of *clinging* that betrays the very idea or aspiration of ethics as transcendence. What is more, could it be that an ethics that bears witness to suffering as such, and a justice that is oblivious to suffering as such because it is both a remedy *and* an agent of suffering, have absolutely nothing in common except the thinker's unbearable yearning for the one to lead to the other? In that case, what is *before* thought and what is accomplished *by means of thought* could never be brought together *by* thought, except in a form that devours itself.

Suffering as Such

What the angel of history sees

Levinas's philosophy of the *I*'s essential being-for-the-other finds common ground with Buddhism in a category that I will call *suffering as such*. 'Suffering as such' names the ever-mounting accumulation of each and every concrete moment of suffering in the world, however justified and whatever its causes and conditions may be. Walter Benjamin's description of the 'angel of history' allows us to catch a glimpse of it. In the ninth of his *Theses on the Philosophy of History*, Benjamin imagines that this angel is like the one that Paul Klee painted in *Angelus Novus*. Eyes staring, mouth open, and wings spread, the angel's face is *'turned toward the past'*, Benjamin says. The description continues:

> Where we perceive a chain of events, he sees one single catastrophe which keeps piling wreckage upon wreckage and hurls it in front of his feet. The angel would like to stay, awaken the dead, and make whole what has been smashed. But a storm is blowing from Paradise; it has got caught in his wings with such violence that the angel can no longer close them. The storm irresistibly propels him into the future to which his back is turned, while the pile of debris before him grows skyward. This storm is what we call progress. (Benjamin 1968: 257–58)

Figure 3.1
Angelus Novus
Paul Klee (1910)

If there really were an angel of history such as the one that Benjamin describes, his main occupation would be to bear witness to *suffering as such*. Not only would this angel see the terrible cost of what history's winners call 'progress', he would also see the many mundane moments of suffering that happen every day, but that somehow never get noticed in the history books or in the halls of government. Little sufferings and big ones, suffering that is someone's fault and suffering delivered out of the blue by an impersonal fate, the mortifications of oppressors called to judgment as well as the agonies of the oppressed, the torments of the unjust and unethical as well as the passions of the righteous: the angel of history would see them all. *'Life is suffering'*, according to the Buddha's First Noble Truth:

> The world is full of suffering. Birth is suffering, old age is suffering, sickness and death are sufferings. To meet a man whom one hates is suffering, to be

> separated from a beloved one is suffering, to be vainly struggling to satisfy one's needs is suffering. In fact, life that is not free from desire and passion is always involved with distress. This is called the Truth of Suffering. (Buddha 1966: 38)

According to Schopenhauer, whose thinking was greatly influenced by his own idiosyncratic understanding of Buddhism, *'the ceaseless efforts to banish suffering achieve nothing more than a change in its form'* (1969: I, 315). *'The mass of men lead lives of quiet desperation'*, observed Thoreau (1950: 7). *'Action is suffering and suffering is action'*, says Thomas à Becket in *Murder in the Cathedral* (Eliot 1963: 21). Willie Loman's suicide, in *Death of a Salesman*, is preceded by his anguished calculation that the proceeds of his life insurance are worth more to his family than he is: thus does art warn philosophy that there are some forms of suffering that make non-existence look like a blessing (Miller 1945: 125–26). Although these examples may seem to elevate suffering into a metaphysical category, one need not be a philosopher to catch sight of its ubiquity. Physical pain is but one of the more obvious modes that transfix us in suffering; the list of nouns that identify the others is impressively long,[1] and a phenomenology of all these modes of suffering that did justice to each of their many ways of appearing would fill the shelves of a good-sized library.

Whether suffering is life's very determination, from the cradle to the grave, or whether it happens only interstitially, amidst an otherwise pleasurable hedonic flow of life, the main point to notice now is that the category 'suffering as such' includes each and every moment of suffering in all of its many forms. What is more, Levinas's ethical philosophy, like Benjamin's angel of history and the Buddha, *practises no discrimination in the face of this suffering*. Non-discrimination in the face of universal suffering is the very meaning of Levinas's notions of the *'the hateful I'*, *'being-for-the-other'*, and *'taking upon oneself the fate of the other'* (2001b: 165). To be responsible, in Levinas's sense, for suffering as such is thus equivalent to being responsible for the suffering of the good and the bad, the just and the unjust, the poor and the rich – as if Wittgenstein's assertion that the world of the happy man is a different one from that of the unhappy man were the exact opposite of the truth (Wittgenstein 1974: 72).

---

1 Here is a partial list, in no particular order: grief, despair, anguish, fear, anxiety, regret, sorrow, revulsion, disgust, bitterness, envy, hatred, jealousy, contempt, longing, disappointment, boredom, agitation, impatience, embarrassment, shock, guilt, hunger, thirst, dizziness, resentment, compassion (suffering for another's suffering), loneliness, panic, shame, helplessness and greed.

Compassion

If suffering as such is a universal category that is accessible to phenomenological inquiry, Levinas interprets compassion for it in the same way. Phenomenally speaking, the phrase 'compassion for suffering as such' represents the *this* and the *how* of a permanent *encounter*. In encountering suffering, a thoroughly radicalised compassion – one that does not differentiate between sufferings, whether according to their causes or on any other ground – meets *all* sufferings that it encounters on an equal footing. The context of any one such compassion (its *now* and *here*, together with its *vision*, all determined on the basis of its *history*) undoubtedly prevents it from recognising everything that another compassion might be able to recognise as suffering. The point is not that a radicalised compassion occupies a neutral and omniscient (or all-feeling) point of view, but that it practises no discrimination among those sufferings that it recognises *as* suffering.

How does this non-discrimination show itself? Consider Walter Benjamin's image of the *'revolutionary killing of the oppressor'* (1978: 298), which allows us to glimpse a feature of the problem of suffering that is ordinarily overlooked or elided by our tendency to discriminate. His image of self-righteous slaughter is a reminder that even the just and necessary desserts of 'bad' people are engines of suffering for someone. Consider the anguish and privation of those innocents who love or otherwise care about the punished one. Where is the justice in the tears of the parents, spouse and children of those who are justly repressed or destroyed? Then there is the intractable problem of those unfortunates who, caught in a web of circumstantial evidence, delay, defensive inadequacy or prosecutorial excess, fall unfairly under the wheels of a system of justice that is inevitably less than perfect. One might even say that convention counts the suffering of both classes of innocents as unavoidable 'collateral damage' in the war that justice wages on injustice. As for the guilty, the case could be made that the justly punished suffer *more* than the unjustly punished for every increment of pain they endure. Martyrs can dilute their torment by entertaining the sublime belief that some day justice will be done on their account. But the just suffering of those who are guilty of injustice, like the supposed pain of those in hell, is unmitigated by any prospect of a better justice to come.

Ethics and justice owe their existence and their respective orientations to the vast ocean of suffering as such. For in a world without the possibility of suffering, or where suffering is always experienced as 'delight and consolation', as Meister Eckhart (1994: 87) would have it, actions and states of affairs would never be felt as affronts, and the curative and redemptive powers of ethics and justice would have no occasion to cure or redeem anything. Undoubtedly this helps explain why those who exercise power over others so frequently respond to suffering by ignoring or minimising it, or by trying to convince sufferers that it does not exist – 'What the eye doesn't see the heart doesn't grieve over' (Wittgenstein 1983: 205). As Gramsci (1971: 161) and Marcuse (1964: 82) both remind us, if people can be convinced that law, politics and economy have solved or are on the way to solving a 'problem of suffering' that is reduced to an abstraction by concepts, the possibilities for social transformation on the basis of radicalised versions of ethics and justice are greatly reduced.

Ideology's power to pacify to the contrary notwithstanding, however, people always seem to *crave* this or that, and in their craving they yearn for relief. Hence, they never seem totally convinced by the various religious and secular versions of Meister Eckhart's thesis that their suffering should aspire to be like God's: 'Suffering is so blissful for him that suffering is not suffering for him at all' (1994: 87). Humans are not like God in at least one crucial respect: we whine, He doesn't. Since people have a tendency to keep on craving things and yearning for relief from whatever unpleasant condition they happen to be in, their suffering remains the ever-renewed raw material, as it were, of both ethics and justice. A curious raw material this is, however, that not only vastly exceeds the capabilities and aspirations of the fabricators that turn their attention to it, but also becomes a distinct by-product of the fabrication process itself.

The scission of suffering

Consider law, the tool that modern conceptions of justice always seem to turn to first in their efforts to describe how to get from the *here* of injustice to the *there* of justice. If we try to take a perspicacious and honest view of law, we ought to be able to see that its *ultimate* task is not to determine and enforce rights, to establish public values, to do the will of the people's representatives, or to create the entitlements that enable the market to function. All of these ends come after law's task is accomplished and are but effects of, or purported justifications for, what law's task is in itself. To put that task bluntly, in its most basic and immediate sense, *law is the practice of dividing human suffering*. In suffering, people are weighed down by the burden of their present unhappiness. They want it to go away. They yearn to transform the future more to their liking, and so sometimes they turn to law as a method of transformation. Just like Jesus's parable of the shepherd dividing the sheep from the goats (Matthew 25: 32), law divides people's suffering into two parts: the suffering that is socially acceptable, and the suffering that is not. Only those whose anguish falls on the latter side of the line are called rights-holders, and only they may invoke law's coercive methods to the end of lessening their pain. Law ignores all the others – those without rights – thus exacerbating their discomfort: for the feeling of being ignored by those with the power to help can create or accentuate the despair that so often accompanies persistent suffering.

Like law, traditional approaches to ethics and justice are unquestionably attuned to *some* forms of suffering. At the same time, however, they remain just as indifferent as law is to the suffering that lies beyond the ambit of their care, and they even seek to justify the infliction, perpetuation, or enhancement of those sufferings that are felt to be right, just, or necessary. Thus, the given is transformed by a relentless negativity, as Hegel would have it, that continually readjusts and reallocates suffering, but does not eliminate it. Being and knowledge hold ethics and justice to account whenever they are in danger of slipping too far into egotism or tyranny, and a rationalised ethics and justice confront being whenever the latter is in danger of apologising for itself too readily. The result is a 'wise balance' between suffering and the good or the right that is achieved and maintained, at any given time, in the supposedly excellent immanence of knowledge and reason.

The idea of peace on the basis of knowledge originates from reason's interpretation of opposition as violence – what Levinas calls the violence of the 'scission of being into Same and Other' (1996: 13). Knowledge seeks to overcome this opposition by healing the scission: by absorbing the Other into the Same in the form of an adequate representation. The idea that all reasonable people have access to the same knowledge leads each to imagine him- or herself as a Same-that-knows-others and an Other-known-by-sames. From this arises the categorical imperative, whereby the norms legislated by every reasonable Same are always the same – both universal and universally immanent. Whenever peace and justice elude the subject who considers himself reasonable (and which one does not?), this *must* be because reason and knowledge have departed from the consciousness of his opponent. Perhaps the apotheosis of this way of thinking is Kant's argument that no matter how peaceful in fact a person may be, if he does not submit explicitly to the law's authority – if he stubbornly persists in living idyllically, in a lawless state of nature – then the threat posed by his proximity alone is enough to justify law-loving people to 'use violent means to compel [him] to enter into a juridical state of society' (Kant 1965: 77).

Thus unfolds, in the West, a history of thought about law, ethics and justice that considers itself to be firmly grounded in ontology and knowledge. Ethics requires that the irremediable despair of the man contemplating suicide go on and on, says Kant, because the categorical imperative shows him, or ought to show him, that the 'principle of self-love' that underlies the practice of suicide contradicts itself when made into a general law (Kant 1993: 187–88). The penalty that stings or even destroys someone is the essence of corrective justice itself, says Aristotle, at least so long as it rectifies a victim's loss and reverses the wrongdoer's gain (1984: II, 1786). Since the suffering in a state of nature (where 'the life of man [is] solitary, poore, nasty, brutish, and short') exceeds by far the suffering that is inflicted by sovereign power, reason shows that the latter is justified as the lesser of two evils, writes Hobbes (1914: 87–90). 'An unjust law has the nature, not of law, but of violence', according to Thomas Aquinas, who thereby casts punishment according to just laws into the unproblematic category of the non-violent (1948: 633). According to a tenet that is common to these various philosophies of ethics and justice, just and necessary suffering, if it is noticed at all, appears in the guise of a natural occurrence, and it asserts no greater claim on the conscience than do the deaths of the animals whose flesh we consume every day.

As these examples indicate, traditional approaches to ethics and justice create a scission of suffering – bad suffering is distinguished from suffering that is ignored or justified – and hence fail to attain a perspective from which it is possible to think suffering as such. To be sure, compassion is an affect that might yield such a perspective, but only if it could be sufficiently radicalised. To be adequate to the task, such compassion would have to be 'reformulated and salvaged from gross humanism and sentimentalism', as Marinos Diamantides puts it (2000: 151), for merely sentimental forms of compassion are always intermittent and conditioned by the winds of fate. For Levinas, as for Buddhism, compassion for the Other's suffering never ceases: it is like the symbol of compassion in Mahāyāna art, the figure of the *Bodhisattva Avalokiteśvara*,[2] who has 1,000 arms extending in all directions. Similar to Buddhism's *karunā* (usually translated tepidly as 'compassion'), Levinas's radicalised conception of compassion shows itself phenomenally as an existential comportment and not merely as a psychological content – a kind of *calling* that claims our motility from the very beginning, before any individualised feelings of guilt arise (Parkes 1987: 257).

How does the category of compassion for suffering as such stand in the tribunal of reason? To ask this question at all is almost to answer it. Even if it were established that there could be a kind of compassion that spreads its net that widely, reason in its traditional modes would undoubtedly spurn or ridicule it as *useless*. Reason 'knows' that the elimination of universal suffering is an impossible pipe-dream, best

---

2 Sanskrit for 'the enlightened one who looks down on high'.

deferred and reduced to that world in heaven, promised by Christian theology, where true believers are transported after they die. Indeed, the imagined torments that the ungodly will experience in hell appear to be precedents for upholding their sufferings while they are alive, as the otherwise congenial mystic Meister Eckhart indicates: 'if someone does not put their trust in God ... then it is only right that they should experience suffering and pain' (1994: 84). Faith and reason thus conspire to restrain worldly compassion, closely rationing it to those cases in which it is both 'right' and 'feasible' to do something about the suffering in question. The widespread belief that another's suffering is sometimes (or even presumptively) *deserved* is a cage that prevents the gentle beast of compassion from leaving the terrain that faith and reason have allotted to it. So too is the thesis that suffering on account of 'bad acts' is the law of nature, as in Leibniz's contention that 'sins carry their punishment with them by the order of nature, and by virtue of the mechanical structure of things itself' (1934: 19). Hence, reason declares the uselessness of compassion for 'necessary' suffering, thereby condemning it to ridicule or worse in a society that judges everything according to the criterion of its usefulness.

Benjamin's 'Critique of Violence'

Only very rarely does thought's awareness rise high enough (or rather, descend low enough) to glimpse the ocean of suffering in its entirety, and even then the thinker almost always falls back into the practice of justification – as if the mere sight of the immensity of *all* the pain that humans experience is more than the thinker can bear without recourse to a certain hard squinting at that portion of suffering that is taken to be justified or necessary. Walter Benjamin is one of the most notable of these rarities. In his essay *Critique of Violence* (1978: 277–300), for example, he was able to look at history without blinking, as it were, and what he found there was nothing but violence and apologies for violence in the age-old march of human law and justice. While most thinkers see only the march, Benjamin steeled himself to look at the corpses and shattered lives of those whose suffering was deemed just and necessary by the marching hordes or their generals. It is as if Benjamin had transformed himself into the Angel of History that he had so eloquently described in *Theses on the Philosophy of History*.

Nevertheless, in *Critique of Violence*, Benjamin re-enacts a figure that has been a mainstay of Western philosophy since Plato's allegory of the cave first brought it on the scene: the thinker's upward journey to the transcendent is followed by his downward return to the world of interested and brutish opinions and actions. The thought that God's 'divine violence' assures a possible end to the historical cycle of interested law-making that Benjamin calls 'mythical violence' is at first an upward journey to a One who is absolutely Other. It represents what I called in Chapter 1 *theological transcendence*: *from* thought's entanglement in the world of interest *to* an infinite One whose 'expiatory power of violence is not visible to men', and who therefore does not and cannot occupy the order of the knowable (Benjamin 1978: 300). Benjamin's moment of transcendence is the ascent of a thinking that somehow 'has' the idea of the infinite without being able (or willing) to reduce it to knowledge.

This brief moment is followed, however, by the descending return of one who would transform transcendence into a use-value in the world of men and women. For as Benjamin puts it, if divine violence exists, this '*furnishes the proof that revolutionary violence, the highest manifestation of unalloyed violence by man, is possible, and by what means*' (1978: 300). God (A) thus silently promises redemption for the suffering that comes with and in the wake of this sanctified violence (B): a conclusion that shows the $A \Rightarrow B$ of logical transcendence working its usual magic on the imagination. That this magic could be made to produce revolting conclusions is the most important point that Derrida makes in criticising Benjamin's essay in light of the Auschwitz that it preceded by 20 years: 'One is terrified at the idea of an interpretation that would make of the holocaust an expiation and an indecipherable signature of the just and violent anger of God', Derrida writes, not unreasonably (1990: 1045). Enchantment with transcendence also helps to explain Benjamin's troubling expression of contempt for the 'false and ignoble' doctrine that the sanctity of life is a value more important than achieving a just existence for human beings (Benjamin 1978: 298): for here is a contempt that signals a chilling inclination to avert the gaze, and thus to suspend compassion, when it comes to such deeds as the revolutionary killing of the oppressor. A compassion radicalised by the acuity of a vision that absorbs the full sweep of history's brutality is thus promised respite from the heavy burden of suffering on account of *all* suffering. The promise comes not from reason's conviction that its norms for distinguishing good suffering from bad suffering are adequate to the task, as in conventional ideas of ethics and justice, but from the hope that God does and will judge at least some sufferings to be expiations. The threads of faith and hope thus save violence in the name of justice from falling into tragedy.

Levinas's 'Useless suffering'

In the essay 'Useless suffering', Levinas reaches a level of thinking about suffering as such that matches or exceeds Benjamin's analysis of violence as such (Levinas 1998: 91–101). The phenomenology that Levinas exhibits there characterises suffering in terms of a passivity that *undergoes* rather than achieves. No longer seen as the attainment of an active consciousness, suffering becomes the very submission or irrelevance of that consciousness. Even sensibility is already a reception that is eager to transmit its data to an active and thematising consciousness, whereas suffering itself is 'more profoundly passive than the receptivity of our senses' (1998: 92). Suffering is a helpless opening to evil, a pure undergoing that rends rather than knits the humanity of the sufferer. We may complain to and take comfort from others, but we suffer alone. Suffering is the tragedy of the *ego*'s impotence. It appears phenomenally as a solitude locked within itself, afflicted and beset before and despite all projects. Thus, Levinas will conclude that 'the least one can say about suffering is that, in its own phenomenality, it is useless: "for nothing"' (1998: 93).

If the moment of suffering as such is for or on account of nothing, Levinas also notices that this moment almost always undergoes a dramatic subsequent transformation in consciousness. Consciousness proceeds to rationalise suffering's brutal phenomenality by making it useful for something: perhaps the sign of merit and a hoped-for reward. The appeal of the eternal rest that awaits sufferers in heaven, and the earthly compensation of wisdom that convention promises to those who suffer and survive, allow the mind to make suffering into the image of a necessary means to a desirable end for the individual. Wittgenstein's idea that ethics has nothing to do with punishment and reward in the usual sense of these terms offers another kind of comfort, for it alleges that reward and punishment for what we do will reside 'in the action itself' (1974: 72). The formulas *'you are getting what you deserve'* and *'let your conscience be your guide'* thus reassure us that the universe is presently justifying whatever we may be feeling as we act. In addition to spinning stories like these that are designed to comfort the individual who suffers, reason also gives suffering a use-value in constructing its political teleologies, as Levinas so acutely describes:

> It is said to be necessary to the teleology of community life, when social discontent awakens a useful attention to the health of the collective body. Perhaps there is a social utility in the suffering necessary for the pedagogic function of Power in education, discipline, and repression. Is not fear of punishment the beginning of wisdom? Do people not have the idea that suffering, undergone as punishment, regenerates the enemies of society and humankind? (Levinas 1998: 95)

The mind thus gives itself a kind of double dose of justification: as the one who is lashed by suffering, the mind reports to itself, 'It'll do me good'; as one who lashes others, the mind's report reads, 'It'll do them good'.

Yet for all of the arguments in favour of suffering there remains something darkly suspicious about the rational practice of justifying its infliction, especially when it comes to making others suffer. *'There is [an] anxiety of responsibility that is incumbent on everyone in the death or suffering of the other'*, Levinas says, and it leaves the ethical *I 'troubled at the prospect of committing violence – albeit necessary for the logical unfolding of history'* (1996: 164). If, as Benjamin contends, the death penalty reveals something 'rotten in law' by showing law's violent nature more transparently than anything else it does (1978: 286), then Levinas too will find a 'strange failure of justice' amidst the oppression of the weak by the strong that is lurking 'behind the rational administration of pain in the penalties meted out by human courts' (1998: 95). It remains to be seen whether, and to what extent, Levinas shares Benjamin's inclination to transform infinity and transcendence into a warrant for worldly suffering. But in *Useless Suffering*, Levinas clearly thinks what I have called suffering as such in a way that no Western philosopher has done before him. When he says there that suffering shows itself, in its phenomenality, as meaningless and malignant beneath all the reasonable forms espoused by the social 'uses' of suffering, he initiates a claim on the *I* that leaps over all reason, and the possibility of ethical casuistry that it contains, to reach an awareness of suffering in its entirety – *suffering as such*. This is the leap of a thinker who would like to exhibit a radically new conception of ethics based on what we earlier identified as theological transcendence.

Ethics and Transcendence

Levinas is aware that the 'attitude of holiness' that he associates with ethics is a reversal of the normal order of things: namely, the ethical order of norms and reciprocal obligations in terms of which we usually express what we owe to others (2001b: 1). Conventional conceptions of ethics ordinarily frame their most pressing problems in terms of what we called *epistemological transcendence* in Chapter 1: how can the ethical subject know the norms that govern his relations with others, and how can he discover the 'facts' that trigger the application of the norms? In contrast, Levinas's extraordinarily saintly picture of the *I*'s boundless ethical responsibility ultimately comes from attachment to the picture of *theological transcendence*. For him, as for Benjamin, transcendence is a going-beyond-oneself that rests on a movement of discrimination between Same and Other; but at the same time this movement is irreducible to any kind of knowledge that would be beholden to the law of identity. Levinas's' transcendence-to-the-Other, like transcendence to God, encounters an Other that is both absolute and unknowable.

Knowledge and immanence

Knowledge also discriminates, of course, but it does so according to concepts that determine and delimit the known as identities according to the pre-given 'as'-structure of beings. The knower's concept subsumes the known as a mere instance of itself – to know of a murder, for example, whatever it may be as the 'thing in itself', is always to know it *as* 'murder'. Knowledge regards the commandment *Thou shalt not kill* as commensurate with the deed – as if God not only issued a general commandment to guide us before the deed, but also made His judgments of the particular deed, once committed, wholly transparent to the objectifying gaze of humans. The idea that holy texts are commensurate with the completed deeds of other people is the font of all forms of fundamentalism, and rests on a secular theory of knowledge that makes even God into a being whose judgments are knowable by those who are willing (or eager) to inflict worldly suffering on others in His name. In this respect, conventional thought treats the laws of God in the same way that legal formalism treats the laws of man: namely, as transparent vessels full of a meaning that is perspicuous to the various apparatuses and procedures of human judgment and enforcement.

In classical theory of knowledge the primary division is between the *being* to be known, as a thing-in-itself that remains indifferent to how it is perceived, while all the while making itself accessible to the knower in the form of an intuition, and the *representation* – the manifold that an act of consciousness gathers in the subject as an object determined by a concept. Representations thus correlate to beings (realism) or intuitions (idealism), and truth consists in a quality of this correlation: knowledge is *adaequatio intellectus ad rem*. One knows a thing when one has an 'adequate' representation of it: not the impossible equality of a mental 'fact' and a natural 'fact', between which there is no common measure, but a mystical *union* of perception and the perceivable in which being orders, as it were, the forms of knowing that are appropriate to it. The ultimate point of the classical theory of knowledge is just this: when one has defeated what Heraclitus calls a thing's 'tendency to conceal itself' (1987: 71), and has brought its secrets enchained into consciousness like a conquered chieftain, then and only then does one truly *know* it. The image of what Levinas calls 'the supposedly exclusive excellence of immanence which is considered the supreme grace of the spirit in the West' (1998: 185) goes back to Parmenides, whose equation of thinking and being was eventually transformed by Western philosophy into two articles of faith: that thought is the repository of the true, and that truth is thought's supreme value.

The classical theory of knowledge excludes Levinas's kind of transcendence in principle. Trying to know, of course, is a kind of going out of oneself to the (as yet) unknown: phenomenologically speaking, there is a *kind* of exteriority – an alien quality – that belongs to the object that one intends. And Heidegger's famous 'ecstases' of past, present and future are undoubtedly transcendence *in another sense*: his version of transcendence accounts for time's ongoing dispersal of the unity of being-in-the-world by characterising *Dasein* as a 'plural' unity – a going out of itself to find itself on the basis of itself (Heidegger 1998: 108). Neither knowledge nor ecstasy as an account of knowing are transcendence in Levinas's sense, however, because both are *for* the knower, and as such always keep the knower in view in order to return to him. Ever since Kant perversely used the term 'transcendental' to name the conditions within the subject that assure that knowledge will never go beyond the subject's experience (Kant 1998: 199-200), the activity called *getting to know something* has been conceived of as a kind of doubling-back movement: at first a grasping reach outside the skin of the self, and then a withdrawal of the grasp and the grasped back within the self. None of this process of doubling-back ever really amounts to a going *beyond* oneself to something utterly alien. The achievement of knowledge lies *in* the knower, who in the end is left with no gap between himself and the known that he could 'climb across' (the literal meaning of *transcendere*, from *trans* (across) and *scandere* (to climb)). In short, the subject-object relation is a movement of and for subjectivity: '*Knowledge is a relation of the Same with the Other in which the Other is reduced to the Same and divested of its strangeness*' (Levinas 1996: 151). The quintessence of this thesis is the triumph of the totality in Hegel. When consciousness finally 'gets rid of its semblance of being burdened with something alien', Hegel wrote, there will arise a radically pure kind of immanence: an absolute knowledge at the end of history that will shed the ideas of radical otherness and transcendence as childish illusions (1977: 56–57).

Hegel's thought locks the human spirit in a dialectical prison of knower-and-known that is identical to being itself. Levinas promises a dubious kind of escape by transcendence beyond being (dubious because of the burden of responsibility that attends it). His version of transcendence requires an uncompromising alterity – an Other that is irreducible to the concept. This Other would somehow tempt or jolt the knower out of himself in a movement whereby he climbs across the gap that separates the order of knowledge from the order of absolute and unknowable alterity, without even the hope of a return in the form of a representation. Here is a journey without destination and without a return ticket. If in reason the *I conquers* the Other's freedom by reducing him to a concept, in transcendence the *I believes* in the Other's freedom by recognising in him that he *is* uniquely himself. If egotism is defined as freedom without responsibility, then Levinas's ethical *I* must be defined as exactly the opposite: responsibility without freedom. *'This way of being, without prior commitment, amounts to the fact of human fellowship, prior to freedom'* (Levinas 1996: 91).

The idea of the infinite

Among other things, Levinas will call the relation that binds the *I* to the Other *'the idea of the infinite'* (1996: 19). The absolutely Other that belongs to the *I*'s (unfree) Levinasian journey outside itself must be infinite in the etymologically precise sense of being not-finite: not determined or constrained by boundaries or limits. If a 'boundary' allows a thing to be what it is, and a 'limit' prevents it from going beyond itself, then Levinas's notion of the infinite negates both of these conceptual determinations of the law of identity. Unbounded and unlimited, the terms of the ethical relation therefore cannot in principle seep, in the form of knowledge, back into the one who is already enmeshed in them, for immanence destroys otherness and infinitude. Logic's depiction of the relational form – *aRb* – already distorts the uniqueness and holism of the ethical relation by generalising it in terms of its constituent parts. Whereas the absolutely Other standing in relation to the ethical *I* must be other without being several: it must be different in *kind* from everything else rather than different in degree or quality, and as a singularity it can only be named and never described.

For Levinas, therefore, the '*I* and *you*' is a relation between two unique and incomparable beings rather than a relation between two identical beings who cannot become intimate, or feel a responsibility born of intimacy, because their very equality makes them transparent to one another. The old saying that *'familiarity breeds contempt'* has more than a grain of truth in it, for it indicates the possibility of a regrettable (and for Levinas impossible) state of affairs in which the triumph of knowledge is so complete that everyone knows everything about everyone else, and therefore no one needs or cares to be in proximity with anyone but himself. But in fact we are, thankfully, not transparent troglodytes to one another in this way. According to Levinas's phenomenology of the face, the *I* perceives another freedom that is *like* its freedom in or behind the face of the Other, but at the same time it perceives that the Other's freedom is utterly *unlike* its freedom, inasmuch as it does not belong to the *I*. The *I*'s freedom stops short at the Other's face in a way that is both unfree and uncomprehending, thereby putting the very idea that the *I* has freedom into question. Here the temptation to kill the Other is confronted by a 'Thou shalt not kill' that was written in the heart before it was ever inscribed on a tablet. In a nutshell, Levinasian ethics is the intimate curiosity and concern of two unequal beings that are drawn to one another almost against their wills, and against all reason.

How lofty and glorious is the phenomenal irrationality of the ubiquitous small kindnesses that pass between strangers before reason has 'explained' them by reducing them to calculations based on short- or long-term reciprocity! For Levinas, even speech – the very means and expression of reason – cannot be adequately explained by reason. In the encounter between Same and Other, the quintessential form of which is speech, the 'sovereign *I*' – so proud of its accomplishments and knowledge – speaks to the Other in a saying that is irreducible to any said. The messiness of speaking to another is confirmed by the surprise of the unanticipated cues that he gives us, and the uneasiness and suspense we feel in finishing what we have to say, only to hear the other respond to us in his own idiom. Speech upsets the *I*'s complacency and discomfits its sense of self-sufficiency and control. In speaking to the Other, the *I* is concerned to *reach* the Other before trying to know him: 'I have spoken to him, that is, I have overlooked the universal being he incarnates in order to confine myself to the particular being he is' (Levinas 1998: 77). Even if the *I* has decided to speak to the Other in order to get something from him, the *I*'s motive recedes in the moment of speaking itself: it explains the approach but not the consummation.

Saying and said

This moment of reaching out from Same to Other leaves a trace of itself in the said (*le Dit*), but in itself is not the same as *what* is said: in the ethical moment 'the subject is affected without the source of the affection becoming a theme of re-presentation' (Levinas 1996: 81). A trace is left by a saying (*le Dire*) that did not mean to signify itself by means of the trace, just as fingerprints left on a pen are usually not meant to communicate anything. Yet in both cases the trace still somehow manages to become a readable sign for those 'detectives' who go in search of what it signifies. As Otto Pöggeler puts it, '*the trace is a small presence of something that is absent*' (Parkes 1987: 70). The strangeness of Levinas's trace thus lies in its very being – namely, in its being precisely *this* knowable trace that somehow correlates to a saying that always remains incommensurable with being and language. If the trace 'signifies' beyond being, as Levinas alleges (2003a: 40), then it yields a monumental paradox: for the trace's correlation with the saying of which it is the trace seems to enable the memory to remember more than it has experienced, just as the idea of the infinite is said to let thought think more than it can contain. There is a big difference, however, between these two paradoxes: Levinas's infinite *touches* the finitude of the *I* in the proximity of the face, even if consciousness is not filled up with a thought of the infinite that equals its theme; whereas memory does not touch alterity – it constructs it. Here is revealed a sort of dead-end for any phenomenology that aspires to uncover an affect that exceeds the intentional correlation of *noema* and *noesis* in consciousness: a remembered event of being touched by otherness is immanent to the one who remembers it, and is not at all the same as the Levinasian transcendence of the *I* as it is *being affected* by the very proximity of otherness itself.

Levinas will therefore contend that any reduction of the moment of saying to a subsequent said negates its essence, which as saying is the horizon of language itself and not any 'propositional content' that belongs within language. Echoing Chapter 1's thesis that justification always justifies *right now*, and never in advance, the past of the Levinasian saying is an 'originating past' that cannot be reduced to the present because it enacts the very horizon of what counts as 'the present' (Levinas 1998: 150). This is *almost* equivalent to saying that, although the now-time always decides what it calls 'now', the moment it announces this another now-time takes its place to say 'now' all over again, and without the benefit of any binding precedent – although this way of putting it does not do justice to the social dimension of time's horizon in Levinas's thought. As we shall investigate more fully in the next chapter, it was Wittgenstein who first clearly established the idea that language has a horizon outside of which it makes no sense to talk 'about' language. But Wittgenstein's horizon was the sense or meaning of propositions that the *I* simply understands without further ado, whereas Levinas's horizon bounds language within the sociality of the speaking situation: '*expression, before being a celebration of being, is a relationship with him to whom I express the expression, and whose presence is already required for my cultural gesture of expression to be produced*' (Levinas 1996: 52).

Levinas's conception of the primordial sociality of the speaking situation does not portray the social as lying 'in' the individual – he does not make the social a 'fact' that is open to determination by thought. Rather, the social is thought's very activity of determining things by speaking to the Other – the saying, as the social, precedes any mere content of a proposition *about* the sociological or philosophical theme of sociality. Although Heidegger too says that the genuine phenomenon of language exists prior to any mere information that is conveyed by means of language, Levinas rejects Heidegger's belief that language is being's way of empowering humans to let the word be uncovered through *logos* beyond and before all asserting and communicating (Heidegger 1995: 109). For Levinas, the intimate sociality of the speaking situation *precedes* the openness of being and its unconcealment through *logos*.

The speaking situation opens the *I* to the Other before all formal analyses of saids begin to close that opening down. Saying thus forms 'a screen between me and the other' that is opaque to knowledge, and that precipitates a moment of ethics 'not founded on any preliminary structure of theoretical thought, on language, or on any particular moment' (Levinas 1996: 148). In the act of saying the *I*'s exposure and nakedness are manifested to the Other, whose face signifies its own vulnerability and nakedness in return. Here is revealed the very possibility of sincerity itself: not the truth of a statement that is in agreement with the facts, but the kind of sincerity that shines forth from the face before the correctness of any proposition is established or refuted. On this view, the fact that people conceal and lie must be interpreted as a *privation* of exposure and sincerity – a merely deficient mode of what is always prior in the structure of intimate sociality. As Levinas was fond of saying, the moment of ethics has a past that never was a present. This means that the present, being the site of what we think is 'in being', is also necessarily the site of what can be made immanent through knowledge; whereas the moment of ethics, including the saying that is its principal mode, has already departed into the past whenever knowledge attempts to circumscribe it with a concept. Here is a goodness that is *'absent from being'* because it is quite literally invisible, and because any attempt to bring it to cognition is already too late.

In the end, Levinas has left us with a conception of ethics in which the *I* carries the full responsibility for suffering as such, like the mythological Atlas carried the earth: to be a 'me' in a world full of suffering others, Levinas writes, *'signifies being unable to escape from responsibility, as if the whole edifice of creation stood on my shoulders'* (2003a: 33). According to the usual way of telling the story of Atlas, Zeus condemned him to carry the earth on his shoulders as punishment for joining in the revolt of the Titans. His burden was relieved only once, when Hercules supported the world on his shoulders so that Atlas could fulfil Hercules's 11th labour – plucking the apples of the Hesperides. After Atlas finished the labour, however, Hercules managed to trick him into retaking his burden forever (Graves 1955: I, 143-45). Poor Atlas! If Levinas's conception of ethics also seems like a kind of punishment – call it the curse of being human – then we shall presently see how the *I* can seem to shift the weight of its ethical burden by making the passage to justice. And if Atlas could be persuaded to retake his burden, we shall also ask whether, and how, the *I* in its role as an agent of justice could ever be persuaded or allowed to make the return passage to ethics.

Justice and Immanence

Derrida alleges that the occurrence of the ethical event as such is 'menaced by its own rigour' in Levinas's thought (Levinas 2001b: 8). By this he presumably means that the *I*'s Levinasian responsibility for suffering as such is so hypertrophic that it threatens to become nonfunctional, like an enlarged heart that stops pumping by virtue of the intemperate demands placed on it by its own size. But there is another menace that presses upon ethical responsibility even more perilously than its own excessiveness: the event of justice. Justice is a necessary evil, as it were, because the very possibility of my hurting or killing the Other is presupposed, as Derrida puts it, 'by the interdiction that makes it impossible' (Derrida 2001: 204). Thus, at a minimum, justice is required because many people shirk or evade the ethical responsibility – the 'Thou shalt not kill' and 'Thou shalt cause the Other to live' – that speaks to them from the proximity of the Other's face. The need to have a system of justice because of ethical 'violations' is a small thing, however, when compared to the need for justice that is created by the sheer existence of *multiple* Others standing face-to-face with the ethical *I*.

The third person

Justice would still be required even if no one ever shirked their ethical duties, because the Other that happens to be in closest proximity to the *I* at any given moment is never the only one in the *I*'s world. Always already present alongside the Other's face is the face of the *third person* (as well as the fourth, the fifth, and so on almost *ad infinitum*). This co-presence of other humans *disturbs* the original and originary intimacy of the binary ethical relation between an *I* and a *you* because the third person is another Other whose face asserts an equal claim on the *I*'s ethical responsibility:

> [T]he third person is himself also a neighbour, and also falls within the purview of the *I*'s responsibility. Here, beginning with this third person, is the proximity of a human plurality. Who, in this plurality, comes first? This is the time and place of the birth of the question: of a demand for justice! This is the obligation to compare unique and incomparable others; this is the moment of *knowledge* and, henceforth, of an objectivity beyond or on the hither side of the nakedness of the face; this is the moment of consciousness and intentionality. (Levinas 1998: 166–67)

The 'third man' (or person) in Levinas's writings represents the entire society or world of other human beings, any one of whom could be the *I*'s Other in the face-to-face encounter of ethics. Given that one's time, resources and motility are always finite, how is one to choose where to discharge one's ethical responsibility for the Other amongst such a formidable plenitude of others? Since Levinas wants to conceive of sociality as independent of the lost unity represented by being as a whole (which includes the knowledge of the 'nature of sociality' as one of its parts), these other Others cannot be conceived collectively, but must be viewed as singularities that are just as unique, ineffable and needy as the original Other. Injustice is annulled by forgiveness within the circle of the ethical relation, but it demands redress when the entrance of the third person ruptures the ethical situation. 'Hence', Levinas will conclude, '*it is important to me to know which of the two takes precedence*' (1998: 104).

It is important to know! Although Levinas says that '*it is always starting out from the Face, from the responsibility for the other that justice appears*', he believes that *justice itself* is accomplished by means of knowledge and immanence: '*In order to be just, it is necessary to know*', Levinas says, '*to objectify, compare, judge, form concepts, generalise, etc*' (1998: 204). Hence, the for-the-other of ethics must recede so that a knowing judgment can be made *between* multiple others:

> [Justice] calls for judgment and comparison, a comparison of what is in principle incomparable, for every being is unique; every other is unique. In that necessity of being concerned with justice that idea of equity appears, on which the idea of objectivity is based. At a certain moment, there is a necessity for a 'weighing', a comparison, a pondering, and in this sense philosophy would be the appearance of wisdom from the depths of that initial charity [of ethics], the wisdom of love. (Levinas 1998: 104)

The immanence of knowledge that is required to effect justice gives affront to the unique alterity of the Other by leaving him 'de-faced [*dé-visagés*]' (Levinas 1999: 170). This is because the *I* who becomes the agent of justice must form an *idea* of the others who stand before it, and because it cannot allow itself to be ethically *affected* by any particular Other while it is in the mode of doing justice.

In the moment of justice the Other's face is hidden behind the various masks which, like the masks of tragedy and comedy in ancient Greek theatre, correspond to the conceptual pairings that delimit the spheres of law and justice: 'just/unjust', 'lawful/unlawful', 'right/duty', 'plaintiff/defendant', 'wrongdoer'/innocent', 'murder/justified homicide', and so forth. The de-facing and masking accomplished by the work of justice is indeed the very meaning of the blindfold in conventional representations of the Goddess of Justice: *Dikē* does not want to *see* the Other's face – she aspires merely to *know* about the Other's actions. Thought *about* the Other is a rupture of the ethical *I*'s unconditional compassion *for* the Other, as if the ethical relation that preceded the moment of justice were not the 'beginning of society, but its negation' (Levinas 1998: 20). The passage from ethics to justice goes from an intimate relation without reciprocity to a structured relation in which reciprocity – conceived politically as the formal equality of all citizens – characterises the *I*'s new attitude and comportment towards others. 'My search for justice', Levinas says, 'presupposes just such a new relation, in which all the excess of generosity that I must have toward the other is subordinated to a question of justice' (1999: 102). The ethical *I* must therefore deny and efface its very essence in order to metamorphose into the agent of justice.

Harshness in the moment of justice

There is more to this process than the 'inner' effacement of the *I*'s feeling of responsibility, however, for after it knows what to do, the agent of justice now faces the task of *establishing* justice among the ethically incomparable ones that appear before it. Levinas is aware that the de-facing accomplished by the work of justice is followed by an affront that is far more palpable and bloody than any mere objectification of the Other within the consciousness of the agents of justice. Like Benjamin, he acknowledges (as indeed he must) *'a certain violence that is implied in all justice'* (1999: 172): a certain *'necessary harshness'* (1998: 203). A justice that would attend to suffering as such is therefore unthinkable, because justice violently intervenes in precisely this or that given situation to cure or assuage some suffering at the cost of ignoring and even creating additional suffering.

The real sufferings in Germany in the 1920s led to *Mein Kampf*, a perverted manifesto of justice for the German *Volk*, and thence to the horrific 'rational solution' that is represented by Auschwitz. Likewise (I will dare to say it) the massive and unconscionable sufferings in the third world today lead to proposals for distributive justice on an international scale that would undeniably *give* what is needed, but that would still have to *take* or *withhold* from others in order to give it. Pascal says that 'we see neither justice nor injustice which does not change its nature with change in climate. Three degrees of latitude reverse all jurisprudence; a meridian decides the truth' (1941: 101). But the foregoing shocking (and perhaps unpardonable) juxtaposition of Auschwitz and international justice for the poor is not offered to prove the shop-worn claim that conceptions of justice are always relative in Pascal's sense, and therefore that they belong to the order of mere opinion. It is offered solely as an expedient means for forcing thought to confront the reality that law and justice *reallocate* suffering, may periodically *increase* or *diminish* overall suffering, but that they can never reach what we have called suffering as such. I will call this insight the deflationary view of justice.

Let me be clear: the deflationary view of justice does not deny or close its eyes to the suffering that is called 'injustice' any more than the deflationary view of language denies that words can be expedient means. Rather, it construes the conventional aspiration for justice as first and foremost a longing to rectify injustice *under the banner of righteousness and necessity*. That this kind of banner-flying can create pernicious ideological effects on society as a whole has been a constant theme of social and legal criticism ever since Marx's essay *On the Jewish Question* showed the contingency and partiality of the bourgeois conception of right (Marx 1964: 3-31). But there is a more narrowly focused and basic phenomenon than this that lurks beneath the ideological effects on society of law's categories and rhetoric: hiding under the banner of righteousness and necessity is, first and foremost, a kind of lie that the agent of justice tells *itself*. If this lie is interpreted in the familiar Western way as an attempt to deny the *I*'s essential freedom and responsibility for the outcome of its actions, someone like Sartre would call it 'bad faith' (1956: 49). But I am interested in going beyond this interpretation to a source that lies far deeper in us than our existential freedom. As we shall see in the next section's account of the phenomenon of distress, the lie that the agent of justice tells itself is a futile attempt to put an end to the agent's *own* suffering by clinging desperately to the image of a ground – a kind of legal authority – for what it does in the name of justice.

According to Levinas, the intimate connection between law and justice testifies to a forgetfulness of suffering as such that *must* attend justice if it is ever to overcome what Derrida calls the 'absolute evil' of another kind of amnesia – the one that lets the unjustly dead bury their own dead, without any notice or attention from the living. It is on account of this evil that 'justice is desirable', says Derrida, '*through* but also *beyond* right and law' (1994: 175). Levinas, too, will say of the trial in France of the infamous Nazi Klaus Barbi, 'Honor to the West!' (1998: 231). Yet both Derrida and Levinas, like Walter Benjamin before them, knew full well that law used as a means of and to justice is also a means to the suffering of 'wrongdoers' and their families. This explains why Benjamin sought, in *Critique of Violence*, to locate the possibility of a radically pure kind of violence that does not reside in the order of means and ends.

There is therefore a strong and potentially troubling kinship between Benjamin's non-opposition to the 'revolutionary killing of the oppressor' and what Levinas said when asked the question 'Does the executioner have a face?' Levinas, the philosopher of the face *par excellence*, replied:

> You are posing the whole problem of evil. When I speak of Justice, I introduce the idea of the struggle with evil, I separate myself from the idea of non-resistance to evil. If self-defence is a problem, the 'executioner' is the one who threatens my neighbour and, in this sense, calls for violence and no longer has a Face. (1998: 105)

The Other who faces the *I* in the ethical encounter has a face: in this situation, Levinas says, '*even the SS man has what I mean by a face*' (1998: 231). As an ethical Other, even a Nazi can procure for the *I* 'an exit from the straightforward grasp and power of consciousness' (Levinas 1996: 19–20). Standing before the agent of justice, however, *the executioner no longer has a face*. While it is doing justice, the *I* returns to itself without any possibility of exit. It follows that a 'justice' that attempted to attend to suffering as such would not be justice at all; it would have to be Levinasian ethics in its starkest form, somehow endeavouring to bind up the wounds of the Other without wounding in any way the other Other who did the wounding. Justice cannot and should not be this compassionate. The passage from ethics to justice is a movement from the pre-theoretical and compassionate, *through the theoretical and the violent,* and thence to justice or its possibility. This does not mean that justice itself is ever present or reducible to knowledge – there is ample indication in Levinas, not to mention Derrida and other postmodern thinkers, that justice in its own right is a 'transcendent' value. Here is revealed the opposition between thinkers such as Aquinas, who would secure justice on the basis of a norm or programme that is commensurate with it (1948: 663), and those for whom justice is never commensurate with the means used to achieve it. But however loudly and often postmodernism characterises justice as an infinite and transcendent value (Balkin 1998: 144), the *means* used to achieve any imaginable justice still stubbornly refuse to transcend violence and the finite order of knowledge.

The glorification of justice

The glorification of justice in Western thought ensures a certain forgetfulness of the relation of justice to violence and suffering. Given its status as a supreme value, the imagined sign and seal of the arrival of justice could only be a certain *rapture* of the just. The hagiology of such a justice would include a passage about this rapture's delight or sublime satisfaction on account of the fact that justice has been or is being done, and that the unjust have been or are being made to pay for their iniquities. Is there not a measure of satisfaction to be found in hearing the despair that is evident in Satan's tale of his fall to the 'unhappy mansion' of hell in Milton's *Paradise Lost*? (1949: 236). Are we not delighted, if only a little bit, by the Foucaultian spectacle of great criminals such as Timothy McVeigh and Ted Kozinski being caught and brought to justice? (Foucault 1979: 32–69). Even thinkers such as Levinas, who take care to characterise justice as ineffable and always to come, still conceive of it as an impossible *end* towards which the means of law and violence are or can be directed. The *I*'s passage from the (non-)being of ethics to its incarnation in being as the sword of justice marks a contamination of the impossible end of justice itself by the actual and violent means used to aspire to it. For it is one of history's most important and tragic lessons that transcendent ends cannot be disentangled from their worldly means without incurring the greatest danger of fanaticism. This is why Levinas will say that 'the just person who knows himself to be just is no longer just', and why he will further stipulate that 'the first condition of the first and the last of the just is that their justice remains clandestine to them' (1996: 17).

Despite the opacity of justice to its agents, however, Levinas still calls for justice *'always to be made more knowing in the name, the memory, of the original kindness of man toward his other'* (1998: 229). You may not know whether you are acting justly, Levinas seems to be saying, but if you always remember the moment of ethics you can at least know that you are on the right track. A justice that is kind is not necessarily just, given the occasional need to be harsh, but a justice that 'remembers' kindness is better than one that does not: what on earth does this mean? *Who or what* is made 'more knowing' in the name and memory of simple goodness and charity, and how can this knowing help but pervert what it names and remembers into a programme or norm from which virtually anything can be deduced? *'It is for your own good that I do this'*: is this saying a manifestation of a humane justice that is 'always to be perfected against its own harshness' (Levinas 1998: 229), or is it the kind of 'tough love' that can lead to outrages that are all the more outrageous for having been cast, however much in good faith, in the guise of ethical concern? Does the ethical attitude of Levinas's agent of justice – *'preferring injustice undergone to injustice committed'* (1998: 32) – lead to the possibility of a better justice, or only a different one? These questions lead us into a decisive encounter with the innermost essence of Levinas's thought.

A Phenomenological Interpretation of Distress

A judge has no neighbours. Justice subordinates and holds in abeyance any feeling of ethical generosity that may arise in the encounter between the Other and the agent of justice. Although the suppression of generosity in favour of sober judgment is necessary for justice to emerge, the moment of justice also necessarily eclipses the just *I*'s awareness of *suffering as such*, as if the agent of justice needed, and craved, a deep shadow to fall on the consequences of its actions. If we credit Levinas's phenomenological acuity with having discovered a pre-gnostic and pre-original phenomenon of care for the other person, we may excuse him for overlooking a phenomenon that is co-original with it. By means of the suspension (*epoché*) of the natural attitude that is required for all rigorous phenomenological research, it is possible to detect in the moment of care for the Other the co-emergence of a different yet intimately linked phenomenon – one that I will call *distress*. Because Levinas stops short of giving a rigorous phenomenological description of the moment of justice as such, he fails to see that with ethical responsibility always arises distress on account of that responsibility, and further, that this distress is connected *essentially* to the craving desire for foundations in accordance with the form of logical transcendence.

To be sure, Levinas himself was aware of something like the phenomenon of distress, albeit in a vague and general sort of way. In the essay *Peace and Proximity*, for example, he describes (or prescribes) an 'anxiety of responsibility that is incumbent on everyone in the death or suffering of the other', and he writes of this anxiety in terms of the ethical *I*'s being 'troubled at the prospect of committing violence – albeit necessary for the logical unfolding of history ... [and] the march of truth' (1996: 164). However, nowhere does Levinas make distress on account of responsibility into a *theme*. Although this section attempts to rectify the omission, I write it with my eyes open, as it were, and not because I think that the phenomenological method gives philosophy some sort of superior access to existential truth. As Levinas himself said, phenomenology is at bottom simply a 'new possibility of moving from one idea to another' (2001b: 31). In keeping with the attitude of Zen that I have attempted to exhibit throughout this book, we will enact a phenomenology of distress here as an expedient means for recognising that Levinas's philosophy of the relations among suffering, ethics and justice, while it is rich and abundant with insight, in the end threatens to become a dark cave of entangling vines for anyone who is tempted to cling to it.[3]

The moment of justice

If, like Dilthey, we take the word 'life' to be the name of a fundamental phenomenological category, it behoves us first of all to clarify and delimit the particular region of life in which the phenomena of distress and the longing for foundations show themselves. The choice of 'life', instead of Heideggerian 'Dasein', is intentionally ambiguous: it reflects a certain indifference to the larger ontological problem of how the being of the human being should be described. To put it bluntly, distress shows itself *however* we characterise the being of the human being.

In identifying the region of life where distress arises we must exclude the adversarial moment of fighting for justice, for this moment is filled up completely with concern that the thrusts and parries of our strategies and discourse will be causally effective. One does not long for foundations in the middle of a fight, except to the extent that the rhetorical strategy of talking in terms of 'foundations' may help one win. Nor is the region we seek to be found in that rather common mode of being in which one unreflectively 'drifts along', content to accept and reiterate unthinkingly

---

3 See page 17 fn 12 for a description of the Zen metaphor of entangling vines.

what 'they' say about the content and nature of foundations for justice. Staying rigorously within the moment of craving desire as such, those who long for foundations dwell outside the comfortable zone of indifference to any questioning or understanding that might hamper their actions or well-being. If, as Kant alleges, we make judgments about the beautiful and about nature's designs according to the principles of order and purpose that underlie all of our judgments in these fields (Kant 2000), then in making judgments in the domain of justice the principles of order and purpose take a back seat, phenomenally speaking, to the feelings of responsibility and distress. In the region of life that we seek, the mind holds itself at a distance from the fray of particular struggles for justice, and it draws back, even if only momentarily, from the levelled-down discourse of everyday talk about why justice is a self-evidently valuable end.

The usual disposition of life is to encounter and be occupied with what is nearest to hand in its care. Care need not, and usually is not, explicit *as* 'care' to a thematising consciousness. Rather, care is a fundamental phenomenological category, first discovered by Heidegger (1962: 225–73), which indicates formally that life is always already concerned with or about *something or other*. In the region of life that we seek to delimit, care encounters an Other towards whom it feels an ethical pull: as the previous exposition of Levinas's thought has shown, the *I*'s care upsurges towards this original Other in the form of *responsibility*. Co-present in this encounter, however, is *distress* on account of this very responsibility, owing to the presence of *other* Others who will or may be affected by the *I*'s responsible actions. Distress, which is itself a form of suffering, is a kind of making-present of the actual and possible suffering of others. In distress (from the Latin *dis-* and *strangere*, 'to bind tight') the Other and other Others are bound tightly together in a care that stands immobilised before a decision. The impending decision (from the Latin *de-* and *caedere*, 'to cut off') is distressful because it will sunder care into a living portion and a dead remainder, cutting its superabundance of generosity in two. These two phenomena – *responsibility* and *distress* – are equiprimordial in the *I*'s encounter with the Other in the region of life with which we are concerned. Any thinking that aspires to uncover the phenomenal relation between ethics and justice must take care (pun intended) to account for both of them.

Along with Levinas, we will call this region of life *the moment of justice*. It is characterised by the more-or-less conscious awareness of an impending decision within the context of a care that remains other-directed at all times. Here, the 'decision' is not to be grasped anthropologically, as a 'free choice of man', but ontologically, as a fateful cutting-off of possibilities. Distress is therefore distressed in the face of an undecided that *will in all events be decided*, for as I said earlier, in distress the *I* is caught in the maelstrom of a care that renders the comfortable stance of indifference impossible. The decision must (and will!) decide between the original Other, to whom the *I* is ethically indebted, and other Others, to whom the *I* is also ethically indebted. For Levinas the moment of justice is filled up with trying to *know* which Other takes precedence, and the procedures and immanence of the knowledge that is required to effect justice give affront to the uniqueness of both Others by leaving them de-faced. However, since Levinas does not identify the phenomenon of distress that precedes the de-facing and violence of justice, he is unable to assess the meaning of this phenomenon, or its significance for his project. Levinas yearns to perfect justice against its own harshness by taking the quest for justice back to its source: one's obligation to the other person. But if distress arises equiprimordially with ethical responsibility in the moment of justice – if the two are locked together in such a way that the longing for foundations is an inevitable modification of them – then Levinas's project would be a chimera. For then the 'obligation with respect to the face' would *mean* that distress would always seek escape from the torment of a decision between others by means of a collapse into one form or other of fundamentalism.

The meaning of distress

Before getting too far ahead of ourselves, I should clarify the precise phenomenological structure of 'distress'. Distress is always *on account of* something. Distress should not be conceived as a psychological 'feeling' that arises within a human whose being and essence have been otherwise determined. For a long time psychology has limited what the word *distress* indicates to a 'condition' that is caused by such mechanisms as cognitive dissonance, and that can or should be subjected to therapeutic transformations. Ontic psychology considers and construes the psychophysical only. Attuned to life *in* a world that is itself taken for granted, it does not investigate what appears *as* the world. In its existential signification, therefore, distress shakes off all purely psychophysical references and takes on the raiment of a genuine *foreboding*. This foreboding (from the Old English word *bēodan*, meaning to proclaim) is the voice of distress proclaiming in advance to the *I* that its decisions in the sphere of justice can and will produce painful consequences, and not just ameliorative ones.

Without distress, ethical responsibility would not be *responsibility*: for who knows whether the charity that I happen to extend to one stranger will not also lead to suffering on the part of another? It is possible that the one whom I succour today may cheat or murder others tomorrow in a way that my tender mercies have made all the more effective, and it is certain that the shirt off my back that I give to a needy person today will not be available for me to give to a needier person tomorrow. Because the phenomenon of ethical responsibility is usually regarded as a good thing, one might even go so far as to applaud the fact that distress is one of the very determinations of being human in the moment of justice, and never merely a symptom. Consider the old English proverb that 'the road to hell is paved with good intentions': does this saying not *warn* responsibility of the consequences of acting on its impulses, and does it not hint (in the way that so many enduring folk sayings do) at the genuine phenomenon of distress that precedes and produces the warning? Distress is no less than an existential comportment: a Heideggerian *Mir-Sein* ('Being-to-me') of distress on account of others that may or may not be explicitly present to cognition (Heidegger 2001a: 103).

Distress should never be confused with the phenomenon of *fear*. In fear one fears for *oneself*. To be sure, in the moment of justice there may also arise fear that the suffering Other's voracious needs will make too great an ethical demand on the *I*, even to the point of exhausting or destroying it. It would be a mistake to underestimate the fear that the *I* feels in the presence of the Other when it lapses from ethical responsibility into the mode of caring for what Heidegger calls 'the myself for which I care' (2001a: 71). The phenomenon of fear undoubtedly gives evidence for Sartre's famous epigram, 'Hell is – other people!' (Bartlett 1980: 865). It also provides a phenomenal basis for the truth of Derrida's previously quoted remark that the event of ethics in Levinas's thought is 'menaced by its own rigour' (Levinas 2001b: 8). But whether or not fear for the self actually emerges in the moment of justice, it is not what I mean by the phenomenon of distress. If *fear* is taken to be a phenomenological basis for the truth of egoism, and *ethical responsibility* to be a phenomenological basis for the truth of altruism, then it must be said that *distress* yields a truth that straddles the age-old opposition between these two points of view. Although distress manifests itself as egoism, in the sense that it is the *I* that suffers distress, it also manifests itself as altruism, inasmuch as distress ultimately comes from the *I*'s feelings of responsibility towards others.

Distress announces itself before action in the urgency of that searing question we sometimes ask ourselves, '*Am I doing the right thing?*' It is revealed in the anguish of Jacob in *Genesis* 32, who, when told that his brother Esau was marching to meet him at the head of 400 men, is described in verse 8 (verse 7 in the Christian Bible) as being '*greatly afraid and anguished*'. According to the great 10th century rabbinical commentator Rashi, although Jacob was *afraid* for his own death, he was *anguished* at the possibility of having to kill (Levinas 1999: 135). Anguish here is for the Other, or rather, for Jacob's complicity in the Other's fate. According to Jewish tradition, the Decalogue's command 'Thou shalt not kill', although absolute in form, does not bear a message of truth that is absolute enough to condemn killing in self-defence. In short, there is an 'exception' to God's law – one that was read into it by early commentators. Yet there is always the chance that a killing believed to be in self-defence will be interpreted by God as an aggression, and hence an affront to the law. The chance of this interpretation-to-come means that '[n]o judgment of the deed can be derived from the commandment', as Benjamin puts it, 'and so neither the divine judgment, nor the grounds for this judgment, can be known in advance' (1978: 298). Jacob's anguish is a perfect symbol of the phenomena of distress and craving desire: the *I* that experiences these phenomena is distressed to recognise that it is about to overbear others and cause them to suffer or die, and as a consequence of its distress it craves a sign that what it is about to do is justified by some higher authority than itself.

Distress shows itself as co-present whenever the *I*'s ethical responsibility for the Other involves other Others, which is to say, virtually always. There is a sense in which every moment of ethics is at the same time a moment of justice, if only because the ethical *I* who feels the tug of responsibility to this particular Other also 'knows' that it could choose to devote its limited time and resources to relieving the suffering of someone else. Distress is not yet a *value* orientation: it is not yet the posing of the question which of these two (or more) Others is most worthy of the *I*'s intervention – a question that is to be decided according to some calculus of worthiness 'known' to the *I*. Value thinking thinks *after* distress has surfaced, and transforms the latter phenomenon into the procedures of justice that are the concrete consequences of distress and longing, whereas distress, like responsibility itself, is pre-gnostic and shows itself in the form of uneasiness or anxiety on account of the *I*'s responsibility being pulled in opposite directions.

In the moment of justice the *I*'s sense of responsibility undergoes a kind of rupture. In the mode of trying to do justice to others, the *I* now encounters both an anxious Other towards whom it feels the ethical pull of a responsibility to do something to help, and more-or-less concrete other Others who will or may suffer on account of the *I*'s intervention in the situation. Reason may later call these injured Others 'wrongdoers' or 'collateral damage', but distress arises before reason intervenes with its panoply of casuistries and justifications. Ethical responsibility to these other Others *presses upon* the *I*'s responsibility to the original Other. Other Others confront responsibility with spectral images and vague stirrings of foreboding on account of what reason will later sanitise by placing it into the categories of just or necessary suffering. The direction of the *I*'s care thus comes to a halt as care itself splits, as if caring-for-others had to come up against itself as an enemy arriving from the opposite direction. The hint of suffering as such *slips in* and threatens to cut short the hyperbole of responsibility that the *I* feels for the original Other. In the phenomenon of distress the Same does not return to itself, as in knowledge and fear but, rather, remains outside itself in a care that has lost its way among many Others.

Nothing is to be gained from trying to decide whether responsibility or distress is the more original phenomenon, for what shows itself in the moment of justice as such is not a sequence. This phenomenology of distress in relation to responsibility therefore does not attempt to make a constituting nature out of a constituted nature, because the very sense of 'constituted' in the sphere of justice comes back to responsibility-and-distress as an absolute origin. As we shall see, the *justification* of pain according to the stipulation $A \Rightarrow B$ is itself a modification of responsibility and distress. Prior to judgment and justification, responsibility and distress arise *together* in the moment of justice, united in the form of a field of forces, as it were, that makes the *I* pause in doubt before acting in a world swarming with many suffering Others. Neither ethical responsibility nor distress should be conceived of as something detached and rigidly autonomous from the concrete mode of temporality that is the moment of justice. Distress and responsibility abide together in a synthesis with its own peculiar form of intentionality: the *cogitatum* of this synthesis is neither this Other nor the other Other, but the emptiness of a freedom that confronts the decision between them.

Freedom and the collapse into foundations

Distress and responsibility, taken together in their synthesis, 'mean' a freedom that is always concretely empty of all content. Although this freedom may be conceived as standing outside the temporal present in the form of its 'possibilities', it nonetheless remains powerless to avoid what springs forth *in* the present as it seizes one possibility to the exclusion of others. In attachment to the images that arise in the moment of justice, freedom as origin folds back on itself in the form of motive, as if freedom were but a flickering shadow cast by the decision just before it arrives. In having a motive the *I* loses its freedom to a ground that it understands and follows so completely that the ground *becomes* its motive. Prior to motive, yet always finding itself eclipsed by its deeds, freedom becomes what Heidegger calls 'the ground of ground' (1998, 134): a gaping 'abyss of ground' whose destiny it is to be constantly filled-up by the present *whatever* it does. 'You can *do* what you *will*', said Schopenhauer, 'but at any given moment of your life you can *will* only one definite thing and absolutely nothing else but this one thing' (1999: 21). The intuition of responsibility that Levinas finds in the phenomenon of the two-person ethical relation would become a kind of mechanistic compulsion were it not for the evidence given by the phenomenon of distress. This phenomenon thus makes comprehensible Heidegger's idea that human life *is* its possibilities. For even if distress offers no solution to the dilemmas of justice, at least it confirms that they *are* dilemmas.

The craving desire for a foundation in the moment of justice is a modification of responsibility and distress. It is a flight from freedom, taken not merely in the sense of the capacity to exercise and resist power, but in the far deeper sense of what Roland Barthes calls the 'capacity to subjugate no one' (Kearney and Rainwater 1996: 366). *For the moment of justice is also always a moment of someone's subjugation.* In founding, the *I* lets that which is attached to it already – namely that in which it is imprisoned as what 'they' expect – run its course. Freedom recedes so that the correctness of derivation and of fitting into an established order may hold sway. The decision becomes decided, as if the *I* had nothing to do with it. Thereafter reason comforts itself by the undeniably correct psychological argument that compassion for universal suffering had to be suffocated so that compassion for particular sufferings could breathe.

The longing for foundations is the anterior portion of a movement into *collapse* – into what Heidegger calls *die Ruinanz* (2001a: 98).[4] In collapse life forms itself out of the movements that it makes within the comfort of a dream world in which the formula 'A $\Rightarrow$ B' seems more real than do A and B themselves, taken in their own right as what is thus. Collapse collapses onto what is said to be the 'basis' of this or that movement, but what in fact shows itself phenomenally as mere images (Zen) or, if you will, 'the nothingness of factical life' (Heidegger 2001a: 108). Collapse is seductive, especially for those who long to end the torment of distress. Collapse allows universal suffering to depart and then re-enter the scene metamorphosed into just and necessary suffering. Collapse allows the questioning of foundations to cease: it is unwillingness to wait, an impatience with all further thinking. It is the temporary defeat of distress by the illusory army of logical transcendence and its founding movement. Distress on account of responsibility is painful, and the *I* that experiences it falls into the business of grounding and constructing itself as a responsible and just person in order to escape from its own suffering. But always prior to this moment of escape through self-grounding, distress and longing arise in the same other-regarding sphere of life as the phenomenon of the face. They are the latter's phenomenological counterweights, so to speak, and they

4 From the Latin *ruo*, meaning 'collapse'.

transpose the Levinasian concept of a 'passage' from ethics to justice from the category of benign aspiration to the category of flight and evasion.

The word 'passage' is ambiguous: it signifies both a *going* and a *way of going*. While going (in a spatio-temporal sense) is undoubtedly an existential imperative for human beings, no *way* of going could ever precede the movement from infinite ethical responsibility to justice. Such a 'way' would have to underlie the actual going in the manner of a path to which the one who goes surrenders himself in advance. A way between ethics and justice thus would be a kind of foundation for going that would betray the very idea of *infinite* (unbounded) ethical responsibility. Such a betrayal is inevitable because a truly unbounded responsibility could never find even its first step on a path that is pre-bounded in principle: a path that ineluctably leads to remedies for one person's suffering in the domain of a justice that is always the engine of suffering for someone else. The 'passage' from ethical responsibility to justice must always occur by means of a sort of callousness. It must always be accompanied by a certain evasive turning-away, not entirely innocent, from the phenomenon of universal human suffering to the phenomenon of this particular Other's particular forms of suffering. When the language of law and politics attempts to justify care's turning away from suffering as such towards particular sufferings, social theory calls it ideology. But prior to becoming ideology it is always the phenomenal consequence of responsibility's confrontation with distress.

Nevertheless: although awareness of suffering as such departs from the *I* during and after its collapse into foundations, it must also be said that this departure shows itself in the mode of *staying away* rather than disappearing into absolute nothingness. The staying away of any attunement to suffering as such that transpires during the *I*'s collapse into foundationalism is, as it were, a peculiar mode of holding sway: the thought of universal suffering is present in its very absence from 'official' (well-founded) discourse and practice. It is the phenomenal basis of Levinas's remark that solitude 'is perhaps better than dispersion in the anonymity of insignificant relations' (2001b: 57), for at least in solitude you do not have to pretend to anyone that everything in the world is as it should be. Universal suffering is a damned bloody tragedy that even the most ardent supporters of justice cannot push out of their minds. Kafka was right when he said that '*no people sing with such pure voices as those who live in deepest Hell; what we take for the song of the angels is their song*' (Banville 2004: 38). You can almost *hear* the universal suffering that law and justice ignore, that they pretend does not exist. It is like the faint sound of moaning that can sometimes be heard on the wind if you open your window, tune out the everyday din of business and play, and really *listen*.

The Problem of the Passage

The failures of reason

Levinas is not simply lacking in rigour by failing to provide a unifying ground for the passage from ethics to justice, or from the order of non-being to the order of being. He is opposed in principle to articulating a ground on which knowledge could achieve a synthesis in being of transcendence and immanence. He also takes great care to avoid defining suffering psychologically, as the mere presence of uncomfortable feelings that occasionally interrupt the hedonic flow. For the presence of suffering, like the presence of pleasurable feelings, or even indifference, would then fall into the realm of being: suffering would be constituted as a mere affective state a 'condition' of the human being conceived as a container for psychological mechanisms. By making suffering a *datum* of consciousness, and placing it in opposition to other affective states where suffering is absent, the metaphysics of presence leads to technologies for measuring, calculating, comparing, and 'curing' particular manifestations of suffering. However much relief psychology and psychotherapy may have brought to individual sufferers, they are predicated on a metaphysics of the presence of suffering that is also tied to historical outrages: to various ideologies of progress and control, and their tolerance for breaking eggs to make omelettes. These technologies orient themselves to an end (the cessation of certain sufferings in the long run) that justifies the means of inflicting other sufferings in the short run: physical or chemical lobotomies and shock treatments, for example, or the violent suppression of certain traditions and traits in 'aberrant' cultures.

No wonder Levinas sought to distance himself from a conception of suffering that would open the door for the rational justification of historical violence. The palpable failures of reason to prevent the countless murders and unspeakable outrages of the past and present centuries give rise to the suspicion that reason has more to account for than just its failures. Reason's active participation must also be suspected: not just reason in the sense of one human faculty among others – the faculty of thinking – but reason in the sense of the reasons that humans give to explain and justify themselves and their world. In *Useless Suffering,* Levinas even goes so far as to say that *'the justification of the neighbour's pain is certainly the source of all immorality'* (1998: 99). For Levinas knows that suffering as such becomes regrettably invisible to knowledge and the social arrangements that it supports, as he so poignantly portrays in the essay *Transcendence and Height*:

> For me, the negative element, the element of violence in the State, in the hierarchy, appears even when the hierarchy functions perfectly, when

> everyone submits to universal ideas. There are cruelties which are terrible because they proceed from the necessity of the reasonable Order. There are, if you like, the tears that a civil servant cannot see: the tears of the Other. (Levinas 1996: 23)

Ethics as first philosophy signals a profound break with all philosophies of being and knowledge precisely because their attitude towards suffering as such is to divide it into parts that can be cured, justified, or ignored. Knowingly or not, these philosophies are made to serve as props for the perpetuation of existing violence, or for incremental or utopian programmes that require the use of future violence.

Surely one of the greatest tragedies of history lies in the amnesia of suffering as such that is experienced by those who succeed in overthrowing unjust and oppressive social arrangements, only to establish new ones that create still other classes of disaffected sufferers. The French Revolution and the Terror; the American Revolution and the genocides of Native American peoples; the Emancipation Proclamation and Jim Crow; the Russian Revolution and Stalinism; the fall of the Berlin Wall and the rise of gangster capitalism in Eastern Europe; Bush's war to liberate Iraq and the Abu Ghraib and Guantanamo prison scandals: is it not possible to read history as one long dialectic between the violence of justice and the violence of injustice? *'Oh, the violence of administration!'*, Levinas exclaims, as if he were keening all of history's post-revolutionary dead (2001b: 51). But all weepiness aside, Levinas also knows that, in a world full of suffering Others, *justice must be done*. Necessary knowledge and violence therefore re-enter Levinas's thought in the form of a justice to which ethics does or can *lead* in the manner of A $\Rightarrow$ B. But what kind of 'leading' is this that cannot be characterised in terms of cause or ground without intensifying the authority of the very managerial and magisterial discourse that Levinas associates with the infliction and the forgetfulness of so much suffering?

The conatus of thinking

Levinas likes to quote Pascal's aphorism 'The *I* is hateful' to elucidate the phenomenon of the *I*'s departure from itself in the transcendence of the ethical relation. He describes this hatefulness in terms of the *I*'s essential guilt on account of its persistence in being (*conatus essendi*, as Spinoza puts it), as if Levinas were implicitly transforming Nietzsche's concept of will-to-power into a kind of psychological trigger for the *I*'s movement from being-for-itself to being-for-another. However, what Levinas could not see was the *conatus* of his own thought. Levinas discovered in the ineffable subject of ethics the A from which the primordial movement ($\Rightarrow$) to the Other (B) is established, and then he discovered in ethics itself the

A of a second movement (⇒) to justice (B). These movements of logical transcendence reassure the reason that always requires reasons, while at the same time seeming to derationalise the terminal points of the movements as a way of distancing Levinas from the very discourse of truth (by means of the principle of rendering reasons) that he was so desperate to avoid. The result is a passage that is comprehensible in form and content only because of thinking's own 'hateful' clinging to its persistence in being. The guilt of the *I*'s *conatus essendi* is thus transformed into a celebration of its discovery of that guilt – a celebration requiring that very same *conatus essendi* in order to celebrate. This situation would be comedic were it not for the awful sorrow of suffering as such that motivates Levinas's journey.

Levinas's pre-theoretical, pre-reflexive, and ineffable *I* is irremissibly locked in the ethical relation, yet it is somehow able or required to shift gears: it is able to *descend* from the transcendence of ethics (where the *I* is not free to be irresponsible) to the immanence of justice (where the agent of justice is not free to follow its heart). Levinas does not want to deny that the ethical *I endures* throughout this movement, for he says that a 'forgetfulness' of the 'source to which the quest for justice goes back [namely, ethical obligation] risks transforming the sublime and difficult work of justice into a purely political calculation – to the point of totalitarian abuse' (1999: 170). But if it is the case that the *I* of ethics is still 'there' behind the procedures of justice, *who or what is the one who effects justice?* If, as Amanda Loumansky says, Levinas's philosophy calls on us to 'whisper in [law's] ear "Remember the other"' (2000: 3000), how am I to whisper into my own ear when I assume the role of the lonely *agent* of law and justice who must transform multiple ineffable Others into knowable others?

The point of these questions is not to reproach Levinas with a transgression of the law of identity, for both he and I would gladly accept the reproach in the interest of his theme. The point is that the ineffable *I*'s effacement or dormancy, required to let knowledge and calculation emerge during the hour of justice, seems to leave no site or milieu for the 'sublime and difficult work of justice', or even for the 'forgetfulness' of ethical responsibility that Levinas says is inconsistent with justice (1999: 170). Only one who is present to himself can forget what he once knew. Therefore, does the ethical *I* retain a kind of dreamy self-identity (if not awareness) during the procedures of justice, akin to that of TS Eliot's '*patient etherised upon a table*'? (1930: 11). Does this *I*, always sensitive to suffering as such, *grieve* on account of the suffering that its own hand must inflict in the name of justice, and if so, does this mean that the agent of justice is a hand that moves itself? The folk cry of compassionate punishment is 'This will hurt me more than it hurts you'. Who is this 'me' that both hurts and is hurt? The one who weeps on account of what he 'must do' to another in the name of justice: who is this one, such that he could become a theme for philosophising?

Remaining attuned to the depth of Levinas's own thinking requires us to admit that between the 'outside of being' that belongs to ethics and the 'in being' of the means of justice lies a domain that cannot properly be classified in terms of the dualism 'being/non-being'. The questions asked in the previous paragraph thus seek to expose the problem of the passage beyond all objectification of who, what, when, and how. *They seek to uncover a certain longing, or suffering, within thinking itself.* So desperate is Levinas to avoid the Scylla of objectifying knowledge and the Charybdis of emotive mysticism that he passes through them blindfolded, tied in desperate hope to the mast of the *image* of a possible passage from ethics to justice. He thereby seeks to overcome through faith and hope what WB Yeats calls the most fundamental of all divisions: 'that between the intellect, which can only do its work by saying continually "thou fool", and the religious genius which makes it all equal'. If thinking about suffering as such is a kind of restless longing for solutions expressed in terms of a passage from one thing to another, then the solution itself is thinking's means of coping with its *own* suffering.

At bottom, the intelligibility of the passage or leap from the infinitude of ethics to the finitude of justice is underwritten, if at all, by the distinction between the finite and the infinite. Although this Levinasian distinction lies on this side of the Cartesian scission of the universe of ideas – the 'idea of substance' *versus* the 'idea of the infinite' (Descartes 1985: II, 24–36) – we must strip the infinite of all its false aura of mystery to be able to see it for what it is. The infinite in Levinas's sense (or any other sense) is neither an extremely great magnitude nor the material or spiritual impossibility of reaching a limit: it is, first and foremost, *a decision*. The decimal expansion of an irrational number, for example, does not go 'on and on forever', for in fact all numerals that are written by the hands of human beings have to stop somewhere. Instead, an irrational number's decimal expansion is infinite because the rule that defines the number stipulates the senselessness of saying that one has at long last written down 'all' of its digits. I raise this comparison now to bring to light an aspect of Levinas's thought that is obvious, but at the same time extremely difficult to appreciate. *The Levinasian ethical relation is infinite because Levinas himself has stipulated that no description of it that would be satisfactory to knowledge could ever be satisfactory to him.* He says '*No!*' to all but the most elliptical and ephemeral discourse about ethics and the moment of justice. At the simplest and most basic level, this is what 'beyond being' and 'beyond knowledge' signify: a decision by Levinas to eschew the language of limits and bounds when talking about what we owe to other people in the moment of ethics. To say that there is more to it than that – to say that the word 'infinite' signifies something about ethics as a thing-in-itself – is to fall into the very metaphysical trap that the idea of infinitude is supposed to escape. For ethics, as Levinas conceives of it, is not any kind of thing-in-itself that *could* be accessible to knowledge and the settled linguistic meanings that serve it.

A Zen conclusion

To conclude our meditation on Levinas's thought we will try to think through his dilemma from a Zen point of view. If the infinite were located in *prajñā* – in awareness (but not in thought!) – as the emptiness of *all* limits and distinctions, then there would be no distinctions to be found anywhere, including no distinction between the finite and the infinite. In that case, the mind would receive any philosophical thesis of infinitude that discriminates between the finite and the infinite as a mere image that attempts to govern our thinking and feed our craving desire for solutions. Being aware of the deflated status of the opposition 'infinite/finite' in this way, the mind would feel no need to cling to the idea of a passage or leap. In such an event, the infinite would show itself as being utterly irrelevant to the idea of a passage – indeed, it would not show itself *as* anything at all. *This* infinite would be the 'site' of all non-discrimination, and the supreme in-difference of a mindfulness (*smrti*, in Sanskrit) that does not differentiate or crave foundations, but that at the same time does care about the suffering of others. That conventional thought would conceive of the impossible unity of indifference and compassion as a contradiction is beside the point. Comportment is never a contradiction: it is just how one is.

Perhaps the most appropriate metaphor for this infinite would be a *mirror of suffering as such* that could never survive the passage into justice without shattering itself. If the body of this mirror occasionally (or even often) uses violence out of compassionate concern for the suffering of others it would never try to lie to itself about what it is doing. This is the nub of another famous (and perhaps shocking) koan from *Book of Serenity*, 'Nanquan kills a cat':

> One day at Nanquan's the eastern and western halls were arguing over a cat. When Nanquan saw this, he took and held it up and said, 'If you can speak I won't cut it'. The group had no reply; Nanquan then cut the cat in two. Nanquan also brought up the foregoing incident to Zhaoshou and asked him; Zhaozhou immediately took off his sandals, put them on his head, and left. Nanquan said, 'If you had been here you could have saved the cat'. (Cleary 1998: 37)

In the context of a similar dispute between contending factions, King Solomon threatened to cut a baby in half because he knew that the true mother would never permit this to happen. Solomon had a 'theory' of judgment and the theory worked: the baby was spared and all of Israel praised the king for the divinely inspired wisdom of his justice (1 Kings 3: 16–28). But no mere theory could have spared Nanquan's cat, for Nanquan possessed no conception of right speech or judgment. By the same token, Nanquan would never have felt the need to invent a convoluted theory to explain why his unpardonable violence to the cat was sanctified by an insight into what must be done that was deeper than someone else's insight. *Nanquan just used violence as an expedient means.* End of story. If this sounds nihilistic and irresponsible, look at the alternative. If Levinas is right in posing the question 'Is it righteous to be?' (2001b) – if there is a certain disquieting violence that we do to others merely by our own relentless existing, consuming, and needing – then surely it must *at least* be open to question whether our practice of constantly garbing our being and actions in words of justification is not a kind of desperate lie born of an equally desperate desire for reassurance.

On the other hand, if the infinite were to be experienced in the way that I have just suggested, it would forfeit all intelligibility. One cannot understand, comprehend, have an idea of, or even touch by thought that which makes no discriminations, and therefore produces no enduring antitheses. That which lies on the other side of the distinction between unity and difference is not beyond being, as Levinas would have it, but beyond 'beyonds', which is to say, at a minimum, beyond intelligibility. This does not mean that the loss of intelligibility in such a case would necessarily be a failure to be regretted. Indeed, it could be the best thing that ever happened. It seems to me that the profundity of Levinas's conception of the face and its role in both ethics and justice fails by virtue of its very legibility to achieve the perspective on suffering as such that it aspires to reach.

At this point it would be more than a little expedient to contrast Levinas's profoundly intelligible words with the following gloriously unintelligible koan about the face, the soul, and language:

> Lin-chi addressed the monks: 'Look at this lump of flesh which is my body. Inside is a soul which has no status. The face is the gateway for the soul, through which the soul goes out and comes in. If any of you are uncertain of this, just look'. A monk asked: 'Describe this soul that has no status'. Lin-chi ran to the monk, took hold of him, and shouted in his face: 'Speak! Speak!' The monk began to speak. Lin-chi pushed him away, exclaiming: 'Why should I listen to a soul with no status?' (Van de Weyer 2000: 11/20)

If anyone *understands* and can *paraphrase* this koan he has missed its point completely. Lin-chi would laugh in your Levinasian 'face' if you tried to express his (or even Levinas's) 'deep meaning'. For meaning resides on the level of mere knowing, and knowing resides on the level of the kind of discriminating mind that attaches itself to its discriminations like a barnacle attaches itself to the hull of a ship. On the other hand, a barnacle, once it is attached, *has* to go wherever the ship takes it, whereas the discriminating mind *lets* itself go wherever its dualisms take it when they are plugged into the formula of logical transcendence, $A \Rightarrow B$.

If there were an understanding beyond understanding, therefore, it would never try to represent itself as a passage to (or from) anything else. Indeed, it would never try to represent itself as anything at all. Such an understanding would simply show itself in the comportment of the one who understands. It would *shine forth*. How painful it would be to experience the death of illusions in this way, and to let go of the yearning to dominate and control others through the violence of language. Yet how liberating this would be! For the deepest liberation has nothing to do with the will's capacity to make and justify decisions, and everything to do with the mind's ability to regain its beginning: to shed its illusions as if they were a chrysalis, and to become mindful, at long last, of what it always already was. If Levinas's philosophy ever does become a set of profoundly intelligible 'guiding words' for negotiating the passage between ethics and justice, this could be the worst thing that ever happened to it.

Chapter 4: Wittgenstein's Noisy Silence

Introducing *A Lecture on Ethics*

The average person would probably agree that a book describing the many kinds of birds there are in the world is not itself a bird. But what would he or she say about a book that not only described the many different uses human beings have for words like 'good' and 'evil', but also asserted that all of these uses are ethically equivalent, at least as far as philosophy is concerned? I think it is clear that the average European or American, at least, would call such a book unethical, if not evil. Of course, nothing is stopping us from calling a book on birds a bird. Our new way of talking, however novel and surprising at first, would in the end simply amount to giving the word 'bird' a new use. But I would be willing to bet that most Westerners would not be surprised – and indeed that they would heartily approve – if the epithets *unethical* and *evil* were applied to a book that compared Hitler's *Mein Kampf* with the Torah, or Hermann Goering's remark that 'right is whatever pleases us' with Jesus's teaching 'blessed are they which do hunger and thirst after righteousness, for they shall be filled' (Matthew 5:6). One can only imagine how much greater an offence they would feel if the comparison led the book's author to aver that all of these texts stand on exactly the same level, ethically speaking.

Nevertheless, there is little doubt that Wittgenstein's *Complete Book of Ethics*, had he ever written it, would have read just this way. According to one particularly telling incident that is recounted by his friend Rush Rhees:

> And once when I mentioned Goering's '*Recht ist das, was uns gefällt*',[1] Wittgenstein said that 'even that is a kind of ethics. It is helpful in silencing objections to a certain attitude. And it should be considered along with other ethical judgments and discussions, in the anthropological study of ethical discussions which we may have to conduct'. (Rhees 1965: 25)

1 'Right is whatever pleases us.'

Wittgenstein's remark about the 'ethics' of the Nazis was not an aberration. Beginning in lectures to his classes in the 1930s (1993: 103–04), then in the *Philosophical Investigations* (1953: 36e) and, finally, in conversations near the end of his life (Bouwsma 1986: 40–41), Wittgenstein consistently maintained that the way to understand the meaning of ethical words is not to try to define them or make theories about them, but to investigate and describe what he called their 'grammar'. To investigate the grammar of a word, for Wittgenstein, is to inquire into the conventions that frame the many different uses that people actually make of the word in daily life. Beginning in about 1932, Wittgenstein frequently compared the uses of language to the playing of games – board games, ball games, children's games, and so forth. Like these games, the various uses we make of language are constituted by rules that are sometimes rigid, sometimes flexible and always subject to historical change. He called these rules *grammar*, and he maintained that the various grammatical rules comprising 'language-games'(*Sprachspiele*) are determined by their role in this or that 'form of life' (*Lebensform*), rather than by the objects to which they may or may not refer. Just as we recognise that there are legal and illegal moves in real games, so too there are meaningful and nonsensical operations (propositions and speech acts) in language-games. Just as the moves in a real game have meaning only in the context of the particular game being played – there is no such move as 'castling' in the game of backgammon, for example – so too language acquires its significance by being always already embedded in the cultural system of which it is a part.

The ways in which people do in fact use words may or may not comport with a metaphysically inclined philosopher's preconceived notions of how they ought to be used, but according to Wittgenstein it represents an important philosophical and moral gain to come to see clearly how the words *are* used. What is more, 'it is not our aim to refine or complete the system of rules for the use of our words in unheard-of ways', he wrote in the *Philosophical Investigations*, 'for the clarity we are aiming at is indeed *complete* clarity' (1953: 51e). Self-deception was for him a cardinal sin and intellectual honesty and clarity were cardinal virtues. His comparison of philosophy to the treatment of an illness (1953: 91e), and his aspiration to make philosophical problems '*completely* disappear' through the painstaking analysis of how people actually use words, are strikingly similar to the way the Zen master Lin-chi described his own teachings. Although *'it is most important that you come to see clearly'*, Lin-chi said to his followers, *'I have no Dharma to give to men. I only cure diseases and undo knots'* (Schloegl 1976: 24, 44). The peace that Wittgenstein sought to give to philosophy through the application of various methods of 'therapy' (his word) was motivated by his belief that metaphysical questions 'tormented' philosophers by bringing philosophy *itself* into question (1953: 51e). For he was convinced from his own example that allowing one's restless thoughts to achieve peace is 'what someone who philosophises yearns for' (1980: 43e). From the standpoint of Wittgenstein's mature thought, therefore, philosophy is merely a method of solving nagging metaphysical puzzles by reducing them to the status of mere confusions about how ordinary grammar works. On this view, the ultimate product of philosophical research really ought to be quite modest: 'a whole cloud of philosophy condensed into a drop of grammar' (1953: 222e).

On the matter of ethics, Wittgenstein came to believe that if we reflect on the multiplicity of examples that are shown us when we first learn the meaning of the word *good*, and look closely at the many different language-games we play with that word, we would find ourselves agreeing with him that 'good' has what he called a 'family of meanings' (1953: 36e). This idea compares word uses with the resemblances between members of a family: just as 'the various resemblances between members of a family – build, features, colour of eyes, gait, temperament, etc etc – overlap and criss-cross', so too the various uses of words such as *good* overlap and criss-cross without showing any *single* aspect or property that unites them all (Wittgenstein 1953: 32e). He thought that the Platonic search for a single essence of words like *good* revealed a 'contemptuous attitude towards the particular case', and he traced this attitude in a rather Buddhistic way to philosophers' misguided '*craving for generality*' (1960: 17–18) and their '*longing for the transcendent*'(1980: 15e). If philosophers could only bring themselves to let go of this craving for generality, he believed, they would then be able to see the plain truth that '*the use of the word "good" (in an ethical sense) is a combination of a very large number of interrelated games, each of them as it were a facet of its use*' (Wittgenstein 1978: 77). Which is to say, Wittgenstein believed that a complete philosophical investigation of the grammar of 'good' would show the investigator that the word not only does not have a single meaning, but that it does not even have a single theme that could be rightly said to run through all the different contexts in which it is used.

But we are getting ahead of the story – or rather, continuing along this line would be a different story altogether. In the rest of this chapter we will be occupied with the text of a lecture about ethics that Wittgenstein gave in 1929 to a meeting of the Heretics Society in Cambridge.[2] Although Wittgenstein was invited to speak by CK Ogden,

---

2 Ray Monk writes that the Heretics 'had previously been addressed by such luminaries as HG Wells, Bertrand Russell and Virginia Woolf' (Monk 1990: 276).

the first English translator of the *Tractatus*, the members of the Heretics Society made up a general audience that had no particular interest or training in philosophy (Wittgenstein 1993: 36). The typescript of Wittgenstein's remarks, written in English and bearing no title, was first published posthumously as *A Lecture on Ethics* in the *Philosophical Review* (Wittgenstein 1965: 3–12), and was later republished in the book *Philosophical Occasions* (1993: 36–44). It represents the only sustained exposition by Wittgenstein of his views on ethics in print, although numerous epigrams and fragments on ethical matters are scattered throughout his other writings.

Surprisingly enough, the lecture is not concerned with laying the groundwork for an investigation of the grammar of ethical words in the sense that his later philosophy would use the term 'grammar'. If one succumbs to the academic temptation to view the lecture as a sort of transitional 'philosophical' text, bridging the youthful thought of the *Tractatus* and the mature thought of the *Philosophical Investigations*, its ethical point would be lost completely. In *A Lecture on Ethics*, Wittgenstein attempts to assert an obscure ethical thesis, however tortured and veiled is his manner of asserting it. Ethics, the way the term is used in the lecture, not only has no relationship to anything that could be investigated, it is also not something the experience of which could ever come to anyone who thought of himself as an *investigator* while he was having the ethical experience. In short, *A Lecture on Ethics* is almost the only instance after the publication of the *Tractatus* in 1921 in which Wittgenstein publicly discarded his otherwise inflexible equation '*philosophy = clarifying linguistic usages*' to announce a dramatic and seemingly mystical *thesis* about ethics.

As a general matter, Wittgenstein refused to let himself be enchanted by anyone's ethical norms or discourse, including especially his own, and in this respect he showed himself to be very much like a man of Zen. To pick one of many possible examples, compare Wittgenstein's famous 'man in a room' remark[3] with an analogous passage from the collected teachings of Lin-chi:

Wittgenstein

> A person caught in a philosophical confusion is like a man in a room who wants to get out but doesn't know how. He tries the window but it is too high. He tries the chimney but it is too narrow. And if he would only *turn around*, he would see that the door has been open all the time. (Malcolm 1984: 44) (emphasis in original)

---

3 Interestingly enough, Heidegger knew of this remark and paraphrased it with approval in the *Heraclitus Seminar* (Heidegger and Fink 1993b: 17).

Lin-Chi

> Followers of the Way, you take the words that issued from the mouths of old teachers, saying 'this is the True Way, this old sage is wonderful; I am but an ordinary fellow and dare not compare myself with such great masters'. Blind fools! Your whole life you hold such views, going against the evidence of your single eye, trembling like asses on ice, your teeth clenched with fear. (Schloegl 1976: 36)

Both Wittgenstein and Lin-chi sought to disabuse people of the feeling that the problems tormenting them were incredibly deep and that they were incapable of solving the problems on their own. Both thinkers wanted people to open their eyes and *just look* at what lies already displayed in full view, right in front of them. Not that they took this to be an easy thing to do: Wittgenstein and Lin-chi also realised (in the words of the former) that '*the very things which are most obvious may become the hardest of all to understand*', and that '*what has to be overcome is a difficulty having to do with the will, rather than the intellect*' (Wittgenstein 1980: 17e).

Of course, at this stage we should all have at least some idea of why the Zen master Lin-chi employed expedient means to help his students enlighten themselves. But why did Wittgenstein, who as far as I am aware knew nothing about Zen, follow a path of teaching that radically deflated language and philosophy? It has been suggested that Wittgenstein's account of the mystical is like the Zen practice of acting with an empty mind (Glock 1996: 253). If that is so, however, why was he so *unwilling* to talk about ethical matters, and why was he so eager to consign ethics to the category of the ineffable? If it was not because of his unconditional compassion for the suffering of others, as in Lin-chi's case, was it because of his own inability to *let go* of his vehement and very un-Zen opposition to certain ways of thinking and talking in philosophy? But perhaps these questions are premature, and I have already said too much by asking them here. At this stage of our thinking the foregoing questions and interpretations must remain mere hypotheses. We have not yet begun really to *think* about the important matters that Wittgenstein's lecture on ethics brings into view. Let us start to do that now by giving the lecture as close and as sympathetic a reading as possible, from start to finish.

Tracing the Movements of the Lecture

Relative and absolute ethics

After making a few preliminary remarks about the difficulties he feels in communicating his thoughts on ethics in English in this particular venue, Wittgenstein begins his lecture by gently leading his audience to a place that must have seemed familiar and comforting to them at the time: he adopts, somewhat disingenuously, the great GE Moore's explanation of ethics as *'the general enquiry into what is good'* (Wittgenstein 1993: 38). But from this familiar place he rapidly proceeds, by way of a rhetorically skilful series of transformations, to take them to an end that he earlier warned them they would not agree with or might not understand. Ethics conceived as 'enquiry into what is good' by an inquiring subject is transformed into ethics conceived as the mystical experience of the ethical. And the use of ethical language undergoes a sort of double metamorphosis: after first being transformed from a particular speaking subject's attempt to describe what is good and bad into humanity's tendency in general to speak in ethical terms, it is then transformed again into an act of witness to the revelation that ethics, in his sense of the term, is ineffable.

The structure of ethics-as-inquiry is maintained until the end of the lecture, when Wittgenstein will step out in front of his text, as it were, and speak to the audience from his heart rather than his head. But he softens them up for what is to come right at the beginning. No sooner does he adopt Moore's definition than he subverts it by introducing certain other expressions that he says are 'more or less synonymous' with Moore's: 'I could have said Ethics is the enquiry into what is valuable, or, what is really important, or I could have said Ethics is the enquiry into the meaning of life, or into what makes life worth living, or into the right way of living' (1993: 38). He even tells them that his 'slightly wider' sense of ethics includes 'what I believe to be the most essential part of what is generally called Aesthetics'(1993: 35), as if living ethically consisted merely in *seeing* the world in the right way – *sub specie aeterni* ('under the aspect of eternity'), as he put it in the *Tractatus* (1974: 71, 73). The effect that he says he is seeking to accomplish by throwing this welter of phrases at his audience is to give them a rough idea of 'what it is that Ethics is concerned with'. But what he actually accomplishes by thus freeing ethics from the constraints of any one definition is to set in motion the lecture's progressive devaluation of any and every imaginable expression of the ethical.

The first kind of expression that Wittgenstein devalues is what he calls the use of ethical words in their 'trivial or relative sense'. Expressions such as 'This is a *good* chair' and 'This is the *right* road' are commonly used to assert that something comes up to a certain predetermined standard that reflects someone's preferences. As Wittgenstein notes, in such cases the thing and the standard can be put together in a synonymous expression of fact, and in such a way that all connotation of moral judgment disappears. The translation of 'This is the right way to Granchester', for example, is 'This is the right way you have to go if you want to get to Granchester in the shortest time' (1993: 39). But not everyone wants to get to Granchester in the shortest possible time – some people like to meander and gaze at the countryside. From the standpoint of a conscientious philosophical observer, therefore, the relative sense of ethical words comes down to saying 'This person believes that *X* is valuable'.

In describing reality, we also describe what we come upon among human beings. People have preferences, and this is a describable fact. But in describing the preferences that people have, one describes only *that* they have them, and not that the preferences that people happen to have are also ethically valid. The possibility that a philosopher's allegedly 'value-free' act of describing other people's preferences might in turn be correctly described by sociologists and psychologists in terms of the philosopher's own unconscious and socially conditioned value preferences does not refute this point. If we look only at the way people actually use language we should be able to recognise that the grammar of the word 'description' differs from the grammar of the word 'evaluation' in most of the language-games that are played with these words. Indeed, this is a truth that psychologists and sociologists themselves implicitly acknowledge by taking advantage of this very distinction to utter their own allegedly impartial 'scientific descriptions' of other people's latent value preferences. Wittgenstein's conclusion that it forms no part of the description of people's preferences that some are more valuable than others does not announce a grandiose (and dubious) metaphysical distinction between Is and Ought. Rather, it is a calculated decision to play the usual 'description *versus* evaluation' language-game as a rhetorical strategy. Wittgenstein wants to lead the audience of his lecture to a point of view that transcends the distinction between Is and Ought, even if that very distinction seems at first glance to deny all possibility of success to the aspiration for ethical transcendence.

The possibility of demystifying ethical words by translating the sentences in which they appear into simple statements of verifiable fact is central to his argument and, like any good advocate, he gets his audience to accept this possibility by concentrating on easy cases first: 'good chairs', 'right roads' and the like. Cases such as these prepare the audience to hear something plausible in his transitional thesis that 'every judgment of relative value is a mere statement of facts and can therefore be put in such a form that it loses all the appearance of value'(1993: 39). The whole point of putting these easy cases first is that they now enable Wittgenstein to draw a sharp contrast between our use of words such as 'good' in their relative sense and our use of them in what he calls an *'ethical or absolute sense'*. In a movement that foreshadows the authority that his later philosophy will constantly draw upon, Wittgenstein does not justify his distinction between the relative and absolute senses of ethical words by saying that it corresponds to a distinction in the metaphysical realm of what is 'really good', but by saying that it reflects the ways in which these words are actually used by people.

For example, he notes that a bad tennis player can defeat criticism of his game by saying that he knows he plays badly, but he does not want to play any better. If this person were now to call his game 'good', we would know exactly what he means: namely, that his tennis game comes up to the idiosyncratic standard of self-satisfaction that he has set for it. But someone we have caught in a lie, Wittgenstein now says, does not meet our objection that he is behaving badly by saying 'I know I behave badly, but then I don't want to behave any better'. The way we commonly use ethical words in *this* context makes it unlikely that we would respond to the liar's remark in the same way we would to the tennis player's syntactically identical remark – that is, by just shrugging and saying, 'Ah, then that's all right'. Our conventions permit us to make another move in the game. They allow us to rejoin to the liar: 'Well, you *ought* to want to behave better' (1993: 39). Our conventions give us the right to expect that the liar's next move will come from a grammatical repertoire that includes expressions like 'You're wrong, I didn't lie' and 'You're right, I'm sorry'. They also give us the right to be surprised and offended if he now gives us a Goeringesque argument that what he ought to want to do is whatever happens to please him. In this the first example he gives of an absolute judgment of value, Wittgenstein the rhetoritician again skilfully appeals to the easy case: for what audience of educated Englishmen in 1929 could fail to appreciate the difference between saying that someone is a bad tennis player and saying that he is a bad man? The obviousness of this difference in commonsense attitudes towards the two cases greatly serves Wittgenstein's rhetorical purpose of getting his sceptical audience of science buffs to acknowledge to themselves that there exists a human impulse to speak about ethical matters in a sense that cannot be reduced to the description of a purely objective relation between conduct and standards.

The big book of ethics

At this point in the lecture Wittgenstein's audience probably expected him to begin speaking about the golden thread of ethics, in its absolute sense, that he had teased out of the otherwise heather-hued tapestry that we humans weave by the plethora of uses we have for words such as 'good'. But instead of gratifying their desire to hear of the absolutely ethical, he now gives them the surprising image of a verbose 'omniscient person' to contemplate. The omniscient person knows 'all the movements of all the bodies in the world dead or alive and ... all the states of mind of all human beings that ever lived', and he writes down all that he knows in a 'big book' (1993: 39). This Big Book contains a description of 'all relative judgments of value and all true scientific propositions and in fact all true propositions that can be made', including a complete description of all of our states of mind. The omniscient person's Big Book would describe a murder, for example, by reporting on all of the things physical and psychological that happened, including even all of the 'pain or rage caused by this murder in other people when they heard of it' (1993: 39–40). But in the pages of the Big Book the '*murder will be on exactly the same level as any other event, for instance the falling of a stone*'. It is not that Wittgenstein wants to *deny* that there is an ethical responsibility not to murder other people; he merely denies that language can express the ethical status of murder in any way that distinguishes it, ethically speaking, from the description of a stone's falling. Which is to say: the omniscient person does not sort his words into categories such as high and low or good and evil – he simply goes on and on describing in a monotone, as it were. His Big Book therefore contains not a single jot of ethics in the absolute sense of the word, but only 'facts, facts and facts' (1993: 40).

Omniscience in a person entails the possibility of his writing down all the facts that human beings ever knew or could know – or rather, all the facts that human beings, given their various historical perspectives, could rightly claim to know. On the other hand, mere scriveners, even omniscient ones, do not *intervene* in the activities they describe. In this respect it is not difficult to recognise that the omniscient person is a figure for Wittgenstein's own conception of philosophy's task. His describes this task in a paragraph of the *Philosophical Investigations* that many of his followers have elevated to the status of a canon:

> Philosophy may in no way interfere with the actual use of language; it can in the end only describe it. For it cannot give it any foundation either. It leaves everything as it is. (1953: 49e)

We will return to Wittgenstein's thesis of non-intervention in a little while. But for now it is enough to say that notwithstanding the philosophy of philosophy that is represented by his image of the omniscient person, *A Lecture on Ethics* is not a treatise on what philosophy should be. On the contrary, Wittgenstein is about to tell his audience that ethics in *his* absolute sense of the word does not correspond to any kind of 'knowing' or philosophising at all. By now the more astute among his audience probably had noticed that the commonsense distinction Wittgenstein had earlier drawn between the relative and the absolute uses of ethical words is not enough to keep either kind of use from falling into the omniscient person's Big Book. All of our actual expressions –

including even those in which we express judgments of absolute value – will be inscribed in the Big Book of facts along with our other expressions, because the omniscient person knows that it is a fact that we said them. Not even the omniscient person himself could *definitively* order ethical words into the ethically good and bad, for omniscience is not the same as omnipotence. This shows the problem that is faced by any ethicist who aspires to have his ethical words excluded from the Big Book on the ground that they alone express the 'truly ethical': that which evaluates does not and cannot evaluate its very own act of evaluating. This point is sufficiently important that we should take a little time to elucidate it by means of one of Wittgenstein's most favourite metaphors: the measuring stick.

According to the most interesting sense of this comparison, ethical discourse can no more assure its own privileged ethical status than a yardstick can represent that it is 36 inches long. A yardstick is what we use to help us say of bodies that *they* are so many inches or feet long. Ethical language is what we use to say of human behaviour that it is good or bad. Just as what we use to measure does not in turn measure itself, so too what we use to praise as good or condemn as bad does not praise or condemn itself. The question 'Is this ethical judgment truly ethical?' *can* be answered, but only in the same sense as the question 'Is my yardstick 36 inches long?' can be answered. This is the most important sense of Wittgenstein's later remark concerning what was then the standard metre-bar in Paris: 'There is *one* thing of which one can say neither that it is one metre long, nor that it is not one metre long, and that is the standard metre in Paris. – But this is, of course, not to ascribe any extraordinary property to it, but only to mark its peculiar role in the language-game of measuring with a metre-rule'(1953: 25e). Thus, I *can* write ethical language about other people's ethical language (or about my own prior ethical pronouncements), just as I can measure my yardstick with another yardstick. *But whatever it is that the second yardstick settles about the length of the first, it settles nothing about itself.* Rather, *I decide* to make the second yardstick the standard of measurement, and without this decision it would make no sense to say that the first yardstick is (or is not) 36 inches long. I hold the second yardstick to the first, and read off the numeral '36' from the second one at the place on its surface to which the first one comes up – *this* is what it looks like when I am measuring one yardstick with another. I read a book advancing a theory of the good, become agitated and angry at what I see written there, and then write a book of my own pointing out how the theory advanced in the first book is rubbish – *this* is what it looks like when I try to write ethics about ethics. The omniscient person has just as much right (and power) to enter a description in his Big Book of my words and deeds in the second case as in the first.

The translation of mundane statements of personal taste containing words like 'good' into statements that so-and-so merely prefers *X* probably did not raise too many hackles in the audience. After all, who would deny that the expression 'This is a good chair' comes down to saying simply that the speaker likes the chair? The Big Book is essentially a vast catalogue of relative ethics, and it begins appearing controversial only when the omniscient person starts filling it with statements of absolute value such as 'Democracy is good' and 'Genocide is bad'. Some people believe that the expressions of their ethical preferences in cases like these *refer* to the good as if it were a describable and verifiable fact. In thinking this way, however, they unfortunately fall prey to a confusion caused by what Wittgenstein will later call the *Bedeutungskörper* ('meaning-body') theory of meaning.

According to this theory, which Wittgenstein first named in 1932, and which the *Philosophical Investigations* associates with the account of language contained in Augustine's *Confessions* (1961: 29), every word has a meaning that is correlated with the word, and this meaning is the object for which the word stands (Wittgenstein 1953: 2e). The logical form of this theory of language can be depicted as *'x' means* □, where the sign '□' signifies an object called the *meaning* of the sign *'x'*. The theory acquires its plausibility from cases in which an ostensive definition is possible, such as calling a dog by its name: it is easy to see that we can point at (and even pet) what the word 'Rover' refers to, although even here we risk confusing the *bearer* of a name with the name's *meaning*. However useful it may be in thinking about the case of names, however, the theory turns our minds to mush when we apply it to concept-words such as 'good', for it leads us to expect (and all too often to invent) a ghostly meaning-body (□) that 'good' refers to: 'some words refer to things, so we create ghosts for other words to refer to' (2003: 384). When we are asked to identify the ghost that we have created, however, all we can do is repeat ourselves: we pound our fist and say 'The absolutely good really, really *does* mean □!' But, of course, this is hardly the same as showing what the sign '□' itself *refers to*. In fact, the puzzle of what ethical words 'refer to' is not the result of some failure of vision or intelligence on our part; it is merely a product of our chosen norm of representation. Some people let the *Bedeutungskörper* picture of meaning take control of their philosophical intelligence and subvert their ability to notice that there is an interesting if not fundamental distinction in the use of language between such practices as calling a dog by its name and saying that genocide is 'bad'.

The idea that words must always mean their meaning-bodies is a variation of logical transcendence, inasmuch as we let our craving attachment to its norm of representation, A $\Rightarrow$ B, make us believe that we *must* account for our ability to understand language by appealing to something like a *meaning* (A) that always *leads* (in the manner of a cause or ground) to our *understanding* it (B). But why *must* it be the case that our ability to use and understand language is always predicated on the 'meaning' of word? Do we always call to mind a dictionary entry or other representation of the word 'fire', for example, before we react to someone telling us that we are in the midst of a 'fire hazard'? In *The Blue Book,* dictated to his class during the 1933–34 school term at Cambridge, Wittgenstein uses the analogous case of giving someone an order to fetch a red flower from a meadow to show that our understanding of language need not *always* (or even usually) be based on the 'meaning' of words. While it is possible to imagine a case where someone actually employs a colour chart to determine the meaning of the word 'red' in the context of such an order, Wittgenstein notes that *'this is not the only way of searching and it isn't the usual way'*. On the contrary, more often than not the following is the case:

> We go, look about us, walk up to a flower and pick it, without comparing it to anything. To see that the process of obeying the order can be of this kind, consider the order '*imagine* a red patch'. You are not tempted in this case to think that *before* obeying you must have imagined a red patch to serve you as a pattern for the red patch which you were ordered to imagine. Now you might ask: do we *interpret* the words before we obey the order? And in some cases you will find that you do something which might be called interpreting before obeying, in some cases not. (Wittgenstein 1960: 3) (emphasis in original)

Wittgenstein's description of the way that we usually obey orders is not rocket science; it is a modest kind of phenomenology that is open to anyone with the will to see clearly what transpires in the course of using language. Nevertheless, the history of the philosophy of language is littered with the corpses of theories that depend for their plausibility on attachment to the *Bedeutungskörper* picture of meaning and its implicit norm of logical transcendence, sometimes to the point of absurdity.

Opposition to the *Bedeutungskörper* picture of meaning suffuses Wittgenstein's lecture in the form of his overt hostility to the claim that people's expressions of ethical preferences refer to objects that reside within some sort of factual realm of the Good. To help persuade the audience that *all* ethical expressions, including even the expressions of absolute ethics, belong together as mundane entries in the omniscient person's Big Book, Wittgenstein offers them a hypothesis that is obviously false. He tells them that if the absolutely ethical were a describable state of affairs – a fact – it would have to be something 'which everybody, independent of his tastes and inclinations, would *necessarily* bring about or feel guilty for not bringing about'. In other words, all the people in the world (including even the omniscient person) would have to agree to the absolute rightness of exactly one way of reacting to ethical situations. Only then could preferences become validities, not because consensus refers to some meaning-body of metaphysical truth that makes them valid, but because literally everyone would *actually read* the entries in the Big Book under the aspect of their universal ethical truth. The distinction between Is and Ought would dissolve, but only because people's linguistic usages would have shifted to obliterate the distinction. Without this kind of universal consensus on the use of ethical language, conflicting ethical expressions break up into mere factoids, and the omniscient person has no option but to enter them all on the same level, as mere preferences.

Since the real world has never exhibited a truly universal consensus on ethical matters, Wittgenstein calls the univocal world that is depicted in his hypothesis a 'chimera': 'No state of affairs has, in itself, what I would like to call the coercive power of an absolute judge' (1993: 40). This way of putting it shows the audience the sense of his earlier assertion that *'all the facts described [in the omniscient person's Big Book] would, as it were, stand on the same level and in the same way all propositions stand on the same level. There are no propositions which, in any absolute sense, are sublime, important, or trivial'* (1993: 39). It is important to recognise that Wittgenstein's conception of the moral equivalence of facts *as such* is not a thesis of 'moral relativism': it is simply a function of the grammar of the word 'fact'. Since our various uses of language actually *do* distinguish statements of what is from statements of what ought to be, Wittgenstein believed that the imperative of intellectual honesty and clarity requires us to acknowledge the difference while we are philosophising.

Towards the end of his life Wittgenstein gave this illustration of how difficult the philosophical task of ignoring the repulsiveness of certain ethical expressions might be:

> Imagine a tribe who when they viewed things that were horrible, loathsome to us, clapped their hands, their faces bright, and now they always uttered the word 'doog'. And now you are to translate the word 'doog'. How will you translate it? Will you hesitate about this? (Bouwsma 1986: 42)

As far as *A Lecture on Ethics* is concerned, the answer to Wittgenstein's question is clear: hesitate or not, we must translate 'doog' as 'good' no matter how much we disapprove of the tribe's conduct, thus signifying (correctly) that *they* approve of what they are doing. Indeed, even if the omniscient person himself tried to pass judgment on the tribe's activities, he would then immediately have to enter a mundane description of his own ethical judgment in the Big Book, right alongside all the other facts that are recorded there. In other words, any feelings of ethical distaste that this *Über*-philosopher might experience cannot be translated into a statement of the 'absolute badness' of the tribe's form of life without becoming just another mundane use of ethical words. A murder and the falling of a stone, the death of a baby and the birth of a sparrow, Auschwitz and what we had for breakfast this morning: according to Wittgenstein, even if it is granted that people's deep-seated values cause them to notice these things, under the aspect of ethical words, once they *are* noticed as facts a philosopher has no more right to say that their *sheer facticity alone* automatically sorts them into some sort of ethical hierarchy than he has to say that a triangle is a circle.

Science and ethics

Propositions say how things are *in* the world, and in doing this they show us what they represent (if anything); but they can express nothing that is 'higher' than what is in the world. For Wittgenstein, absolute ethics is higher. But if ethics in its absolute sense is higher than the world, and if nothing meaningful can be said about it, this does not imply that Wittgenstein scorned ethical discourse. On the contrary, in general he thought that the pseudo-propositions of ethics (as opposed to those of metaphysics and the philosophy of mathematics) belong to the category of *important* nonsense. Hence, in *A Lecture on Ethics* he did not summon the authority of the facts set down in the omniscient person's Big Book in order to put an end to his audience's nonsensical attempts to express the ethical; *he summoned them to preserve that very discourse from the onslaughts of a scientific world-view*.

He had already hinted at this theme near the end of the *Tractatus*, where he wrote: 'We feel that even when all *possible* scientific questions have been answered, the problems of life remain completely untouched. Of course there are then no questions left, and this itself is the answer' (1974: 73). But this hint was not taken by most of the analytic philosophers who were attracted to the *Tractatus* in the 1920s. By the end of that decade the logical positivists had taken over the *Tractatus*'s position that there can be no meaningful ethical propositions, but they did not do this because they thought that ethics is something that is 'higher'. Rather, they maintained that ethical discourse is full of latent nonsense because the foundation of value on which ethical expressions rest cannot be verified – cannot be compared with reality and found to be true or false. Gordon Hunnings succinctly describes the view on ethics that was held by many members of the Vienna Circle as follows: '[T]he majority of ethical statements either express one's own feelings or are designed to influence the feelings of others. The rest were at worst simply meaningless, or, at best, misconceived attempts to prescribe a moral order that traded upon the logical slight of hand of moving from statements about how the world *is* to statements about how the world *ought* to be' (Hunnings 1988: 77–78).

In sweeping ethical language under the rug, the logical positivists completely dropped Wittgenstein's idea that ethics is a matter of paramount importance, for they considered it to be an unfortunate and embarrassing manifestation of his tendency towards mysticism (Glock 1996: 110). It thus seems very clear that Wittgenstein used the opportunity afforded by his lecture to the Heretics Society to distance himself from this aspect of a movement with which he was publicly associated, at least at that time. It is true that Wittgenstein was going through his most dogmatic 'verificationist' stage at or around the time of the lecture. According to this point of view, the meaning of a proposition is determined by the methods that we use to verify its truth: 'The verification is not *one* token of the truth, it is *the* sense of the proposition (Einstein: How a magnitude is measured is what it is)' (1975: 200). But for Wittgenstein the nonsensicality of *ethical* expressions was never a function of our inability to verify them. If facts cannot be compared with values according to the true-false propositional calculus, this does not mean that ethics is *a priori* of no interest to philosophy, as the logical positivists claimed. For the very attempt to expel ethics from philosophy is itself a value-based (ethical) act. In *A Lecture on Ethics*, Wittgenstein took great pains to articulate a conception of absolute ethics that could never be mistaken for positivism. And one could say that the distance between him and the logical positivists on this matter is measured, as it were, in terms of mystical miles.

Wittgenstein had already told the audience in his introductory remarks that he did not intend to give them a lecture on logic – that is, a lecture that would have gone over the problems concerning the logical form of language that had preoccupied him in the *Tractatus* (1993: 37). And now, at the mid-point of the lecture, he begins to reveal tendencies that many, if not most, people in this audience of science-lovers must have interpreted as being distinctly unscientific, if not downright incomprehensible. It appears that Wittgenstein had hypothesised the presence of meaningful propositions of fact in the omniscient person's Big Book in order to set up yet another opposition: for he quickly proceeds to put the expressible fact that people constantly *do* try to say something about the absolutely ethical up against what, in his final series of remarks, he will characterise as the inexpressible *experience* of the ethical.

The exploding book of ethics

If whatever we say or do can be reduced to a factual description in the Big Book, Wittgenstein now tells his audience flatly that absolute ethics itself could never be deflated in this way: '*Ethics, if it is anything, is supernatural and our words will only express facts; as a teacup will only hold a teacup of water [even] if I were to pour out a gallon over it'* (1993: 40). It begins to emerge that Wittgenstein is not offering his audience a theory or dogma on the limits of language in order to silence people's tendency to express ethical judgments in terms of absolutes. Rather, he wants to silence only a certain *kind* of discourse about absolute ethics – the kind that would reduce it to an objective scientific report:

> And now if I contemplate what Ethics really would have to be if there were such a science, this result seems to me quite obvious. It seems to me obvious that nothing we could ever think or say should be *the* thing. That we cannot write a scientific book, the subject matter of which could be intrinsically sublime and above all other subject matters. I can only describe my feeling by the metaphor, that if a man could write a book on Ethics which really was a book on Ethics, this book would, with an explosion, destroy all other books in the world. (1993: 40)

Although Wittgenstein began the lecture by adopting Moore's definition of ethics as the inquiry into the good, by now the more philosophically knowledgeable among his audience would have understood that he was aggressively confronting and contradicting Moore's conception of ethics as a kind of 'science' (Moore 1993: 55). Wittgenstein, like Heidegger and Derrida, saw himself as someone who destroys, subverts, and goes beyond philosophical tradition. Did he not say that if his name is remembered in philosophy, this would be analogous to remembering the name of the person who burnt down the library of Alexandria? (Wittgenstein 2003: 73). And did he not mutter to himself, in the course of characterising his philosophical work, 'I destroy, I destroy, I destroy'? (1980: 21e). Wittgenstein took up Moore's claim that the word 'good' is indefinable only in order to completely radicalise it. As Hans-Georg Glock puts it, Wittgenstein thought that ethics is deep precisely *because* any attempt to say it inevitably transgresses the limits of language (Glock 1996: 109).

The above-quoted passage on the exploding book of ethics suggests that Wittgenstein's criticisms of metaphysics, like Kant's, were meant to draw limits to human understanding in the interest of something else: if for Kant this something else is faith, then for Wittgenstein it is ethics (Ayer 1985: 31). Although the audience must have already sensed that Wittgenstein had a deflationary view of science, he now proceeds to bring that view to a head by posing yet another strange thought experiment. After dryly noting that in ordinary life we say that a *miracle* 'is simply an event the like of which we have never seen yet', he asks the audience to suppose that one of them suddenly grew a lion's head and began to roar. Although this would undoubtedly strike us as an extraordinary and amazing event, Wittgenstein avers that after we had recovered from our initial surprise we would probably want to fetch a doctor and have the case scientifically investigated, perhaps even to the point of vivisecting the unfortunate lion-man. But if this would be our reaction, he asks, then 'where would the miracle have got to?' Unless we think that a miracle is merely an event that has not yet been explained by science, Wittgenstein remarks, 'it is clear that when we look at it in [the scientific] way everything miraculous has disappeared'. The ultimate point of the thought experiment is *not* that it proves miracles do not exist, or that science has proven there are no miracles. The only thing it truly shows, Wittgenstein tells them, is that '*the scientific way of looking at a fact is not the way to look at it as a miracle*'. Only the values and perspective of the viewer can determine the ethical significance of facts, *any* facts, and this means that 'imagine whatever fact you may, it is not in itself miraculous in the absolute sense of that term' (1993: 43).

Wittgenstein's striking image of a book of ethics that, in order to *be* a book of ethics, necessarily would destroy all other books in the world is reminiscent of another imaginary apocalypse of texts that we discussed once before in this book, namely, Derrida's image of a 'worldwide burning of libraries'(1962: 94). You will recall that Derrida invented this image, in his *Introduction to Husserl's Origin of Geometry*, to intervene in Husserl's project of trying to guarantee the survival of the objective truth of geometry by locating its absolute ideality in the possession of a worldly custodian: the transcendental subject who is able to 'reactivate' geometric truth simply by reading the graphic signs in which historical human beings have inscribed it. But Derrida's rhetorical purpose in invoking the possibility of a worldwide catastrophe of tangible signs is to force the objectivity of geometry to a level at which the defenders of its privileged metaphysical status, especially Husserl, must agree that 'if geometry is true, its internal history must be saved integrally from all sensible aggression'(Derrida 1962: 95). Whereas Wittgenstein's underlying purpose is not to expose and explode his audience's metaphysical prejudices, but to bring into view the *experiences* that give rise to his own temptation to say that ethics in the absolute sense exceeds all the worldly sounds and pen-scratchings that human beings could ever make. To prepare the way for this transition from the abstract sphere of facts and propositions to concrete sphere of experiences, Wittgenstein asks his audience yet another rhetorical question. If it is true that all facts are equal, and that anything we could possibly say about ethics is just a fact like other facts, 'then what have all of us who, like myself, are still tempted to use such expressions as "absolute good", "absolute value", etc, what have we in mind and what do we try to express?'(1993: 40).

Experiences of the absolute and trying to describe them

The answer, Wittgenstein tells them, is that we sometimes have experiences that tempt us to say that they (the experiences themselves) have absolute value. Wittgenstein observes that each person is inclined to offer his own stock example of such an experience, thereby continuing to destabilise any residual belief that our particular feelings of absolute value are necessarily universal. Having thus briefly de-universalised our feelings of absolute value, Wittgenstein now proceeds, albeit with great diffidence, to share two of his own favourite examples of an experience with the absolute. First, he confesses to having had the experience of wondering at the existence of the world.[4] Secondly, he tells them about an odd feeling he sometimes has that he is absolutely safe, no matter what happens.[5] When he has the first experience, he admits, he is inclined to utter such phrases as *'how extraordinary that the world should exist'*; when he has the second, he wants to say things such as *'I am safe, nothing can injure me whatever happens'*(1993: 41). In Wittgenstein's descriptions of these experiences, the audience does not see him ethically involved with other people, as in Levinas's writings about the experience of absolute alterity. Rather, they see him standing alone in the face of an utterly *impersonal* absolute other. On the other hand, just like Levinas's phenomenological descriptions of the ethical encounter between the *I* and the face of the Other, Wittgenstein's narration of his encounters with the absolute is not meant to give his audience any concrete ethical guidance for conducting their lives. One might say that in both cases the ethical experience *par excellence* is displayed as an unteachable mode of living itself.

In one of the most trenchant passages of the *Tao Te Ching*, Lao-tsu wrote that *'one who knows does not say it; one who says does not know it'*(Lao-tsu 1994: 21). As if heeding Lao-tsu's advice, Wittgenstein quickly

---

4 Wittgenstein's near gushing about the existence of the world is uncharacteristic, and it has a distinctively Heideggerian flair. Indeed, it is probably the case that around this time Wittgenstein had been reading or at least thinking about Heidegger's work. In a passage labelled *Apropos of Heidegger*, Friedrich Waismann quotes Wittgenstein as saying, on 30 December 1929: 'To be sure, I can imagine what Heidegger means by being and anxiety. Man feels the urge to run up against the limits of language. Think for example of the astonishment that anything at all exists' (Waismann 1979: 68). Michael Murray notes that all references to Heidegger in this passage were deleted (and thus possibly intentionally suppressed) when the *Philosophical Review* published some of Waismann's notes in 1965 to accompany *A Lecture on Ethics* (Murray 1974: 501–03).

5 William Bartley traces this example to an experience that Wittgenstein had in 1910, when he attended, and apparently was deeply affected by, Ludwig Anzengruber's play 'Die Kreuzelschreiber'. The play contains a scene in which one of the characters expresses the same feeling of absolute safety that Wittgenstein mentions in the lecture (Bartley 1985: 189).

proceeds to undercut the validity of his own expressions after having just confessed to the audience that he is sometimes wracked by the desire to blurt out sentences like the ones he had just quoted to them. Almost as though he were ashamed of having revealed them, he withdraws all of their authority by saying: *'And there the first thing I have to say is that the verbal expression which we give to these experiences is nonsense'* (1993: 41). They are nonsense, he tells them, because what they try to say lacks an antithesis. To experience wonder at the existence of the world, for example, does not mean to wonder at the world being this way as opposed to some other way – it means to wonder at the world being no particular *way* at all, but rather just being *whatever* it is. Likewise, to have the experience of *absolute* safety does not mean to feel that it is physically impossible for certain hurtful, but imaginable, things to happen – it means to feel safe no matter what happens, even if all imaginable dangers come to pass.

Bipolarity

Wittgenstein once summed up his entire philosophical method as a transition from the question of truth to the question of sense (Wolcher 1997: 57). On this view, an expression is not capable of being either true *or* false until it has first earned the right to be called true or false by *making sense*. Patent nonsense such as 'Flitry is the Goomring's feragrove' is neither true nor false, for example – it is merely gibberish. We would not even know how to *begin* deciding whether it is true or false. In addition to obvious cases like this, there is much latent nonsense, especially in philosophy, which people take for true or false when they should be classifying it as nonsense (*Unsinn*). It is important to understand that 'nonsense' is not a value judgment: it is a logical classification that follows from Wittgenstein's all-important criterion of 'bipolarity'. As he defined it in an early letter to Bertrand Russell, the criterion of bipolarity holds that 'we only understand a proposition if we know both what would be the case if it was false and what if it was true' (1995: 47), or, as he put it elsewhere, 'Language can only say those things that we can also imagine otherwise' (1975: 41). This criterion leads to the conclusion that expressions such as *'how extraordinary that the world should exist'* and *'I am safe, nothing can injure me whatever happens'* are nonsense because the negation of what they seem to assert does not represent an imaginable state of affairs.

For example, since we know what a unicorn would look like if it did exist, the proposition *'Unicorns exist'* makes sense, as does its antithesis. But a pseudo-proposition such as *'The law of non-contradiction is true'* is nonsense because no one knows what it would look like for this proposition to be false. I mean, what state of affairs could I even be *trying* to represent if I said *'Two plus two is four* and *two plus two is not four'*, such that we are justified in saying that the negation of this alleged proposition is 'true' in the same way that the proposition *'There are no unicorns'* is true? This example shows why Wittgenstein classified the laws of logic as grammatical rules rather than as genuine propositions. *'The laws of logic, for example, excluded middle and contradiction, are arbitrary'* he told one of his classes, adding:

> This statement is a bit repulsive but nevertheless true. ... A contradiction is a proposition of the form *p and not-p*. To forbid its occurrence is to adopt one system of expression, which may recommend itself highly. This does not mean that we cannot use a contradiction. In fact it is used, for example, in the statement 'I like it and I don't like it'. (Wittgenstein 1979b: 71)

Propositions that take the form of a contradiction sometimes have a use. Thus, the example that Wittgenstein gives – *'I like it and I don't like it'* – is a perfectly good way of expressing ambivalence. Since one can imagine both the state of affairs of being ambivalent *and* the opposite state of affairs (being certain), this shows that even a proposition that takes the form of a contradiction can be bipolar.

In contrast, Wittgenstein held that statements of *absolute* possibility or impossibility are always latent nonsense. A good example of this from the domain of legal theory is Stanley Fish's assertion that *'formalist or literalist or four corners' interpretation [of legal texts] is not inadvisable ... it is impossible'* (Fish 1991: 56). In this passage Fish is not saying that there is a kind of literalist interpretation of the law that is imaginable and representable, but that is empirically impossible. His sentence does not play the same kind of role in his writing and thinking as the following sentence would, for example: *'It is impossible for George Bush to lift a 1,000-pound boulder over his head'*. We can imagine and represent, in words or pictures, what it would look like for George Bush to lift a 1,000-pound boulder over his head, and it is precisely *this* imaginable state of affairs that such a sentence would exclude as impossible. But anyone who is reasonably familiar with Fish's work knows that he is not saying that there is some describable practice that the term 'literalist interpretation' stands for, and that engaging in this practice is so extremely difficult for human beings to do that it comes down to being impossible in fact. No, Fish is trying to say that there is *absolutely* no such thing as a literalist interpretation of legal texts. But this is just what he does not do: he does not (and will not) describe *what* he is excluding as impossible.

Wittgenstein's favourite expressions of absolute ethics (his wonder at the existence of the word and his feeling of being absolutely safe) are similar to Fish's statement that literalist interpretation is absolutely impossible. Grammatically speaking, imagination is tied to the ability to represent *what* is imagined. This is why Hollywood 'idea-people' are paid millions to bring the most bizarre and fanciful imagined worlds and states of affairs to the motion picture screen. If what cannot be imagined cannot be represented, it follows from the criterion of bipolarity that its antithesis cannot be represented either. Thus, Wittgenstein tells the audience of his lecture that *'it is nonsense to say that I wonder at the existence of the world, because I cannot imagine it not existing'* (1993: 41–42). Whenever we try to imagine the nothingness that is conventionally taken to be the antithesis of being, we always find ourselves imagining *something* that exists – a limitless black void, for example. Yet this *imagined* nothingness is somehow never the same as what we think we really mean when we philosophise about the possible 'non-existence of the world'. Likewise, it would be a misuse of the word 'safe' to say that I would be safe even if every imaginable destructive event were to happen – for I have no idea what it would look like for me to *be* (existentially) safe even if something happened that utterly and violently destroyed me. It would seem to be the case that Wittgenstein's favourite expressions for describing his experiences with the absolute say absolutely nothing at all.

Metaphors

Having introduced his audience to the sense-killing operations authorised by the criterion of bipolarity, Wittgenstein now turns his rhetorical guns on our tendency to use metaphors and similes to talk about our experiences of the absolutely ethical. He does so by introducing yet another kind of experience that inclines us to describe it in terms of absolute value: feeling guilty. People sometimes characterise their experiences of feeling guilty by saying that God disapproves of their conduct. This way of putting it employs a *simile*: people depict God as though He were a 'human being of great power whose grace we try to win, etc, etc' (1993: 42). But a simile, like a metaphor, is a kind of comparison of something with something else, and this suggests that what is compared could also be described in other terms – terms that do not rely on the metaphorical comparison. A meteorologist, for instance, is capable of giving a prosaic description of sunrise that does not rely one whit on Homer's metaphor of the 'rosy fingered dawn'. If we drop the comparison of God to a person who is capable of disapproving, however, we find ourselves unable to describe 'Him' in language that is non-metaphorical. We can discover this for ourselves simply by looking at the grammar of the word 'God': we often speak of God's eyes, mouth and hands, but we never talk about His other body parts (Wittgenstein 2003: 211). Although it may sound unpardonably crude to say it, the fact that we never ask 'Does God have an anus?' ought to tell us that God is not really a disapproving person after all.

All of this implies that even metaphorical expressions of the absolutely ethical – including such remarks as 'God disapproves our conduct'– are types of nonsense too. Or rather, I should say that Wittgenstein does not read these expressions as trying to *describe* anything at all. Wittgenstein tended to view religious expressions as speech acts – proclamations or manifestations of faith rather than propositions with a sense. Thus, they serve a function in religious life that has nothing to do with indirect (metaphorical) description: 'In religion talking is not *metaphorical*, either; for otherwise it would have been possible to say the same thing in prose' (Waismann 1979: 117). To explain a metaphor by saying 'I'm using this as a metaphor *for* what I can't otherwise say' amounts to exactly the same thing as saying that what I am *really* trying to say, underneath the metaphor, cannot be said at all.

Wittgenstein's treatment of metaphors in *A Lecture on Ethics* makes a strong distinction between metaphorical description and description by other (non-metaphorical) means, as if a metaphor merely compared something present with something absent, whereas non-metaphorical language was capable of directly naming and revealing the present thing without any impure admixture of the other, absent thing. To the extent this represents a theory of metaphors, the distinction is highly dubious from the point of view of thinkers such as Heidegger and Levinas, who maintain that significations of all sorts always precede givens and illuminate them *as* what they are. This view, which reflects what Heidegger called the 'as'-structure of experience, asserts that in using language we always implicitly compare the given (and present) with the pre-given (and absent) as a way of allowing what is present to signify itself as something intelligible. Thus, Homer's 'wine dark sea' would no more compare the sea to the darkness of wine than it would compare wine to the darkness of the sea: darkness is not, to paraphrase Levinas, an exclusive prerogative of either wine or seas; it is an element of a predicating act that *'lies at the confluence of countless semantic rivers'*(Levinas 2003a: 11). The later Wittgenstein will recognise something like this point in the form of his concept of the language-game embedded in a 'form of life' without, however, abandoning the position articulated in *A Lecture on Ethics* that the absolutely ethical is unsayable. This later development of Wittgenstein's thought makes it easier to see what may be obscured by the lecture's questionable distinction between the metaphorical and the non-metaphorical: it suggests that the reason Wittgenstein's experiences of the absolute are unsayable is not because no 'direct' (non-metaphorical) descriptions of them are available, but because Wittgenstein *chose* to remain silent about them.

Although Wittgenstein would undoubtedly have dismissed Levinas's voluminous discourse about the category of interpersonal *ineffabilia* as a nonsensical distortion of language, he sides with Levinas on one crucial point. Both thinkers subscribe to the thesis that the realm of the knowable (the realm of facts) and the realm of the sayable codetermine one another. On the one hand, we can say perfectly well what we 'know', as in Levinas's conception of a justice that can and must know and objectify relations between 'citizens'. However, on the other hand, we cannot describe what we cannot and do not know, as in Levinas's conception of the face-to-face ethical encounter as such. Thus, the Cartesian self-evidence of Wittgenstein's experience of seeing the world as a miracle, while as undeniable in its own way as Levinas's experience of 'facing', underwrites neither knowledge nor any kind of sensible proposition about it. So much for Heidegger's *Seinsfrage*, as far as Wittgenstein is concerned: '*This astonishment [at there being something rather than nothing] cannot be expressed in the form of a question, and there is also no answer whatsoever*' (Waismann 1979: 68). What is more, our experiences of the absolutely ethical involve no question *in principle* of any sort of antecedent wishing or willing that the experiences arise, for wishing and willing are grammatically linked to a describable 'what' that is wished for or willed. Experiences of the absolutely ethical just arise, and when they are gone the world – including even our memories of the experiences – no longer appears miraculous to us. That which is most important about these ephemeral experiences therefore escapes the net of thought and language in much the same way that interpersonal acts of *saying*, as Levinas notes, cannot be *said* without distorting and reducing them to caricatures.

Absolute ineffability

One could say with some justification, therefore, that by his own lights Wittgenstein the lecturer should have kept his big mouth shut when it comes to the matter of these inexpressible experiences. For even to say that certain experiences are 'really, really inexpressible' is illicit by Wittgenstein's own criterion of bipolarity: if we *can* imagine what it would be like to express the inexpressible, then we ought to be able to express it after all; and if we cannot imagine this, then it follows that we also cannot meaningfully say that 'it' is inexpressible. Wittgenstein knew that when it comes to the sense of negative propositions like 'absolute ethics is *not* expressible' the criterion of bipolarity requires that one must be able to express the *positive* sense of what is not the case. Otherwise no one can know what it is that the proposition excludes:

> If a picture [or proposition] presents what-is-not-the-case … this only happens through its presenting *that* which *is* not the case. For the picture says, as it were: '*This* is how it is *not*', and to the question '*How* is it not?' just the positive proposition is the answer. (Wittgenstein 1984: 25e)

The idea that the sense of not-*p* always depends on the sense of *p* is what the Vienna Circle's Otto Neurath meant when he exposed the formal contradiction contained in the concluding remark of the *Tractatus*. '*What we cannot speak about we must pass over in silence*', Wittgenstein had written, to which Neurath dryly rejoined: 'one must indeed be silent, but not *about* anything' (Ayer 1985: 32). And Wittgenstein himself clearly knew that it was windy nonsense to go on saying, of the inexpressible, that it is inexpressible. Barely a month after the lecture he told the members of the Vienna Circle that 'anything we might say [about being or ethics] is *a priori* bound to be nonsense', adding that this 'running up against the limits of language' is always a perfectly hopeless endeavour (Waismann 1979: 68–69).

Wittgenstein therefore should have stopped the lecture at the point where he said that 'a certain characteristic misuse of our language runs through *all* ethical and religious expressions'(1993: 42) – he should have stopped, that is, *if* he meant the words 'misuse' and 'nonsense' as criticisms. Thus, if he truly thought that ethics includes aesthetics, as he had told the audience earlier, one might have expected him to end the lecture with a remark like the one he put in his notebook a few years later: '*In art it is hard to say anything as good as: saying nothing*'(Wittgenstein 1980: 23e). The Zen equivalent of this point is the old saying that a good thing is never as good as nothing. Whether or not this is good advice, however, Wittgenstein did not stop talking, and now, nearing the end of the lecture, we see him almost beginning to gush. He assumes the uncharacteristic position of coming right up to the verge of canonising, not any particular text, not even texts in general, but the very fact that there *are* texts: '*Now I am tempted to say that the right expression in language for the miracle of the existence of the world, though it is not any proposition* in *language, is the existence of language itself*' (1993: 43–44).

Lest the audience of his lecture had failed to hear the word 'tempted' clearly enough, Wittgenstein immediately retreats from the verge of a coronation of being and the language that expresses it. In what can only be described as an extraordinary public display of *philosophicus interruptus*, he says: 'For all I have said by shifting the expression of the miraculous from an expression *by means of* language to the expression *by the existence* of language, all I have said is again that we cannot express what we want to express and that all we *say* about the absolute miraculous remains nonsense' (1993: 44). What he was about to canonise as being the right expression for the absolutely ethical, in other words, he leaves on the altar without a priest to officiate at the ceremony of its reception into the canon. He cannot bring himself to criticise others for gushing, but at the same time he cannot bring himself to gush. '*Kneeling means one is a slave*', he wrote elsewhere about the usual way people receive religious or other discourse that moves them and strikes them as being deep (2003: 219). And even though he clearly *wanted* to be deep, Wittgenstein had such a profound fear of losing himself to authority that he knew he could never bring himself to kneel: *'I cannot kneel to pray because it's as though my knees were stiff,'* he wrote in 1946, *'I am afraid of my own dissolution, should I become soft'*(1980: 56e). Gender theorists could have a field day with this remark, and I will leave that aspect of Wittgenstein's complex personality to them. I will only say here that Wittgenstein *qua* thinker was apparently unable, for whatever reason, to appreciate that yielding is sometimes the most expedient thing to do.

The lecture is now drawing to a close. Wittgenstein's undoubtedly confused audience probably wondered by now where the feeling had gone that there is something *deep* in the distinction between relative and absolute ethics. If he thought that the existence of deep ethical feelings in people were just a fact like other facts, those of his audience who still were following him might have expected him to agree with the argument that reason ought to be capable of finding 'the correct logical analysis of what we mean by our ethical and religious expressions' (1993: 44). But not only does he anticipate and reject this argument at the end of the lecture, he expresses his disagreement in a way that bears witness to a kind of revelation or epiphany. When the fact-monger's argument for the describability of Wittgenstein's sense of absolute ethics is urged against him, he says, *'I at once see clearly, as it were in a flash of light, not only that no description that I can think of would do to describe what I mean by absolute value, but that I would reject every significant description that anybody could possibly suggest,* ab initio, *on the ground of its significance'* (1993: 44). While Wittgenstein thus acknowledges to his audience that there is something deep in the ethical realm, he also pugnaciously sets his face in advance against any ethical expression that anyone could ever say or write in an effort to tie that deepness down.

The Lecture as an Ethical Deed

Wittgenstein's lecture classifies the ethical dimension of our relationships with other people (the social), our individual feelings of guilt, and the *I*'s lonely musings about the wonder of existence all under a single heading: *ethics in the absolute sense*. In one broad stroke he obliterates the distinction, so carefully maintained and nurtured by Levinas, between a being-centred philosophy like Heidegger's and a philosophy that is 'beyond being' in its radical insistence that the two-person ethical relationship is prior to ontology. But the fact that Wittgenstein is being unorthodox (if not unsubtle) in giving such a broad scope to the category of ethics is immaterial to us here. For our purposes, it is far more significant that he takes great pains to prove to his audience that *any* experience with the absolute, however it may be conceived, is ineffable, and that it is ineffable to a degree that Heidegger and Levinas either did not know or could not appreciate.

To be sure, the latter two thinkers devalued scientific language, including the language of traditional metaphysics, for the same reason that Wittgenstein did: namely, because of its tendency to reduce being and ethics to calculations that strip these themes of all of their mystery and profundity. But on the other hand, Heidegger and Levinas both embraced what they took to be a different and more excellent kind of discourse: Heidegger touted poetry and the language of *alētheia* (unconcealment), and Levinas invented a quasi-theological kind of phenomenological discourse. Although Wittgenstein, too, draws a distinction between *types* of language about ethics – the relative *versus* the absolute – he does so with an enormous caveat that is completely missing from the work of the other two philosophers. For Wittgenstein, not even the most elegant expressions of the absolute are up to the task. Unlike Heidegger and Levinas, Wittgenstein appears to turn away from language as such, language in any of its possible forms and permutations, when it comes to saying anything meaningful about the absolute. This turning-away is not *itself* absolute, however, as we shall see.

Important nonsense

On the one hand, Wittgenstein desperately wanted the audience of his lecture to understand that his idea of absolute ethics is something very important, perhaps even the most important thing of all. But, on the other hand, he also tried to prove to them that nothing meaningful can be said about this ethics – including even his own pet examples of the absolutely ethical. Frank Ramsey once wryly remarked that for Wittgenstein to describe ethical language as *'nonsense but important nonsense'* was a little too much like having one's cake and eating it too (Grayling 1988: 55). Ramsey's critique invites us to read the lecture as a mystical but ultimately cowardly thesis *about* ethics: one that employs the criterion of bipolarity to put ethical expressions behind an impenetrable barrier of nonsensicality, while at the same time seeking to immunise ethics against science by mysteriously (or incoherently) distinguishing between *types* of nonsense. It is hard to know how to distinguish important from unimportant gibberish without having at least some idea of what either kind of expression is even *trying* to say. Since Wittgenstein's concept of 'nonsense' rules out the possibility of such an idea in principle for those statements that are classified under it, the operation of distinguishing the important from the unimportant in the realm of nonsense is left without a rudder. Now in the end we will be giving an interpretation of the lecture that is similar to Ramsey's when we turn our attention to the strategic aspects of Wittgenstein's posture of silence in the face of the absolute. But to interpret the lecture as announcing *any* kind of programmatic thesis would be premature at this stage, for we have not yet finished reading all that the text has to say.

Contrary to Ramsey's allegation that Wittgenstein was trying to advance a problematic thesis about ethics in the lecture, it would appear that Wittgenstein himself thought that at least some of his statements were Austinian performatives rather than mere elements of a speech 'about' ethics. In other words, there is a sense in which Wittgenstein took the lecture to be an ethical *deed*. Strong evidence for this can be found in the last four sentences that he spoke to the audience:

> My whole tendency and I believe the tendency of all men who ever tried to write or talk Ethics or Religion was to run against the boundaries of language. This running against the walls of our cage is perfectly, absolutely hopeless. Ethics so far as it springs from the desire to say something about the ultimate meaning of life, the absolute good, the absolute valuable, can be no science. But it is a document of a tendency in the human mind which I personally cannot help respecting deeply and I would not for my life ridicule it. (1993: 44)

In a conversation that he had with Friedrich Waismann and Moritz Schlick in Vienna on 17 December 1929, exactly one month after the lecture, Wittgenstein described what was on his mind as he spoke the foregoing words to the audience:

> At the end of my lecture on ethics I spoke in the first person. I think this is something very essential. Here there is nothing to be stated any more; all I can do is step forth as an individual and speak in the first person. ... All I can say is this: I do not scoff at this human tendency in man; I hold it in reverence. And here it is essential that this is not a description of sociology but that I am speaking *about myself*. (Waismann 1979: 117–18) (emphasis in original)

An almost schizophrenic picture of Wittgenstein begins to emerge if one puts the text of his lecture as a whole together with his own interpretation of his final remarks. On this view, Wittgenstein-the-philosopher spoke from his head in resolutely maintaining that ethical discourse is essentially nonsense, but Wittgenstein-the-*Mensch*[6] spoke from his heart to express unqualified respect for the general human tendency to use words such as 'good' and 'bad' in their absolute sense *despite* their nonsensicality. Wittgenstein-the-*Mensch* is the one I would like to consider now. It seems to me that this person's apparently undifferentiated respect for the fact that people misuse language in

6 I use the Yiddish word *Mensch* to connote the kind of person who tries to be upstanding and decent.

ethical contexts raises certain troubling issues. I am not referring to the paradox that can be produced when one hoists Wittgenstein-the-philosopher on his own petard, as it were, by applying the criterion of bipolarity to his assertion that absolute ethics is absolutely ineffable.[7] No, what really troubles me about Wittgenstein-the-*Mensch* is the shameless *profligacy* of his respect for ethical discourse.

The problematic character of a general respect for ethical discourse

Wittgenstein's unqualified expression of respect for our tendency to misuse ethical language is analogous to the sort of thing that troubled Derrida about Walter Benjamin's essay *Critique of Violence*. According to Derrida, Benjamin's eagerness to understand historical violence as a possible manifestation of divine violence is more than a little problematic in light of the nightmarish events that occurred after 1920, when *Critique of Violence* was first published. Even the most tentative dance with history's executioners comes at a terrible cost: one always gets blood on one's hands. Thus, it is perfectly understandable that Derrida succumbed to the temptation to describe Benjamin's essay in terms of *terror*: 'one is terrified at the idea of an interpretation that would make of the holocaust an expiation and an indecipherable signature of the just and violent anger of God' (1990: 1045). A critique that is terrified at certain unpleasant (if not horrific) interpretive possibilities can also be directed at *A Lecture on Ethics*. Thus, if it is true that Wittgenstein attached absolute ethical value to his very act of saying to the audience, in 1929, that he deeply respected people's inclination to talk about ethics, then what is to stop his passionately expressed *neutrality* about particular ethical statements from sliding into applications in the moral sphere that are at least as troubling as those that Derrida associates with Benjamin's text? If the impulse to speak ethical nonsense is a universally valid and respectable human tendency, as Wittgenstein seems to be saying, then it would appear that a Nazi's remark to the effect that 'Genocide is good' stands on exactly the same level as the statements of his victims that 'Genocide is evil'. If this conclusion seems too harsh, then I would ask you to remember the fact, brought out at the beginning of this chapter, that Wittgenstein was prepared to classify the Nazi aphorism '*Recht ist das, was uns gefällt*' together with all the 'other ethical judgments and discussions, in the anthropological study of ethical discussions which we may have to conduct' (Rhees 1965: 25).

---

7 Namely: if saying that something is unsayable is to have any sense, then it must be possible to say *what* it would be like to be able to say it in the first place, in which case it would not be unsayable after all.

On the one hand, Wittgenstein knew what Zen also knows: namely, that language does not *have* to produce consequences, and that people *let* it have consequences through their acts and omissions. However, on the other hand, he also knew that nonsensical expressions sometimes go hand-in-hand with unspeakable outrages precisely because people are deluded by their obsessive attachment to texts. In their suffering, people are inclined to worship the god of texts. How could Wittgenstein care less about the consequences of this text-worship than he did about keeping his own peculiar sense of intellectual integrity safely above the possibility of serious philosophical criticism? Without suggesting that we should attempt to psychoanalyse him here, it would not be irrelevant to note what Wittgenstein once wrote in his diary: '*there is nothing I am more afraid of, nothing I want to avoid so unconditionally as ridiculousness*' (2003: 123). Despite the affront that seeming to be ridiculous would have given to his vanity, however, how *could* Wittgenstein bring himself to say, as late as 1945, that 'it isn't sensible to be furious even at Hitler; how much less so at God'? (Wittgenstein 1980: 46e). As the following example suggests, sometimes being furious and seeming ridiculous are the most expedient things to do, even if every philosopher on earth stands up and laughs at you:

> As things now stand, everything is up for grabs. Nevertheless: Napalming babies is bad. Starving the poor is wicked. Buying and selling each other is depraved. Those who stood up to and died resisting Hitler, Stalin, Amin, and Pol Pot – and General Custer too – have earned salvation. Those who acquiesced deserve to be damned. There is in the world such a thing as evil. Sez who? God help us. (Leff 1979: 1249)

No philosopher would read Arthur Leff's sentences as well grounded arguments; indeed, Wittgenstein would say that if they were well grounded they would be ethically worthless. Explicitly groundless remarks such as Leff's are more like a philosopher's *act of witness*: just the kind of compassionate engagement that Wittgenstein's lecture rules off limits to himself as a matter of principle. It is as if *A Lecture on Ethics* had revised Voltaire's famous aphorism to say 'I approve of your speaking nonsense against what you think is evil, but I will not defend to the death your right to say it'– the exact opposite of what Voltaire wanted it to say.[8]

Wittgenstein's ideal

At around the time he gave his lecture on ethics, Wittgenstein wrote: 'You cannot lead people to what is good: you can only lead them to some place

---

8 The real quotation reads: 'I disapprove of what you say, but I will defend to the death your right to say it' (Bartlett 1980: 344).

or other. The good is outside the space of facts' (1980: 3e). Among other things, this remark makes the important point that ethical words have the power to lead people who want to be led. To what place, then, was Wittgenstein leading the audience of his lecture? If the good exceeds or transcends the facts, his lecture on ethics shows that Wittgenstein's all-too-human yearning to express it did not. Sometime in 1929 he had written: *'My ideal is a certain coolness. A temple providing a setting for the passions without meddling with them'* (1980: 2e). But how could Wittgenstein have failed to know and appreciate, at the time he wrote of his ideal, that there can be murder in the cathedral as well as sacrament? For the terrible events that are reflected in the following lines from Yeats' poem *The Second Coming* had already long since begun to unfold into still more terrible events:

> The blood-dimmed tide is loosed, and everywhere
> The ceremony of innocence is drowned;
> The best lack all conviction, while the worst
> Are full of passionate intensity. (Yeats 1989: 187)

I have always thought that the last two lines of Yeats's poem make an excellent description of Wittgenstein-the-person: as a *thinker* he was passionately intent on purging philosophy of all opacity and flimflamming, but as a *Mensch* he was too diffident to express any particular moral conviction beyond the egocentric imperative that a thinker should never delude himself. Thus, it would be perfectly understandable (I do not say 'true'!) if someone were to say that Wittgenstein embodied the best *and* the worst in Western philosophy.

Wittgenstein's expression of deep respect for the human tendency to use ethical language to express the absolute was a passionate act *within* the temple – and thus was a failure to live up to his own ideal of moral coolness. He did not, of course, *say* that his respect extended to remarks such as Hitler's, in *Mein Kampf*, that 'those who want to live, let them fight, and those who do not want to fight in this world of eternal struggle do not deserve to live' (Hitler 1943: 289), and it would be utterly unfair to argue that any *particular* expression of his ethical respect could ever have extended that far. On the contrary, Wittgenstein (three of whose grandparents were Jewish) joined the British war effort as a hospital volunteer, and it is clear that he was no friend of modernity in any of its forms.[9] But if this is so, what was the *point* of his saying that he respected

9 For example, in 1930 he wrote the following sentence in an early draft of the foreword to a book that would be posthumously published as the *Philosophical Remarks*: *'The spirit of this civilisation makes itself manifest in the industry, architecture and music of our time, in its fascism and socialism, and it is alien and uncongenial to the author'* (1980: 6e). On the other hand – and this is what can be so maddening about Wittgenstein's stance on ethics – he apparently felt the need to apologise for his intrusion, as it were, by saying in the very next sentence, *'This is not a value judgment'*.

the undifferentiated human tendency to express the ethical, if he was not also prepared to say that he respected some human uses of ethical words more than others? Even if one grants Wittgenstein his thesis that the ethics of someone like Goering and the ethics of someone like Jesus emerge from the same source – the urge to speak nonsense in the face of something deep – it is not immediately obvious why a thinking person should either feel or succumb to the urge to respect equally the tendencies that both men felt. Borrowing from his philosophy-to-be, one almost feels entitled to ask Wittgenstein: just what language-game *were* you playing in the lecture?

If, as Wittgenstein intimated to his friend Ludwig von Ficker, saying what can be said in a sense *shows* the ethical from within, by showing the limits of the expressible (Engelmann 1967: 143-44), then perhaps it is what we choose to say *and* be silent about that shows what is ethical within us to other people. Perhaps the fact that in his later philosophy Wittgenstein never attempted to give a comprehensive description of the language-games that we humans play with ethical words says something ethical about *him*. Amidst the nightmare of the Second World War, for example, one of his students asked him why he never discussed politics in his lectures. According to the student, Theodore Redpath, 'he said he *could* not do so but that one day he would give a lecture or talk explaining *why* he could not' (Wittgenstein 2003: 354). As Redpath correctly reports, Wittgenstein never did give such a lecture or talk. *Why not?*

There is a sense in which the lecture on ethics was Wittgenstein's first acknowledgment that there could be such a thing as a language-game with ethical words, for the fact that ethical language is ruled nonsense by the criteria of the *Tractatus* was not enough to stand in the way of Wittgenstein's seeing and reporting the fact that people just *do* constantly go on talking this way. But he himself apparently could not do this, and it is this quality in him – what Newton Carter aptly calls his 'ethic of acquiescence'(Carter 1994: 143) – that creates such a strong temptation to judge his lecture on ethics as wanting in something – something ethical. Heaven knows that Heidegger has been taken to task enough for remaining silent about the moral abominations of Nazism and the Holocaust. Even though Wittgenstein loathed Nazism and did not personally embrace it the way Heidegger did (however briefly), he did occupy a position in Western thought that would have lent his voice considerable credibility had he chosen to speak out against the awful things that were happening in the world during the 1930s and 40s. So many writers have given tongue-lashings to Heidegger for his membership in the Nazi party, his acceptance of the rectorship at the University of Freiburg, and his post-war silence about the crimes of the Nazis.[10] Should we not follow their lead and take Wittgenstein to task for his silence about the great moral questions of his day?

We should not. Regardless of what other thinkers may do or want to do, we will not further succumb to the temptation to judge Heidegger and Wittgenstein here, for that would be to wallow unthinkingly in the very trough from which we are trying to extricate ourselves: attachment to the fetish of logical transcendence. The temptation to condemn Wittgenstein and Heidegger stems from the prejudice that a philosopher's ideas (A) must necessarily *lead* somewhere in particular, and that where they lead can best be determined by looking at the way the philosopher lives his own life (B). From the Zen standpoint that has informed our meditations throughout this book, this prejudice is a manifestation of attachment to a mere norm of representation, $A \Rightarrow B$. The various texts that comprise Heidegger's philosophy of being and Wittgenstein's philosophy of ethics (A) no more *had* to lead to these men's behaviours (B) than the text of a legal rule always has to lead to its 'correct' application. It would even be a mistake for us to obsess about what we take to be certain 'affinities' connecting the written work of either philosopher to morally questionable 'tendencies'. *In the context of this book, we simply do not care about the alleged moral dangers that conventional thought finds lurking in philosophical texts.* Rather, we are trying to understand or experience what it would be like not to become attached to *any* text at all.

While we could throw rocks at Wittgenstein and Heidegger all day long on account of their ethical lapses, this would not allow us to make any progress in our own journey. Something is revealed by Wittgenstein's silence on questions of ethics that is far more important than any merely personal predilections of Wittgenstein the man. I am referring now to his thesis that since we cannot talk meaningfully about absolute ethics, the only proper course for a philosopher with integrity is to remain silent in the face of the unsayable. It would appear that Wittgenstein's lecture on ethics rather noisily announces a *strategy* of silence. It is the very possibility of such a strategy that will allow us to take our critique of logical transcendence to the next level.

---

10 To cite two examples from the many instances of Heidegger-bashing in the literature, consider Manfred Stassen's scathing introduction to the volume on Heidegger in *The German Library* series (Heidegger 2003c: ix–xxxiii) and Richard Cohen's only slightly less vitriolic remarks about Heidegger in his introduction to Levinas's *Humanism of the Other* (Levinas 2003a: xiv–xxv).

A Zen Reading of Wittgenstein's Thesis of Silence

There comes a point near the end of *A Lecture on Ethics* where Wittgenstein elevates the nonsensicality of ethical expressions to the status of an essence – an essence *of* something important that is neither rational nor irrational, but rather pre-rational. The relevant passage reads as follows: '*I see now that these nonsensical expressions were not nonsensical because I had not yet found the correct expressions, but their nonsensicality was their very essence*' (1993: 44). When read in the context of the lecture as a whole, this sentence says that we do not *deform* language when we speak ethical nonsense to one another; rather, we adhere to its very purpose in our lives. In other words, most people don't *want* to reduce the absolute to verifiable propositions of fact, for if they did that they would be completely abandoning the spiritual or mystical side of life in favour of an unqualifiedly scientific world-view. Wittgenstein's remark about the 'essence' of ethical language thus suggests a strange, if veiled, sort of Platonic thesis. If it is true that Plato erred in thinking that there is (and must be) a single essence of the Good, then it would appear from Wittgenstein's lecture that Plato was right to believe that all absolute uses of the word 'good' have at least *some* kind of essence. Wittgenstein seems to be saying that it is fitting and proper that absolute ethics is unsayable *because that is its essence* – or rather, that is the essence we want it to have – and that while ineffability is perhaps a strange kind of essence to have, at least it is some kind of essence.

Mysticism in Western thought

This reading of the lecture uncovers an aspect of mysticism in Western thought that is paradoxical when seen from the standpoint of Zen. One thinks of the typical mystic as foreswearing all noise making *about* the mystical in order to wallow in experiences *of* the mystical: the 'sensation of eternity' or 'oceanic feeling' about which Freud expresses such puzzlement in *Civilisation and its Discontents*, for example (1962: 11). But in that case the quintessentially silent mystic would never be able to show himself to the world *as* a 'mystic'. To acquire that status, he has to take a mystical position *vis-à-vis* others. Yet the minute he brings his mystical experiences to language in the form of a *thesis* of ineffability that is followed by a *posture* of silence, he threatens to betray his own mysticism by aggressively distinguishing the sayable from the unsayable. Nothing could be more harmful to the mystical impulse than attempting to divide the world into categories. Indeed, the mystic who aspires to show his mysticism in this way falls into one of the most pernicious kinds of ordering: the kind that wrongly thinks it dissolves *all* forms of ordering in the cauldron of mystical insight. Despite their mystical pretensions, thinkers who occupy this level of ordering covertly articulate a distinctly unmystical (if not analytical) distinction that they believe *leads*, in the manner of a cause or ground, to the necessity of silence. This is what *The Blue Cliff Record* means when it compares talking about silence to a broom sweeping away dust: '*though the dust is removed, the tracks of the broom still remain*' (Cleary 1992: 461). The main problem with most forms of Western mysticism is that they share with their antithesis, rationalism, that most fundamental of all intellectual cravings: the need to *account* for oneself in terms of the norm A $\Rightarrow$ B.

Wittgenstein was just this kind of mystical thinker, inasmuch as he stressed, perhaps more fervently than any other philosopher before or since, the importance of showing that there is a limit to what can be said, and of maintaining that limit by interposing silence in the face of what lies beyond it. As we have seen, on the sayable side of the limit stand all of our many practices of using words in this way and that. Our uses of words in various contexts, together with the criteria we employ to decide whether we understand a particular use of words, are matters that can be observed and described. Overtly noisy philosophers, however, often tie themselves into knots trying to answer questions that ignore the organic development and radical heterogeneity of the language that they must borrow from everyday life in order to make themselves understood.

The Heideggerian question '*What is being?*', for example, violently homogenises a word ('being') that, like the word 'ethics', exhibits many different kinds of uses in daily life. Wittgenstein thought that a comprehensive catalogue of these kinds of uses would give as complete an answer as anyone will ever meaningfully get to the question 'What is being?' Even if a thinker tried to whittle away all merely ordinary uses from the surface of the word 'being' as an indirect strategy of approaching something loftier, from Wittgenstein's point of view all that this thinker would get for his trouble is a pile of shavings at his feet and a handful of nonsense left over – a naked and useless sign. To put it bluntly, a word that has been torn loose from its natural home in a particular form of life is good for nothing but babbling. When you boil metaphysical questions down, he once remarked, 'what evaporates is what the intellect cannot tackle', and what remains is a saucepan full of plain grammatical conventions. If I may be permitted to switch metaphors one more time, for Wittgenstein the 'question of being' is like the city of Oakland was for Gertrude Stein: there's no there there.

Nevertheless, certain philosophers (Heidegger and Levinas, for instance) remain chronically unsatisfied by the prospect of assembling the kind of tedious tome of language-games that Wittgenstein recommends as the only proper product of philosophy. Indeed, Wittgenstein was occasionally willing to denigrate his very own philosophical output for its lack of sizzle, calling it a set of 'homely' remarks and a bunch of 'stale truisms' (Glock 1996: 297). Since his philosophy of language seems to offer up a rather grim diet, lacking in food for the soul, the more soulful type of thinker can be excused for yearning to go beyond the mundane task of cataloguing everyday uses of words such as 'being' and 'ethics'. Philosophers like this want to come into contact with something deeper. Although *A Lecture on Ethics* shows that Wittgenstein was not completely unsympathetic to this kind of yearning, in general he had things like this to say to all metaphysically inclined thinkers:

> The correct method in philosophy would really be the following: to say nothing except what can be said, ie propositions of natural science – ie, something that has nothing to do with philosophy – and then, whenever someone else wanted to say something metaphysical, to demonstrate to him that he had failed to give meaning to certain signs in his propositions. Although it would not be satisfying to the other person – he would not have the feeling that we were teaching him philosophy – *this* method would be the only strictly correct one. (1974: 73–74)

After reading the foregoing remark from the *Tractatus*, and others like it that are scattered throughout Wittgenstein's *oeuvre*, a sensitive reader – especially one who is attuned to the Western philosophical tradition as a whole – might be excused for exclaiming, '*How unduly narrow Wittgenstein conceives the philosopher's task to be!*' As I tried to show in the previous section, Wittgenstein's famous proscription that '*what we cannot speak about we must pass over in silence*' is much less a convincing conclusion than it is a dogmatic personal *announcement*. It announced, in a rather noisy and preachy way, the advent of what would become 30 years of silence, from the particular thinker whose name was Ludwig Wittgenstein, about ethical questions that he took to lie beyond the limits of language.

Silence as a strategy

Now Heidegger is unintentionally on to something quite important about the nature of Wittgenstein's kind of silence when he says, in his lectures on Parmenides: '*"To keep silent" is not merely to say nothing. Without something essential to say, one cannot keep silent*' (1992a: 73). This way of talking about philosophical silence has the advantage of bringing out an important feature of *all* modes of Western thought, whether it takes the form of rationalism or mysticism, and whether it belongs to the kind of thinking that builds systems or the kind that tears them down. Namely, Western philosophy tends to be unbelievably pretentious and combative at the same time – as if something incredibly important depended on whether words such as 'being' and 'ethics' appear in scholarly books that hardly anybody ever reads or understands anyway. This kind of attitude is displayed most obviously, of course, in the work of philosophers such as Heidegger. However, even when a thinker keeps silent in the manner of Wittgenstein, he clings to that silence as an equally aggressive mode of *taking a stand*.

Wittgenstein was at heart the kind of mystic who *wanted* something to happen in the world. First of all, he wanted to give himself peace from the torment of trying to answer questions that have no definitive answers. But he also wanted to protect the domain of the ineffable – the 'mystical', as he put it in the *Tractatus* (1974: 73) – from the relentless onslaught of the same scientific world-view that troubled Heidegger, albeit for different reasons. The means that Wittgenstein employed was to demote language from the privileged position it has occupied in philosophy since the beginning of Western thought. As far as Wittgenstein's philosophy of language is concerned, words such as 'being' and 'ethics' stand on exactly the same level as words like 'oatmeal' and 'haemorrhoid', and in this respect he was very much a man of Zen. On the other hand, Alexandre Kojève rightly uses the active voice to characterise silences such as Wittgenstein's when he says that a philosophy of trying to set limits to what can be said inevitably obliges one 'to go beyond Discourse through a *silence* – "mystical", "ecstatic", "algorithmic", "sonorous", or otherwise' (Kojève 1980: 108). For it is the very *effort* to set limits that sends philosophers like Wittgenstein into motion, even if they do sometimes maintain their silence while they are moving. Kojève's way of putting the movement from speech to silence shows that there are thinkers who use silence as a strategy. They want their inaudible silence to be *legible*. They want their silence to be understood as making a point in well-ordered opposition to the projects of those people who blab on and on in philosophy, as if there were nothing of importance that human beings could not say.

Wittgenstein's kind of silence is to speech as the formless is to form: the pole of each opposition is *obsessed* with negating its contrary. Zen thought, on the other hand, tends to be quasi-Hegelian in pointing out (in the words of Lin-chi) that 'all movement of thought goes to a contrary end' (Schloegl 1976: 50). That is, if you aggressively support the thesis *X* you always implicitly preserve and dignify the antithesis not-*X* by keeping it alive and nurturing it in the realm of your obsessions. As if it had been written directly in response to Wittgenstein's thesis of silence about the absolute, the following passage from *The Blue Cliff Record* neatly summarises the reason why I devoted this entire chapter to a reading of *A Lecture on Ethics*:

> Some say the meaning lies in the silence; some say it lies in the pause, that speech illumines what cannot be said, and speechlessness illumines what can be said – as Yung Chia said, 'Speaking when silent, silent when speaking'. But if you only understand in this way, then past, present, and future, for sixty aeons, you will still never have seen it, even in dreams. (Cleary 1992: 507)

What is it that someone like Wittgenstein cannot see, even in dreams? If pouring over the meaning of a holy text or an important philosophical argument is like putting a clod of dung in one's mouth, as Lin-chi puts it (Schloegl 1976: 53), then maintaining a defiant posture of silence in the face of the absolute is like spitting the dung out in disgust: neither form of thinking is a stranger to the scatological. Neither form of thinking can break through to the possibility of recognising that there are ultimately no enduring distinctions between the high and the low, the mystical and the ordinary, and speech and silence. *This* is what ineffability-mongers such as Wittgenstein cannot see.

Please go back and look again at Figure 1.2 (page 25), which shows Kanzan and Jittoku laughing at the moon's reflection. Kanzan and Jittoku do not imagine that they are seeing the moon-in-the-water as it *really* is through eyes that have shed all linguistic and cultural incrustations. On the other hand, neither do they imagine that it is the semblance, the illusion or the aporia of the moon's reflection that they see. That is because Kanzan and Jittoku do not *imagine* anything at all in this picture. Interpreting the painting as a kind of philosophical parable, I would say simply that they are just looking at the moon's reflection. *And taking a short rest from language.* I like to think that this is why they are laughing, for they realise that when they return to language they must always be prepared to say something to prevent their silence from being misinterpreted as obduracy or indifference. For silence like Wittgenstein's, earnestly maintained in the face of a direct question that is heard and understood, is a kind of mimesis: it imitates the *absence* of fixity and form. Any thinker who loudly proclaims that he will remain silent in the face of certain kinds of questions projects (and in Wittgenstein's case *clings to*) an image of the absence of images.

What does an image of the absence of images look like? As a way of answering this question, we will compare Wittgenstein's kind of silence to Figure 4.1, a photograph of a recent installation entitled 'The Empty Museum' in the SculptureCenter in New York City. This piece, constructed by the conceptual artists Ilya and Emilia Kabakov, consists of a room-sized museum gallery installed inside a museum, complete with dark red walls, wood mouldings and benches for contemplation, but without any paintings hanging on the walls. The programme accompanying the installation further describes the installation this way:

Figure 4.1
Ilya and Emilia Kabakov
The Empty Museum, 2004
Installation view, 'Ilya and Emilia Kabakov: The Empty Museum'
SculptureCenter, 11 January – 11 April, 2004
Photo Credit: Hermann Feldhaus
Courtesy of SculptureCenter, NY.

'on the walls, where one would expect paintings to hang, are pools of light, as if the paintings had just recently been removed'. Speaking philosophically, to depict paintings by their absence falls into the same category as depicting them by their presence: they are both forms of *depiction*. A gallery that is full and a gallery that is intentionally left empty both want to be *seen* in relation to the human practice of painting. In the same way that 'The Empty Museum' is no stranger to the art of painting, Wittgenstein's strategy of silence is no stranger to language and the suffering that causes us to become pathologically attached to it. Wittgenstein was able to recognise and address the pathologies of text-worship better than any other Western philosopher before or since, and this is no small feat. But he was unable to recognise the equally pernicious pathology of silence-worship, including the kind of attachment that consists in dogmatic opposition to the use of language in certain spheres.

Vimalakirti's silence

The relation between speech and silence, including the pathologies of both, is the most important theme of *The Vimalakirti Sutra*, one of the most ancient and influential works in the Mahāyāna canon. In this text Manjushri[11] poses a question – 'how does the bodhisattva go about entering the gate of non-dualism?'– to a roomful of deities. Thirty-one very intelligent and insightful aspirants give profound, but wordy, answers, and these make up the bulk of the sutra. But the text goes on to record that the layman Vimalakirti himself *'remained silent and did not speak a word'*. It is very important to realise that in this context Vimalakirti's silence does not consist in the mere absence of sound. He means for this particular silence to make a point. In case readers of the sutra might not grasp what the point is, Manjushri goes on to say *'Excellent, excellent! Not a word, not a syllable – this truly is to enter the gate of non-dualism!'*(Watson 1997: 104–11). In short, Vimalakirti's kind of silence is as noisy in its own way as the noisiest speech, an argument that a brief interpretation of the sutra in *The Book of Serenity* makes when it refers to *'Vimalakirti's teaching of non-duality [and] Manjushri's verbal excess'* (Cleary 1998: 259). If Vimalakirti's silence taught the thesis of non-duality better than Manjushri's words about that silence, this nonetheless implies that both forms of teaching are forms of *teaching*. Although Wittgenstein, like Vimalakirti, was also trying to teach us something by remaining silent about the absolute, there is one major difference between them: using silence as an expedient means is not the same as advocating a philosophical thesis of silence.

Considered from the standpoint of Ch'ing-yuan's third view of mountains and rivers, true silence has nothing to do with teaching some enduring truth about the ineffability of being or ethics. Clinging to a thesis of ineffability that is maintained through silence is just as much a manifestation of craving desire as clinging to any other doctrine. The mind suffers because it cannot find intellectually defensible words for a situation, and so it generalises its inability in the form of a doctrine that allows it to remain mute as a matter of principle. But if someone like Wittgenstein writes a doctrine of ineffability (A) that seems to authorise his subsequent silence about ethics (B), is he really any different from

---

11 Manjushri is one of the great mythical or celestial *bodhisattvas* in the Mahāyāna canon.

someone like Kant, who wrote a doctrine of ethics (A) that seems to authorise his subsequent verbosity (B)? In both cases the thinker seeks to justify something particular by appealing to something general; and in neither case is the most important aspect of the relation between doctrines and deeds – the alleged passage from A to B – made into a problem. This comparison sheds new light on why I was keen to reproduce the picture of Hui-Neng tearing up a sutra in Chapter 1 (Figure 1.1, page 10): rather than seeking to canonise the picture's message, I wanted to suggest that attachment to texts, and attachment to their absence, are *both* impediments. Indeed, if I could somehow reach out of these pages to tear up Figure 1.1 before your very eyes, I would do so right now. To violate the law of the excluded middle by neither holding on to words nor abandoning them is not the same as adopting a *posture* of loquacity or taciturnity: it is simply to be one's ordinary self.

When Kanzan and Jittoku return to language after laughing at the moon's reflection, as they know they must, they will do so earnestly. When they take up language to affirm something, they will affirm it totally; when they take up language to deny something, they will deny it totally; and when they keep silent there will be no hidden message in their silence. Unselfconsciousness is the essence of ordinariness: language and silence are elements of Zen practice because this is just how people go about relating to one another. They are of no importance in themselves. Kanzan and Jittoku know that the use of language and the use of silence stand on the same level, and that both kinds of uses have predictable consequences. But if there are consequences, this is because people *let* their speech and silence have what they call 'consequences'. In doing all of the ordinary things that people do with language, Kanzan and Jittoku will have just as much occasion to speak and remain silent as any other person. But they will never *settle down* in affirmation or denial, or in silence for that matter, for they know that the only task of words and silence is to paint images for the occasion. And who in his right mind would ever choose to settle down inside a picture?

Chapter 5: The Third Mountain

The Two Mountains that Henry Adams Saw

Hardly anyone reads it anymore, but *The Education of Henry Adams* is still one of the most interesting autobiographies ever written (Adams 1931). Although the author came from one of America's most illustrious families – he was a grandson and great-grandson of presidents – he learned the hard way that his privileges could not protect him from grief and its consequences. At one particularly acute point in the book, he writes about his feelings shortly after having watched his beloved elder sister die a grisly death from tetanus. Travelling in Europe at the time, the 30-year old Adams set out to Ouchy, in France, in order to 'recover his balance in a new world', as he puts it, 'for the fantastic mystery of coincidences had made the world, which he thought real, mimic and reproduce the distorted nightmare of his personal horror'. He writes of wanting to 'restore the finite to its place', and in the end the beauty of Lake Geneva and the Alps helped him to overcome his anguish and set the world aright. But healing takes time, and there came a moment when, looking at Mont Blanc, Adams glimpsed what he took to be a very hard and pitiless reality. He writes:

> For the first time in his life, Mont Blanc for a moment looked to him what it was – a chaos of anarchic and purposeless forces – and he needed days of repose to see it clothe itself again with the illusions of his senses, the white purity of its snows, the splendor of its light, and the infinity of its heavenly peace. Nature was kind; Lake Geneva was beautiful beyond itself, and the Alps put on charms real as terrors. (Adams 1931: 289)

Henry Adams looked at Mont Blanc and, for a moment, saw it *as* chaos. The mountain signified, as it were, the absence of all significations – for Adams's initial glance at the mountain found not even a speck of comprehensibility in it. This does not mean, however, that he saw something chaotic that never once had any possibility of being other than chaotic, for he mentions the mountain's charms as well as its terrors. Adams saw the mountain under the aspect of a *pair* of concepts that run, like two threads intertwined, throughout the entire fabric of Western thought. For a thinker, concepts always connote their opposites – the contrasting background of what they are not that allows them to shine forth as what they are – and for the sake of brevity I will call the opposite of chaos 'order'.

Chaos, as the term is used here, is not the mere appearance of disorder within a system (as in chaos theory) for, to paraphrase Levinas, this kind of disorder is always just another possible order that is waiting to be discovered by thematising thought (Levinas 1996: 81). Primordial chaos, in the pre-Socratic sense that I am using it here, is the antithesis of all order, actual *or* potential. Here is an antithesis that by definition eludes the grasp of thematising thought, including any sort of synthesis with its opposite into the Hegelian unity of a new concept that would occupy a 'higher order' of truth. In Hesiod's *Theogony*, for example, chaos logically and historically *precedes* the gods and their ordered cosmos (Atchity 1996: 24). Hesiod's chaos, like the chaos described in the Pelasgian and Olympian creation myths (Graves 1955: I, 27–33), is the *origin* of order – that from which nature, the gods, and all other beings, in their mutual differentiation from one another, spring, or are born. As an origin (A) of the originated (B), chaos is related to, yet essentially other than, any imaginable order. It is this absolute sense of chaos, standing in a truly radical opposition to order, that I would like to draw out for inspection in this final chapter. The chaos that emerges from *this* opposition could never be an object of analysis for philosophy or science. Moreover, *this* chaos can be very, very scary, as Henry Adams knew full well.

Chaos and order: although they twine together in Western thought, they do so in such a way that each is maintained *as* itself – I mean in its own unique self-identity – according to the command of a tyrannical master called the law of the excluded middle. In thought, this implies that the world, in its essential nature, is *either* chaotic *or* ordered – it cannot be both, and it cannot be neither. In attitude, the law of the excluded middle often comes out as the feeling that another person cannot be taken seriously as a philosopher if he has not decided, or at least is not on the path towards deciding, whether the world *makes sense* – whether its essential nature is that of order or chaos, in other words. After all (reason asks), how *could* there be a third possibility that is not also, overtly or covertly, a form of revelation or mysticism lying beyond the realms of sense and reason, and hence beyond the kindred realms of decision and action?

Choosing Order Over Chaos

It was the death of his sister that pushed Henry Adams into seeing Mont Blanc as 'a chaos of anarchic and purposeless forces'. This kind of experience, which is hardly an idiosyncrasy of his, brings out the important question of how death stands in relation to the conceptual pair chaos/order. It is obvious that the prospect of death presents a serious problem for the project of deciding between these two. For how can there be either chaos or order in the world if there always hangs, just above our heads, the sword of an event that threatens to sunder us immediately from the possibility of any and all relations, however they may be characterised? Like it or not, we are all hurtling towards the same end, death. Since a relation implies at least two terms, it would seem to follow that the dead are incapable of coming into a relation with either chaos or order. Chaos and order can fit into the relational form (aRb) because they are both something; but when we are dead we are no longer anything at all. If what we are all on the way to becoming cannot sustain a relation with either chaos or order, then it does not seem possible for the beings that we are now to decide between them with any degree of enduring certainty.

Since death dissolves community, the distinctively social aspect of the problem to which I refer is usually addressed by the creation of an institutional narrative that explains death – that puts the individual's death in its proper place within the formula '$A \Rightarrow B$'. One thinks immediately of the Christian narrative that transforms death into an event of liberation: the moment of transition between living finitely in an imperfectly ordered temporal world and living everlastingly in a perfectly ordered eternal one. The transmigration of souls, or the analogous immortality of the deceased's accomplishments on earth, or the better world the dead leave behind as fallen soldiers in the army of progress: these stories, too, offer the prospect of dampening death's horror and making it bearable. In short, ideologies about what happens *after* one dies attempt to restore social order even, or rather especially, in the omnipresent face of death and its prospect. After all, you can't motivate people to build a beautiful cathedral or a Brave New World for you if they are always moping and whining about the absolute nothingness that follows on the heels of the Grim Reaper. The ugliness of death must be cast in the form of an A that *leads* to a B that is pleasant, or at least worthwhile.

Death does more than simply end our community with the living, however. It also dissolves the selfhood of the very *I* before which are thrown all forms of objectivity and truth. The problem of death therefore exhibits an existential aspect for the individual, and especially for the person who does not accept the comfort of believing in a soul, or in great works that live on forever after the body is dust, or in the inevitability of humanity's upward march of progress. The existential aspect of the problem, which concerns what happens *before* death, is sometimes poignantly evoked by the question '*What is the meaning of my life?*' It is usually addressed by creating a narrative that offers the hope of explaining one's life as a whole – a narrative that puts one's life in its proper place. Here, for example, belong theories like Sartre's, to the effect that *'man is condemned to be free'*, and hence responsible for every aspect of the world that he creates while he is alive (Guignon and Pereboom 1995: 274). The payoff for this way of thinking is supposed to come from the recognition that humans (A) are compelled to decide the meaning of being (B) – compelled, in short, to give order to their lives.

The beguiling image of a courageous person (or a Sartean *pour soi*, or a Heideggerian *Dasein*, or whatever) striding forth into the future not just to *be*, in the manner of a rock or an animal, but to *decide* something called 'meaning' or 'grounds', thus promises to reassure and restore order to at least some minds. I refer especially to the kind of mind that cannot bring itself to believe in God, but also cannot endure the thought that the life of a human being is essentially a ship without a rudder. For the desire to explain the meaning of one's life – to give it order – obtains most of its energy from the struggle to repress the gnawing suspicion that one's life in the end will have amounted merely to a chaotic series of meaningless biological spasms. It gets its energy from the suffering of *anomie*, in other words. Like Moriarty and Sherlock Holmes wrestling atop the Reichenbach Falls (Doyle 1967: II, 317), it would seem that chaos and order are locked in a hateful embrace that always manages to launch both of them over the precipice.

Choosing Chaos Over Order

It should come as no surprise that the usual emotional reaction to the conceptual pair of chaos and order, at least in the West, is to abhor chaos and adore order. Even when a thinker's feelings run the other way, the cracked eggshell of order almost always remains stuck to the chick of chaos that emerged from it, despite the fact that the thinker would have liked to decide *completely* in favour of chaos. Here the possibility is revealed of a different kind of ordering than simply choosing order as such. To be sure, order-loving thinkers such as Hegel may decide definitively in favour of a reasonable world that will be captured like a fly in the amber of absolute knowledge at the end of history. But the renegade thinker who chooses chaos also makes a definite decision, and he makes it within a context that already pre-orders the possibility of the decision and the range of images that surround it as its horizon. The renegade makes his stand in ordered opposition to the one who chooses order. Expressed in semiotic terms, the sign 'order' signifies the same, and at the same level of intensity, for both kinds of thinkers: order-lovers locate the signified of 'order' in the principle of discrimination as such –

the *this* divided from the *that* – while chaos-lovers locate the signified of 'chaos' in this selfsame division, albeit negated or effaced. (One writes 'order' on the chalkboard; the other erases it.) The two are united, to paraphrase Heraclitus, by an opposition that they both *accept* as their master (Heraclitus 1987: 15).

Consider Nietzsche, whose fate-loving ideal of the *Übermensch* is one who artfully creates a life for himself only because he knows that the true character of the world is ever-recurring chaos. Deeply indebted to the metaphysics of Heraclitus, Nietzsche's fundamental metaphysical position projects the essence of the world as a ceaseless flux of inherently unknowable becoming. '*Consequently "knowledge" must be something else: there must first of all be a will to make knowable, a kind of becoming must itself create the deception of beings*' (Nietzsche 1968: 280). What is unknowable probably also cannot be put into words, and Nietzsche confirms this hypothesis: '*linguistic means of expression are useless for expressing "becoming"; it accords with our inevitable need to preserve ourselves to posit a crude world of stability, "things", etc*' (1968: 380). In his mature philosophy, Nietzsche always reasoned from the premise that we human beings, conceived in terms of will-to-power, require the illusion of stability in order to grow and flourish. Thus: '*to impose upon becoming the character of being – that is the supreme will to power*' (1968: 330). But note that Nietzsche makes order into an anthropological necessity – and an artefact of power-relations – that can be called 'illusion' only in comparison with what he takes to be the *true* character of the world, namely, chaos.

In all of this, Nietzsche's thinking exhibits a well-ordered decision in favour of the truth of chaos. The self-identity that will-to-power must possess (A) in order to be what Nietzsche thinks it is *explains* (⇒), for him and his followers, why we humans impose order on a world whose true nature is chaos (B). Hardly anyone who thinks these days is not a follower of Nietzsche in some sense. Consider the ubiquitous and sometimes all-too-glibly pronounced truths that all reality is socially constructed, and that there is no standard for point-of-viewlessness that is not already somebody's particular point of view. Both of these theses require, as a condition of their very intelligibility, let alone their truth, something having the same kind of self-identity that Nietzsche gives to will-to-power, however hazily and diffidently it may be conceived and expressed. Even Marxian and Hegelian dialectics (the grandparent and great-grandparent of these theses) presuppose the identity, however transient it may be, of every moment that acts back on every other moment in the course of the dialectical movement. Nietzsche himself interprets the reason for this kind of presupposition as follows: '*If we did not hold ourselves to be unities, we would never have formed the concept "thing"*' (1968: 338). But since this sounds a little too much like the factual report of an historical anthropologist to capture what I am trying to say, I will amend Nietzsche's remark by adding only this: without *some* notion of unity (and hence order), there would be absolutely nothing to construct the world, and absolutely nothing to occupy a point of view, in the *mental pictures* of 'constructing' and 'viewing' that these two arguments bring with them as their gift to thought. On this view, language does not describe things that would exist independently of will-to-power; rather, it is a relation of words to the *images* that we create for ourselves.

To summarise: Nietzsche makes a noisy decision *inside* the framework of the conceptual pair 'chaos/order'. As the Zen master Nan-ch'üan (747–834) might have put it, Nietzsche thinks that 'knowing is merely deluded consciousness', but his own way of knowing the nature of chaos is through negation – 'it is but *non*-differentiation' (Foster and Shoemaker 1996: 98). To put it another way, Nietzsche's category of ineffable becoming attempts to differentiate itself from human differentiation: an impossible task. Just as the totalitarian state needs to expose conspiracies, whether or not they really exist, so too the one who shrieks 'All is chaos!' needs to preserve and represent something like the ghostly image of order, as a negative connotation of the sign 'chaos', in order to show that the mighty truth of chaos has risen triumphant *over* something else – something untrue that it itself is not.

Rejecting the Dualism of Chaos and Order

What I have just said about the antithesis between order-choosing philosophers and chaos-choosing philosophers points towards a still deeper level of thinking about the dichotomy between chaos and order. Before proceeding to that level, however, I would like to consolidate my gains. When Milton's Satan says 'Better to reign in Hell than serve in Heaven' he *accepts* the division between hell and heaven, and thus gives the world as a whole the kind of order that Milton thought he needed to express his own particular vision of Christian theology (Milton 1949: 240). And Nietzsche's acceptance of the distinction between chaos and order stands on exactly the same level, because this antithesis under-girds his project of expressing what he holds to be the truth of will-to-power. Nietzsche's example therefore suggests the following thesis: *to take a stand* within the opposition between chaos and order is itself to impose order, regardless of where one elects to stand.

If I am right about this characterisation, then the possibility emerges of yet another antithesis. This new antithesis would manifest itself as a thinker's noisy refusal to take *any* kind of stance within the opposition – or, to put it in the usual academic jargon, the thinker would 'reject the terms of the debate'. In contemporary Western philosophy, there is probably no better example of such a thinker than the late Jacques Derrida. And one of the best examples of this example is Derrida's refusal, at the outset of his monumental essay *Force of Law*, to accept the terms implied by the title of the academic colloquium in which he had been invited to speak (1990: 920–23). The colloquium's title, at Cardozo Law School, was '*Deconstruction and the Possibility of Justice*'. But in *Force of Law* Derrida famously repudiates the idea that there is a decidable relation between deconstruction and justice, and he takes great pains at the outset of his remarks to avoid becoming entangled in the dangerous web of 'either/or' that he sees lurking ominously in this title.

The law of the excluded middle implies that either deconstruction is consistent with the possibility of justice or it is not. To borrow an old advertising slogan from one of America's more lurid newspapers, inquiring minds want to *know* which it is, so they can make a *decision* about deconstruction. But Derrida himself decides and announces that he will not play that kind of game:

> That is the choice, the 'either/or', 'yes or no' that I detect in this title. To this extent, the title is rather violent, polemical, and inquisitorial. We may fear that it contains some instrument of torture – that is, a manner of interrogation that is not the most just. Needless to say, from this point on I can offer no response, at least no reassuring response, to any questions put in this way ('either/or', 'yes or no'), to either party or to either party's expectations formalised in this way. (Derrida 1990: 923)

In this refusal to play the game of either/or one can hear the voice of a man who has decided in favour of the undecidable *against* the decidable. In these words, not to mention 1,000 other kindred sentences that Derrida wrote and spoke, I cannot fail to hear the insistent 'No' of a man who does not want to find himself trapped on the flypaper of any sort of discourse that lesser minds might take to be definitive.

What terrible bogeymen Derrida seems to have made of these paltry bits of ink and paper! The interpretation of Derrida that I am putting forward here is not meant to deny a well known essential movement of his work – namely, his desire not to privilege any thesis that might emerge from the unity of what is taken to be a self-enclosed conceptual pair. One could rightly say that Derrida rejects the 'either/or' model of discourse in favour of a 'both/and' model – a model that could, in itself, be simultaneously done and undone *ad infinitum*. However, such an interpretation, while undoubtedly 'correct' from the standpoint of a normal academic exegesis of Derrida's work, is really quite beside the point here. What is most striking about Derrida's rejection of the language of 'either/or' for our purposes is that it *is* a rejection – that it feels and succumbs to the need to oppose itself to a certain other way of thinking and talking. This very opposition – of attitude, if you will – creates order at the level of what I will call *'the project'*.

A decision not to play the game of either/or frames an ordered opposition to the decision in favour of playing it. It cuts between this game and that game, and between our kind of player and their kind. The *Lankavatara Sutra* calls this kind of decision having a *'view of views'*: a mode of attachment that the Zen master Sheng-yi (b 1922) characterises as *'putting one head on top of another'* (Pine 2001: 423). By way of example, consider the rather strong view of views that Derrida seems to express in the following passage on law from *Force of Law*:

> The whole axiomatic of responsibility, of conscience, of intentionality, of property that governs today's dominant juridical discourse and the category of decision right down to its appeals to medical expertise is so theoretically weak and crude that I need not emphasise it here. And the effects of these limitations are massive and concrete enough that I don't have to give examples. (Derrida 1990: 965)

This text allows us to notice a very important distinction: it is one thing to care about a suffering humanity by attending to the discursive conditions and delusions that lead to its suffering; it is something else to despise or have contempt for those conditions – to put one's head above the heads of others. It is therefore important to understand that *having a project*, in the sense I am using the term here, is not the same as opposing this or that injustice. Rather, it is to become attached to opposition as such. Within the context of the opposition between chaos and order, Derrida serves as an excellent example of the kind of thinker who takes his preference for order to a brand new level. Thinkers such as Nietzsche, who characterise the truth of the world as chaos, necessarily accept the well ordered opposition between chaos and order, and thus show what I call the second level of preference for order. But there is a third level of preference for order, and it is manifested by those who loudly refuse to play the name-game at all. These thinkers reveal their preference for order by accepting a well-ordered opposition between their projects and the projects of those who *do* play the game.

Besides Derrida, the previous chapters on Heidegger, Levinas and Wittgenstein afford three other quintessential examples of ordering at the level of the project. Consider Wittgenstein's adamant refusal to play the language game of talking about the absolute, on the ground that anything he could say would be nonsensical according to the criterion of bipolarity. That people do in fact talk nonsense about the absolute is understandable, said Wittgenstein, but since it is *'a priori certain'* that any definition of the good would miss the mark, he himself resolved to say nothing on the subject (Waismann 1979: 69). Or take Levinas, who stood outside of and against the mainstream practice of conceiving of ethics as the discipline of deciding right conduct towards other people according to moral norms. In describing the relationship to the Other as *'a category that falls neither into the being-nothingness opposition, nor into the notion of the existent'*, Levinas firmly opposed his project of thinking ethics as transcendence to any mere calculation in the moral sphere according to binary formulas like duty/no duty and violation/no violation (1989: 50). For Levinas, the passage from the dualism-transcending state of ethics to the dualism-establishing state of justice represents a necessary but tragic descent – a sort of fall from grace. Lastly, and perhaps most vehemently, Heidegger, too, nurtured a project of opposition to those philosophers who decide according to conceptual dualisms created by his shibboleth, 'representational thinking'. What is more, common sense also tends to decide within the framework of the 'either/or', and that is why Heidegger thought that it is completely 'inadequate' to his project of thinking being as such (1985: 81).

I do not raise these examples in an effort to demonstrate that Derrida, Wittgenstein, Levinas and Heidegger are somehow philosophically 'wrong' in their criticisms of the discourse of either/or, but rather simply to illustrate a subtler kind of attachment than attachment to one side or the other of a conceptual dualism. As I see it, in having a project there is the original mind that we all have, there is the thinking of dualistic thoughts that are allowed to float across the mirror of this mind like passing clouds, and then, at the last moment, there is *clinging* to the image of opposition to less enlightened ways of thinking. Clinging to lines and divisions is a kind of order even if the thinker eschews succumbing to the violence of all merely conceptual dualisms, for the word 'order' in this case signifies the stance and attitude displayed by the thinker, rather than the mere conceptual content of his thought. *This* is what I mean by a thinker having a 'project'. A project in this sense is prior to all work, all strategy and all calculations of means and ends. It is characterised by the continuity of pictures and feelings to which there is clinging.

For Derrida, Wittgenstein, Levinas and Heidegger, it is as if submission to the word, in the sense of what ordinary people take to be the everyday word's power to describe, would have inflicted a monumental loss. It is as if they were locked in a wrestling match with words, and for them to fall down before a vulgar description in the order of mere information would entail the humiliation of losing the match and the prize that goes with it. As if they would lose, or at least lose sight of, something overwhelmingly important if they allowed themselves to be pinned down by mundane sentences such as *'Deconstruction is a method of reading texts that disrupts people's settled expectations about what the texts mean'* (Zen Derrida); *'Absolute ethics means compassion'* (Zen Wittgenstein);

'The "face" means you really ought to love your neighbour' (Zen Levinas); and 'Ereignis *is a force of unknown origin that pushes time and being together'* (Zen Heidegger). As if shop-worn words such as 'method', 'compassion', 'love' and 'force' were but teacups in relation to the gallons of meaning at which the words 'deconstruction', 'absolute ethics', 'the face' and *'Ereignis'* can only hint or gesture. As if these latter words were fingers pointing at a moon that is so indistinct that it can only be experienced, and never made into a theme. But what and where is this moon at which these fingers could even *try* to point? The ordinary moon, after all, is just the moon – can't you see it up there, in the sky? And as for efforts to describe it: isn't the most enlightened course simply to laugh at any of its reflections, like Kanzan and Jittoku did (Figure 1.2, page 25)?

We cannot seem to rid ourselves of the feeling that to let go of all attachment to the pictures that organise our thought, speech and projects is either impossible or unwise. We forget that if letting go of pictures is impossible for us to realise in thought, then this implies that it is also impossible for us to realise chaos in thought. For what is our idea of chaos if not the absence of all pictures – the absence of all orientation – the absence of all clinging? My earlier definition of order as the antithesis of chaos is therefore a little misleading. For as a concept, chaos is privative: it is the absence of any and all order. Yet the minute we try to think this concept we impose order on it and thereby annihilate chaos in its essence. As Levinas says, 'if the Other is presented to the Same, the co-presence of the Other and the Same in a phenomenon forthwith constitutes an order' (1996: 68). This paradox is dissolved, if at all, only by the unthematic *experience* of chaos – our being thrown into chaotic situations, for example, where there is no question or even possibility of thinking. The example offered at the beginning of this chapter – John Adams's crazed reaction to his sister's death – suggests that primordial chaos shows itself phenomenally in the form of completely unstructured, and usually very unpleasant, experiences. I say unpleasant because even if we think that it is possible to let go of all our attachments, we just can't seem to shake the fear that letting go would make us fall down, into an abyss that is and must be terrible.

Most thinking people recognise that there is much terrible suffering in this world. We want to change the things that lead to suffering – to correct injustice – and since most of us are not professional revolutionaries, we look around for one of the egghead's usual suspects, such as 'ideology', or 'mainstream modes of thinking and talking', or 'the metaphysics of presence'. In making this move, however, we reveal something essential, and in a way embarrassing, about ourselves: namely, that we are letting the norm of logical transcendence (A $\Rightarrow$ B) lead us around by the nose. Whenever we impute the world or any aspect of it to beliefs, to patterns of thought, to semiotic relationships, or to whatever, we think just like Leibniz thought, even though at some level we also know, from having seen language deconstructed or from deconstructing it ourselves, that there is absolutely no *necessary* connection between sign and signified, words and deeds, beliefs and actions.

The principle of sufficient reason was the engine that drove the famous monadology of Leibniz, who explained all change on the basis of a speculative (and unknowable) metaphysical property internal to the irreducible monads that he thought made up the stuff of the world (Leibniz 1934: 3–20). Don't we do the same kind of thing whenever we assert that people are steered to act the way they do because of what they believe in, or the way their patterns of language divide up experience? To say that our behaviour *must* be rooted in causes or grounds is almost the same as saying that we exist only if we can render reasons for our existence. But surely this is untrue, as the case of Angelus Silesius's rose indicates:

> The rose is without why: it blooms because it blooms,
> It pays no attention to itself, asks not whether it is seen.
> (Heidegger 1996b: 35)

Nevertheless, we sophisticates continue to project the requirements of our theories of the world onto the world, and then steel ourselves to hear no nay saying. What rigid beings we humans have let ourselves become! If only we could loosen up a little, and become more like the rose.

To be more like the rose is not the same as vegetating. Nor is it the same as refusing ever to ask or answer the question 'Why?' It is more like being able, *quite naturally*, to put down what we pick up, and to pick up what we put down. This odd metaphor comes from the last koan that I will tell you about in this book:

> Venerable Yen-yang asked Chao-chou, 'What should one do when one does not take up a single thing?' Chao-chou replied, 'Put it down'. Yen-yang asked, 'When you do not take anything, how can you put it down?' Chao-chou replied, 'Then carry it with you'. (Foster and Shoemaker 1996: 188)

Yen-yang's first question to Chao-chou sensibly seeks a description of what it is like – and how one should behave – after all the illusions that bedevil ordinary mortals have been shed. But instead of describing the code of behaviour of those who occupy this illusionless state, where one does not take up a single thing, Chao-chou perversely replies 'Put it down'. But the only thing that a person without illusions *could* put down is his true and right way of seeing the world, a way that is neither an illusion nor a way of seeing illusions, but instead just the way he *does* see the world, and correctly at that! One cannot put down what one is, and surely one should not put down a correct way of seeing the world.

So Yen-yang presses Chao-chou by asking him a question that shows the illogic of his answer: 'When you do not take anything, how can you put it down?' Here Yen-yang's reason tells him that it is foolishness to advise an empty-handed person to put down what he is carrying. Chao-chou wisely yields, but he does not yield to the force of the argument. His reply, 'Then carry it with you', cuts off Yen-Yang's tongue.

The Narrow Drum

Up to this point, I have attempted to display three modes of thinking about the relation between chaos and order, and I have said that, in one way or other, a thinker's essential preference for order is revealed in all of them. Some thinkers opt for order as such, as it is opposed to chaos. Other thinkers choose chaos as such, but only because they accept an order that already imposes the conceptual dualism of chaos and order. Lastly, some thinkers reject the conceptual dualism, but affirm – and in affirming make order out of – their own linguistic projects as opposed to the linguistic projects of others. What all three modes of thought have in common is their *overt* expressiveness: they all use language to take a stand. As the previous chapter's discussion of Wittgenstein's silence indicates, there is even a fourth level of ordering in the Western tradition. Thinkers who occupy this level loudly foreswear all noise making: they *covertly* express themselves, as it were, by keeping silent. Having merely exhibited the differences between these various modes of ordering, however, the time has now come to unite them.

Let me come right out and say it: *being and beings, ethics and ontology, the sayable and the unsayable, being and becoming, the decidable and the undecidable, my project and your project, speech and silence, either/or and both/and, right and wrong, good and bad – in short, X and not-X in all of its forms – are always narrow drums beaten on both sides.*

You will recall that I compared dualisms to a narrow drum once before, in Chapter 1. The metaphor comes from a single line in the *Book of Serenity*: *'Right and wrong – a narrow drum beaten on both sides'* (Cleary 1998: 70). By bringing it up again, I do not want to imply that oppositions within language are in some sense bad or inferior vehicles for thinking and conveying meaning, for I have no other means to offer. Nor do I mean to reproduce Paul Ricoeur's enchanting formula that the job of philosophy is always *'to keep open the width of language'* (Pyke 1993: portrait of Ricoeur), for there are times when it feels absolutely right to close that width down. Moreover, I am almost certain that it is impossible to gain any width in philosophy without at the same time sacrificing some depth, somewhere. And I certainly do not want to reiterate the shop-worn truth that people's continued adherence to the form of the conceptual dualism grows out of a fallen or contingent metaphysics of presence, thereby leaving the impression (like perfume in the air from a departed guest) that some other way of talking, or keeping silent for that matter, is more in tune with whatever summons us to speak in the first place.

No, when I say that X and *not-X* are a narrow drum beaten on both sides, all that I really mean is that they make a kind of *noise*. Language makes noise. We literally make noise when we speak, of course, but it is also the case that our written words, like a compact disk in relation to a CD player, always stand ready to make noise in the minds of our readers. There is nothing inherently right or wrong, good or bad – in short X or *not-X* – about making noise. Human beings have been doing it for a long time, and they will probably continue doing it for a long time to come. But what is most important about our noise making is not that we do it, or even how we do it. What matters most is our *attitude* towards it – I mean whether or not we *cling* to the pretty (or ugly) pictures that are evoked by the noises we make and hear. Here I am using the words 'what matters most' in a sense that is very unacademic, very personal, and even intimate. What is at stake is the very possibility of breaking through the ancient Western identification of wisdom and discourse. What is at stake is the possibility that getting all the way to the bottom of language – either your own noise or that of others – requires that you neither grasp it nor reject it. The Old French word *attacher*, meaning to fasten with a stake, is almost literally true in the case of what is 'at stake' in our attachment to words and images, sound and form. It indicates that for those who are attached, even the most appropriate or profound statement is, as *The Blue Cliff Record* puts it, '*a stake at which to tether a donkey for ten thousand eons*' (Cleary 1992: 257).

It seems to me that those who never forget to be intelligent for even a second inevitably burden their essential nature. I don't mean 'essential nature' in the Western sense of quiddity, or whatness. I use the term 'essential nature' to evoke the possibility of experiencing what already lies or, if you will, lies absent, *at the beginning*: right in front of us, utterly quiet and still, before all essences and natures. I know this may sound flaky and mystical, and I truly do not want to advocate a mystical thesis here. I want to stay within the realm of the obvious and the simple, and thereby try to avoid what Kierkegaard calls the 'martyrdom of being uncomprehended' (1954: 68). I want to invite you to experience what requires no supernatural beliefs to be seen – what anyone can see, in fact, lying right before their eyes, if only they would just *look*.

The Three Mountains

The first mountain

'When I first began to practise, the mountains and rivers were simply mountains and rivers. ...'

In the beginning, a mountain is just a mountain to us. We think in order to get along and enhance ourselves in a world where objects stand ready, in the manner of Heidegger's 'standing reserve', to be used and manipulated. Whether behaving altruistically or egoistically, we attempt to ground our actions and reactions in well founded and perspicacious rules, norms and principles. We praise the book on religious holidays, we honour the law on Law Day, and we follow the rules on all days. We look for our answers in self-help manuals, 'great books' and the words of the wise. We think instrumentally in this or that manner. Sign and signified become tools of work, as in law's violent overcoming of the given. We bend things and other people to a will that posits ends and means in the service of an appetite that craves. A grieving Henry Adams used Mont Blanc in this way, once he could bring himself to see it as charming. And what could be more natural? Who among us has not thought and behaved in this manner? Who among us will not continue to do so?

The Second Mountain

'... After I advanced in my practice, the mountains and rivers were no longer mountains and rivers. ...'

There comes a time, however, when we look at a mountain and what shows itself to us is no longer a simple mountain. Henry Adams saw Mont Blanc in this way – as a chaos of anarchic and purposeless forces – if only for a short while. But those of us who have attained the sophisticated standpoint of mature thought and speech know that the object world really does or should dissolve in the medium of a kind of thinking that devalues and transcends all mundane positing of *X* or *not-X*. We think deeply and profoundly in this or that manner. We discover essential truths, including the essential truth that there are no essential truths except those that we ourselves posit. And then even positing itself dissolves for some of us, on the basis of the essential truth that what manifests itself in language is nothing more than a play of images. Sign and signified become tools of play and strategy, as in the free play that constitutes the movement of deconstruction. While standing atop the second mountain we cling tenaciously to the deepness of our hard-won insights. In fact, we cling to them just as tightly as we used to cling to the shallowness of the object-world that we exploited when we stood on the first mountain.

On the second mountain we reject simple declarative sentences because of the inadequate and claustrophobic dualisms they imply. But we nonetheless accept the dualism between accepting and rejecting, and this activity of rejecting, this *project*, is what keeps us from falling into the abyss. We cling to the impossibility of a person saying or showing who he or she is (really), and what the world is (really): *that* is our project. And we put our project in order by opposing it to the projects of those who likewise cling, but to the contrary possibility of saying or showing who they really are, and what the world really is. We cling to the image of the second mountain's essential *superiority* over the first.

The Third Mountain

> *'... But when I reached the end of my practice, the mountains and rivers were simply mountains and rivers again.'*

One day, after a very long and difficult journey, we lift our eyes to the mountain and finally see it as it really is. At long last we see that a mountain is, has always been, and will always be, just a mountain after all. Now there is no going back. Henceforth the most abstruse profundity is only just as deep as the thinnest of commonplaces. As a thinker, one loses the feeling that behind every sentence lurks either the possibility of liberation, or the threat of a boundary or prison. Does someone want to deconstruct the word 'Stop' on a traffic sign to display what is ghostly and contingent inside of this and every use of language? – then let him, for one no longer clings to the feeling that texts must have a core meaning or range of meanings. Does someone else want to peddle the possibility of absolute knowledge? – then let him, for there is no longer any clinging to arguments that, at one time, had so utterly convinced us of the thesis that objectivity and universal truth are chimeras.

No longer do words convince us, except at the surface of things. No longer do they threaten us, except on the flip side of that surface. A sign and its signified become no more (or less) real and important than the marks left in the sky by the wings of passing birds. One learns the greatest lesson: that there is no enduring duality between the real and the conventional, and that the heart really can let go of the relentless compulsion to inflict the violence of language or silence, to disrupt and overcome others, and to convince others of the superior wisdom of our insights. The third mountain is, equally, *letting go* of all compulsion to intervene, and not making any *understanding* of this letting-go. To let go without making an understanding of letting go is to have no view of views. As Hui-neng said, *'although no school of instruction exists without its expedient tools, essentially there is nothing to hold on to'* (Pine 2001: 370).

If there is nothing to hold on to, where does this leave our duties to others?

On the first mountain, one faithfully heeds commandments such as *Thou shalt not kill*. Here black is black, white is white, and never the twain shall meet.

On the second mountain, texts such as 'Thou shalt not kill' lose all of their previous clarity; they become mere *texts* that break up into a multiplicity of possible interpretations, including Levinas's 'Thou shalt cause the other to live'. Here black and white is always grey.

But on the third mountain black *is* white – there is no other black. Here, forbearing from killing, like acting to let others live, *constitutes* the precept and its interpretations. To paraphrase Sheng-yi: On the third mountain, there is no precept or interpretation *against* killing (or *for* letting-live) besides just not killing and letting-live (Pine 2001: 291).

Of course, none of this implies that one does or should never intervene. For now it seems both natural and appropriate to look at useful things and see what is *merely* useful. Is there something more to do in the world? Well, if there is, then *just do it*. Now one looks at true and false statements and never sees more than what is *merely* true, or *merely* false. Does something nonetheless call on us to speak? Well, if there is more to say, then *just say it*. On the third mountain, the dualism between theory and practice no longer *abides* – not because one pretends that all dualisms are dissolved by an ecstatic experience or state, but because one has let go of the compulsive need either to accept *or* to reject the language of dualisms. That boundless compassion for all forms of suffering accompanies this way of being is not a provable 'entailment' on the third mountain – for idea A never *really* leads to idea B, except on the first and second mountains – but that's how I imagine that it feels to those who have succeeded in scaling this last and most difficult summit.

This book has been a meditation on the possibility, however remote, of the third mountain.

Bibliography

Adams, H (1931) *The Education of Henry Adams*, New York: Modern Library

Alighieri, D (1994) *The Inferno of Dante*, Pinsky, R (tr), New York: Farrar, Straus and Giroux

Aquinas, T (1948) *Introduction to St Thomas Aquinas*, Pegis, A (ed), New York: Modern Library

Arendt, H (2003) *Responsibility and Judgment*, Kohn, J (ed), New York: Shocken Books

Aristotle (1984) *The Complete Works of Aristotle (2 vols)*, Barnes, J (ed), Princeton: Princeton University Press

Atchity, K (ed) (1996) *The Classical Greek Reader*, New York: Henry Holt

Augustine (1961) *Confessions*, Pine-Coffin, RS (tr), New York: Penguin Books

Aurelius, M (1945) 'The meditations of Marcus Aurelius', in Edman, I (ed), *Marcus Aurelius and His Times*, Roslyn, NY: Walter J Black

Ayer, AJ (1985) *Wittgenstein*, New York: Random House

Bachelard, G (1969) *The Poetics of Space*, Jolas, M (tr), Boston: Beacon Press

Badiou, *Infinite Thought: Truth and the Return of Philosophy* (2003), Feltham, O and Clemens, J (trs), London: Continuum

Bancroft, A (2000) *The Buddha Speaks*, Boston: Shambhala Publications

Banville, J (2004) 'The human stain', 278 The Nation (18 October)

Bartlett, J (1980) *Familiar Quotations* (15th edn), Beck, E (ed), Boston: Little Brown

Bartley, W (1985) *Wittgenstein* (2nd edn), LaSalle: Open Court

Biemel, W and Saner, H (ed) (2003) *The Heidegger-Jaspers Correspondence (1920–1963)*, Amherst: Humanity Books

Benjamin, W (1999) *The Arcades Project*, Eilland, H and McLaughlin, K (trs), Cambridge: Belknap Press

Benjamin, W (1978) *Reflections*, Jephcott, E (tr), New York: Schocken Books

Benjamin, W (1968) *Illuminations*, Zohn, H (tr), New York: Schocken Books

Berger, P and Luckmann, T (1967) *The Social Construction of Reality*, New York: Anchor Press

Bergson, H (1910) *Time and Free Will: An Essay on the Immediate Data of Consciousness*, Pogson, FL (tr), Kila, MT: Kessinger Publishing

Borradori, G (2003) *Philosophy in a Time of Terror: Dialogues with Jürgen Habermas and Jacques Derrida*, Chicago: University of Chicago Press

Bouwsma, OK (1986) *Wittgenstein: Conversations 1949–1951*, Craft, JL and Hustwit, R (eds), Indianapolis: Hackett Publishing

Boxer, S (1998) 'Giving memory its due in an age of license', The New York Times (28 October)

Brooks, EB, and Brooks, AT (trs), *The Original Analects: Sayings of Confucius and His Successors*, New York: Columbia University Press

Buber, M (2000) *I and Thou*, Smith, R (tr), New York: Scribner Classics

Buddha (1995) *The Middle Length Discourses of the Buddha*, Ňánamoli, B and Bodhi, B (trs), Boston: Wisdom Publications

Buddha (1966) *The Teaching of Buddha*, Tokyo: Kosaido Printing Co

Carter, N (1994) *This Complicated Form of Life: Essays on Wittgenstein*, Chicago: Open Court

Cleary, T (tr) (2001) *Classics of Buddhism and Zen: The Collected Translations of Thomas Cleary (5 vols)*, Boston: Shambhala Publications

Cleary, T (tr) (1999) *The Taoist Classics (4 vols)*, Boston: Shambhala Publications

Cleary, T (tr) (1998) *Book of Serenity*, Boston: Shambala Publications

Cleary, T and Cleary, JC (trs) (1992) *The Blue Cliff Record*, Boston: Shambhala Publications

Corbin, A (1960) *Corbin on Contracts (15 vols)*, St Paul: West Publishing

Deleuze, G (1990) *The Logic of Sense*, Lester, M (tr), New York: Columbia University Press

Derrida, J (2003) *The Problem of Genesis in Husserl's Philosophy*, Hobson, M (tr), Chicago: University of Chicago Press

Derrida, J (2001) *The Work of Mourning*, Brault, P-A and Naas, M (trs), Chicago: University of Chicago Press

Derrida, J (1994) *Specters of Marx*, Kamuf, P (tr), New York: Routledge

Derrida, J (1991) *A Derrida Reader: Between the Blinds*, Kamuf, P (ed), New York: Columbia University Press

Derrida, J (1990) 'Force of law: the "mystical foundations of authority"', 11 Cardozo Law Review 920–1045

Derrida, J (1989a) *Edmund Husserl's* Origin of Geometry: *An Introduction*, Leavey, J (tr), Lincoln: University of Nebraska Press

Derrida, J (1989b) *Of Spirit: Heidegger and the Question*, Bennington, G and Bowlby, R (trs), Chicago: University of Chicago Press

Derrida, J (1981) *Positions*, Bass, A (tr), Chicago: University of Chicago Press

Derrida, J (1978) *Writing and Difference*, Bass, A (tr), London: Routledge

Descartes, R (1985) *The Philosophical Writings of Descartes (2 vols)*, Cottingham, J, Stoothoff, R and Murdoch, D (trs), Cambridge: Cambridge University Press

Diamantides, M (2000) 'The subject may have disappeared but *its* sufferings remain', 11 Law and Critique 137–66

Douzinas, C and Warrington, R (1994) *Justice Miscarried: Ethics, Aesthetics and the Law*, Hemel Hempstead, UK: Harvester Wheatsheaf

Doyle, AC (1967) *The Annotated Sherlock Holmes (2 vols)*, New York: Clarkson N Potter

Dworkin, R (1991) 'Pragmatism, right answers, and true banality', in Brint, M and Weaver, W (eds), *Pragmatism in Law and Society*, Boulder, CO: Westview Press

Dworkin, R (1977) *Taking Rights Seriously*, Cambridge: Harvard University Press

Eagelton, T (2004) 'Human, all to human', 278 The Nation (10 May)

Eckhart, J (1994) *Selected Writings*, Davies, O (tr), New York: Penguin Books

Eco, U (2000) *Kant and the Platypus*, McEwen, A (tr), New York: Harcourt Brace

Eliot, TS (1963) *Murder in the Cathedral*, New York: Harcourt Brace and World

Eliot, TS (1930) *Selected Poems*, New York: Harcourt Brace Jovanovich

Engelmann, P (1967) *Letters from Ludwig Wittgenstein, with a Memoir*, Furtmüller, L (tr), Oxford: Basil Blackwell

Finch, H (1977) *Wittgenstein – The Later Philosophy: An Exposition of the 'Philosophical Investigations'*, Atlantic Highlands: Humanities Press

Fish, S (1991) 'Almost pragmatism: the jurisprudence of Richard Posner, Richard Rorty, and Ronald Dworkin', in Brint, M and Weaver, W (eds), *Pragmatism in Law and Society*, Boulder, CO: Westview Press

Foster, N and Shoemaker, J (ed) (1996) *The Roaring Stream: A New Zen Reader*, Hopewell, NJ: Ecco Press

Foucault, M (2003) *'Society Must Be Defended': Lectures at the Collège de France, 1975–76*, Macey, D (tr), New York: Picador

Foucault, M (1979) *Discipline and Punish: The Birth of the Prison*, Sheridan, A (tr), New York: Vintage Books

Frege, G (1980) *The Foundations of Arithmetic*, Austin, JL (tr), Evanston: Northwestern University Press

Freud, S (1962) *Civilization and Its Discontents*, Strachey, J (tr), New York: WW Norton

Glock, H-J (1996) *A Wittgenstein Dictionary*, Cambridge: Blackwell

Gramsci, A (1971) *Selections from the Prison Notebooks*, Hoare, Q and Smith, G (trs), New York: International Publishers

Graves, R (1955) *The Greek Myths (2 vols)*, Baltimore: Penguin Books

Grayling, AC (1988) *Wittgenstein*, Oxford: Oxford University Press

Green, J (1998) *The Recorded Sayings of Zen Master Joshu*, Boston: Shambhala Publications

Grossman, Vasily (1986) *Life and Fate*, Chandler, R (tr), New York: HarperCollins

Guignon, C and Pereboom, D (eds) (1995) *Existentialism: Basic Writings*, Indianapolis: Hackett Publishing

Hadas, M (ed) (1961) *Essential Works of Stoicism*, New York: Bantam Books

Harris, P (ed) (1999) *Zen Poems*, New York: Alfred A Knopf

Hegel, GWF (1977) *Phenomenology of Spirit*, Miller, AV (tr), Oxford: Oxford University Press

Hegel, GWF (1975) *Hegel's Logic*, Wallace, W (tr), Oxford: Oxford University Press

Heidegger, M (2004a) *On the Essence of Language: The Metaphysics of Language and the Essencing of the World*, Gregory, W and Unna, Y (tr), Albany: State University of New York Press

Heidegger, M (2004b) *The Phenomenology of Religious Life*, Fritsch, M and Gosetti-Ferencci, J (trs), Bloomington: Indiana University Press

Heidegger, M (2003a) *The End of Philosophy*, Stambaugh, J (tr), Chicago: University of Chicago Press

Heidegger, M (2003b) *Four Seminars*, Mitchell, A and Raffoul, F (trs), Bloomington: Indiana University Press

Heidegger, M (2003c) *Philosophical and Political Writings*, Stassen, M (ed), New York: Continuum

Heidegger, M (2002a) *Identity and Difference*, Stambaugh, J (tr), Chicago: University of Chicago Press

Heidegger, M (2002b) *Supplements*, Van Buren, J (ed), Albany: State University of New York Press

Heidegger, M (2002c) *The Essence of Human Freedom*, Sadler, T (tr), London: Continuum

Heidegger, M (2001a) *Phenomenological Interpretation of Aristotle*, Rojcewicz, R (tr), Bloomington: Indiana University Press

Heidegger, M (2001b) *Zollikon Seminars*, Mayr, F and Askay, R (trs), Evanston: Northwestern University Press

Heidegger, M (2000) *Elucidations of Hölderlin's Poetry*, Hoeller, K (tr), Amherst: Humanity Books

Heidegger, M (1999a) *Contributions to Philosophy (From Enowning)*, Emad, P and Maly, K (trs), Bloomington: Indiana University Press

Heidegger, M (1999b) *Ontology – The Hermeneutics of Facticity*, van Buren, J (tr), Bloomington: Indiana University Press

Heidegger, M (1998) *Pathmarks*, McNeill, W (tr), Cambridge: Cambridge University Press

Heidegger, M (1997a) *Kant and the Problem of Metaphysics* (5th edn), Taft, R (tr), Bloomington: Indiana University Press

Heidegger, M (1997b) *Phenomenological Interpretation of Kant's* Critique of Pure Reason, Emad, P and Maly, K (trs), Bloomington: Indiana University Press

Heidegger, M (1997c) *Plato's* Sophist, Rojcewicz, R and Schuwer, A (trs), Bloomington: Indiana University Press

Heidegger, M (1996a) *Hölderlin's Hymn 'The Ister'*, McNeill, W and Davis, J (trs), Bloomington: Indiana University Press

Heidegger, M (1996b) *The Principle of Reason*, Lilly, R (tr), Bloomington: Indiana University Press.

Heidegger, M (1995) *Aristotle's* Metaphysics θ 1-3: *On the Essence and Actuality of Force*, Brogan, W and Warnek, P (trs), Bloomington: Indiana University Press

Heidegger, M (1993a) *Basic Concepts*, Aylesworth, G (tr), Bloomington: Indiana University Press

Heidegger, M and Fink, E (1993b) *Heraclitus Seminar*, Seibert, C (tr), Evanston: Northwestern University Press

Heidegger, M (1992a) *Parmenides*, Schuwer, A and Rojcewicz, R (trs), Bloomington: Indiana University Press

Heidegger, M (1992b) *The Concept of Time*, McNeill, W (tr), Oxford: Blackwell

Heidegger, M (1991) *Nietzsche (4 vols)*, Krell, D (ed), San Francisco: HarperCollins

Heidegger, M (1988) *Hegel's Phenomenology of Spirit*, Emad, P and Maly, K (trs), Bloomington: Indiana University Press

Heidegger, M (1985) *Schelling's Treatise on the Essence of Human Freedom*, Stambaugh, J (tr), Athens, OH: Ohio University Press

Heidegger, M (1984) *The Metaphysical Foundations of Logic*, Heim, M (tr), Bloomington: Indiana University Press

Heidegger, M (1977) *The Question Concerning Technology and Other Essays*, Lovitt, W (tr), New York: Harper & Row

Heidegger, M (1975a) *Early Greek Thinking*, Krell, D and Capuzzi, F (trs), New York: Harper & Row

Heidegger, M (1975b) *Poetry, Language, Thought*, Hofstadter, A (tr), New York: Harper & Row

Heidegger, M (1972) *On Time and Being*, Stambaugh, J (tr), New York: HarperCollins

Heidegger, M (1971) *On the Way to Language*, Hertz, P (tr), San Francisco: HarperCollins

Heidegger, M (1968) *What is Called Thinking?*, Gray, G (tr), New York: Harper & Row

Heidegger, M (1966) *Discourse on Thinking*, Anderson, J and Freund, EH (trs), New York: Harper & Row

Heidegger, M (1962) *Being and Time*, Macquarrie, J and Robinson, E (trs), New York: HarperCollins

Heidegger, M (1959) *An Introduction to Metaphysics*, Manheim, R (tr), New Haven: Yale University Press

Heisig, J (2001) *Philosophers of Nothingness: An Essay on the Kyoto School*, Honolulu: University of Hawaii Press

Heraclitus (1987) *Fragments*, Robinson, TM (tr), Toronto: University of Toronto Press

Higham, TF and Bowra, CM (1938) *The Oxford Book of Greek Verse in Translation*, Oxford: Clarendon Press

Hitler, A (1943) *Mein Kampf*, Manheim, R (tr), Boston: Houghton Mifflin

Hobbes, T (1914) *Leviathon*, London: JM Dent

Holmes, O (1897) 'The path of the law', 10 Harvard Law Review 61

Horkheimer, M and Adorno, T (2002) *Dialectic of Enlightenment: Philosophical Fragments*, Jephcott, E (tr), Stanford: Stanford University Press

Hume, D (1977) *A Treatise on Human Nature (Volume I)*, New York: Everyman's Library

Hunnings, G (1988) *The World and Language in Wittgenstein's Philosophy*, Albany: SUNY Press

Husserl, E (1999) *Cartesian Meditations: An Introduction to Phenomenology*, Cairns, D (tr), Dordrecht: Kluwer Academic Publishers

Husserl, E (1991) *On the Phenomenology of the Consciousness of Internal Time*, Brough, J (tr), Dordrecht: Kluwer Academic Publishers

Husserl, E (1962) *Ideas: General Introduction to Pure Phenomenology*, Gibson, WR (tr), New York: Macmillan

Inwood, M (1999) *A Heidegger Dictionary*, Oxford: Blackwell Publishers

Janik, A and Toulmin, S (1973) *Wittgenstein's Vienna*, New York: Simon & Schuster

Kafka, F (1983) *The Complete Stories*, Muir, W and Muir, E (trs), New York: Schocken Books

Kafka, F (1975) *The Diaries: 1910-1923*, Brod, M (ed), New York: Schocken Books

Kafka, F (1937) *The Trial*, Muir, W and Muir, E (tr), New York: Modern Library.

Kant, I (2000) *The Critique of Judgment*, Bernard, JH (tr), Amherst: Prometheus Books

Kant, I (1998) *Critique of Pure Reason*, Guyer, P and Wood, A (trs), Cambridge: Cambridge University Press

Kant, I (1996) *Practical Philosophy*, Gregor, M (tr), Cambridge: Cambridge University Press

Kant, I (1993) *The Philosophy of Kant*, Friedrich, C and Meredith, J (trs), New York: Modern Library

Kant, I (1965) *The Metaphysical Elements of Justice*, Ladd, J (tr), Indianapolis: Bobbs-Merrill

Kaufmann, W (ed) (1956) *Existentialism from Dostoevsky to Sartre*, Cleveland: Meridian Books

Kearney, R and Rainwater, M (ed) (1996) *The Continental Philosophy Reader*, London: Routledge

Kennedy, D (1986) 'Freedom and constraint in adjudication: a critical phenomenology', 36 Journal of Legal Education 518–62

Keown, D (2003) *A Dictionary of Buddhism*, Oxford: Oxford University Press

Kierkegaard, S (1993) *The Diary of Søren Kirkegaard*, Rohde, P (ed), New York: Carol Publishing

Kierkegaard, S (1954) *Fear and Trembling and The Sickness Unto Death*, Lowrie, W (tr), New York: Doubleday & Company

Kojève, A (1980) *Introduction to the Reading of Hegel*, Nichols, J (tr), Ithaca: Cornell University Press

Kristeva, Julia (2001) *Hannah Arendt*, Guberman, R (tr), New York: Columbia University Press

Lao-tzu (1994) *Tao Te Ching*, Lau, DC (tr), New York: Alfred A Knopf

Leff, A (1979) 'Unspeakable ethics, unnatural law, 1979 Duke Law Journal 1229–49

Leibniz, G (1934) *Leibniz: Philosophical Writings*, Morris, M (tr), London: JM Dent & Sons

Levinas, E (2003a) *Humanism of the Other*, Poller, N (tr), Chicago: University of Illinois Press

Levinas, E (2003b) *On Escape*, Bergo, B (tr), Stanford: Stanford University Press

Levinas, E (2001a) *Existence and Existents*, Lingis, A (tr), Pittsburgh: Duquesne University Press

Levinas, E (2001b) *Is it Righteous to Be?* Robbins, J (ed), Stanford: Stanford University Press

Levinas, E (1999) *Alterity and Transcendence*, Smith, M (tr), New York: Columbia University Press

Levinas, E (1998) *On Thinking-of-the-Other: Entre Nous*, Smith, M and Harshav, B (trs), New York: Columbia University Press

Levinas, E (1996) *Basic Philosophical Writings*, Peperzak, A, Critchley, S and Bernasconi, S (trs), Bloomington: Indiana University Press

Levinas, E (1993) *Dieu, la mort et le temps*, Paris: Grassett

Levinas, E (1989) *The Levinas Reader*, Hand, S (ed), Oxford: Blackwell

Loumansky, A (2000) 'Me voici, here I am, here I stand, I can do no other', 11 Law and Critique 287–300

Luke, D (ed) (1964) *Goethe: Selected Verse*, London: Penguin Books

MacKinnon, C (1983) 'Feminism, Marxism, method, and state: toward feminist jurisprudence', 8 Signs: Journal of Women in Culture and Society 635–58

Malcolm, N (1984) *Ludwig Wittgenstein: A Memoir* (2nd edn), Oxford: Oxford University Press

Marcuse, H (2001) *Towards a Critical Theory of Society*, Kellner, D (ed), London: Routledge

Marcuse, H (1964) *One-Dimensional Man: Studies in the Ideology of Advanced Industrial Society*, Boston: Beacon Press

Marx, K and Engels, F (1998) *The Communist Manifesto*, London: Verso

Marx, K (1986) *Karl Marx: A Reader*, Elster, J (ed), Cambridge: Cambridge University Press

Marx, K (1964) *Early Writings*, Bottomore, TB (tr), New York: McGraw-Hill

Merleau-Ponty, M (1992) *Phenomenology of Perception*, Smith, C (tr), London: Routledge

Miller, A (1958) *Death of a Salesman*, New York: Viking Press

Milton, J (1949) *The Portable Milton*, Bush, D (ed), New York: Viking Press

Monk, R (1990) *Ludwig Wittgenstein: The Duty of Genius*, New York: Penguin Books

Moore, GE (1993) *Principia Ethica* (2nd edn), Cambridge: Cambridge University Press

Morrison, T and West, C (2004) 'Blues, love and politics', 278 The Nation (24 May)

Murray, M (1974) 'A note on Wittgenstein and Heidegger', 83 Philosophical Review 501–03

Nietzsche, F (1995) *The Gay Science*, Polt, R (tr), Indianapolis: Hackett

Nietzsche, F (1968) *The Will to Power*, Kaufmann, W and Hollingdale, RJ (trs), New York: Vintage Books

Nietzsche, F (1954) *The Philosophy of Nietzsche*, Zimmern, H (tr), New York: Modern Library

Nishida, K (1990) *An Inquiry into the Good*, Abe, M and Ives, C (trs), New Haven: Yale University Press

Oates, W and O'Neill, E (eds) (1938) *The Complete Greek Drama (2 vols)*, New York: Random House

Parkes, G (ed) (1987) *Heidegger and Asian Thought*, Honolulu: University of Hawaii Press

Parmenides of Elea (1984) *Fragments*, Gallop, D (tr), Toronto: University of Toronto Press

Pascal, B (1941) *Pensées and the Provincial Letters*, Trotter, WF and M'Crie, T (trs) New York: Modern Library

Pine, R (2001) *The Diamond Sutra: Text and Commentaries*, Washington, DC: Counterpoint

Pitkin, H (1972) *Wittgenstein and Justice*, Berkeley: University of California Press

Plato (1961) *The Collected Dialogues*, Hamilton, E and Cairns, H (eds), Princeton: Princeton University Press

Plotinus (1991) *The Enneads*, MacKenna, S (tr), London: Penguin Books

Proudhon, P-J (1994) *What is Property?*, Kelley, D and Smith, B (eds), Cambridge: Cambridge University Press

Pyke, S (1993) *Philosophers*, Manchester: Cornerhouse Publications

Rhees, R (1965) 'Some developments on Wittgenstein's view of ethics', 74 Philosophical Review 17–26

Rorty, R (1998) *Achieving our Country*, Cambridge: Harvard University Press

Rorty, R (1979) *Philosophy and the Mirror of Nature*, Princeton: Princeton University Press

Rosenzweig, F (1985) *The Star of Redemption*, Hallo, W (tr), Notre Dame: University of Notre Dame Press

Safranski, R (2002) *Nietzsche: A Philosophical Biography*, Frisch, S (tr), New York: WW Norton

Sartre, J-P (1995) 'The Humanism of Existentialism', in Guignon, C and Pereboom, D (eds), *Existentialism: Basic Writings*, Indianapolis: Hackett Publishing

Sartre, J-P (1956) *Being and Nothingness*, Barnes, H (tr), New York: Washington Square Press

Sawa, Y and Shiffert, E (trs) (1978) *Haiku Master Buson*, South San Francisco: Heian International

Schiller, D (1994) *The Little Zen Companion*, New York: Workman Publishing

Schloegl, I (1976) *The Zen Teaching of Rinzai*, Berkeley: Shambhala Publishing

Schopenhauer, A (1999) *Prize Essay on the Freedom of the Will*, Payne, EFJ (tr), Cambridge: Cambridge University Press

Schopenhauer, A (1974) *On the Fourfold Root of the Principle of Sufficient Reason*, Payne, EFJ (tr), La Salle, IL: Open Court

Schopenhauer, A (1969) *The World as Will and Representation (2 vols)*, Payne, EFJ (tr), New York: Dover Publications

Shanker, SG (1987) *Wittgenstein and the Turning-Point in the Philosophy of Mathematics*, Albany: State University of New York Press

Singh, S (1997) *Fermat's Enigma: The Epic Quest to Solve the World's Greatest Mathematical Problem*, New York: Walker and Company

Sorel, G (1999) *Reflections on Violence*, Hulme, T and Jennings, J (trs), Cambridge: Cambridge University Press

Spengler, Oswald (1928) *The Decline of the West (2 vols)*, Atkinson, C (tr), New York: Alfred A Knopf

Spinoza, B (1955) *Ethics*, White, W (tr), New York: Hafner Publishing

Stevens, W (1997) *Collected Poetry and Prose*, New York: Library of America

Suzuki, DT (1964) *An Introduction to Zen Buddhism*, New York: Grove Press

Tanahashi, K (1999) *Enlightenment Unfolds: The Essential Teachings of Zen Master Dōgen*, Boston: Shambhala Publications

Thoreau, H (1950) *Walden and Other Writings*, Atkinson, B (ed), New York: Modern Library

Tolstoy, L (1997) *The Gospel in Brief*, Hapgood, I (tr), Lincoln: University of Nebraska Press

Van de Weyer, R (ed) (2000) *366 Readings from Buddhism*, Cleveland: Pilgrim Press

Waddell, N (tr) (1999) *Wild Ivy: The Spiritual Autobiography of Zen Master Hakuin*, Boston: Shambhala

Waismann, F (1979) *Wittgenstein and the Vienna Circle*, Schulte, J and McGuinness, B (trs), Oxford: Blackwell

Watson, B (tr) (1997) *The Vimalakirti Sutra*, New York: Columbia University Press

Watts, A (1957) *The Way of Zen*, New York: Vintage Books

Weber, M (1978) *Economy and Society (2 vols)*, Roth, G and Wittich, C (eds), Berkeley: University of California Press

Weber, M (1958) *From Max Weber: Essays in Sociology*, Gerth, HH and Mills, CW (eds), New York: Oxford University Press

Weber, M (1949) *The Methodology of the Social Sciences*, Shils, E and Finch, H (trs), New York: Macmillan

Whitehead, AN and Russell, B (1910) *Principia Mathematica*, Cambridge: Cambridge University Press

Whitman, W (1891) 'Song of myself', in Walt Whitman, *Leaves of Grass*, New York: Random House-Grabhorn Press

Wittgenstein, L (2003) *Public and Private Occasions*, Klagge, J and Nordmann, A (eds), Lanham: Rowman & Littlefield

Wittgenstein, L (1995) *Cambridge Letters*, McGuinness, B and von Wright, GH (eds), Oxford: Blackwell

Wittgenstein, L (1993) *Philosophical Occasions 1912-1951*, Klagge, J and Nordmann, A (eds), Indianapolis: Hackett

Wittgenstein, L (1990) *Last Writings on the Philosophy of Psychology (2 vols)*, Luckhardt, CG and Aue, M (trs), Chicago: University of Chicago Press

Wittgenstein, L (1989a) *Wittgenstein's Lectures on Philosophical Psychology 1946–47*, Geach, PT (ed), Chicago: University of Chicago Press

Wittgenstein, L (1989b) *Wittgenstein's Lectures on the Foundations of Mathematics: Cambridge 1939*, Diamond, C (ed), Chicago: University of Chicago Press

Wittgenstein, L (1988) *Remarks on the Philosophy of Psychology (2 vols)*, Anscombe, GEM (tr), Chicago: University of Chicago Press

Wittgenstein, L (1984) *Notebooks 1914–1916*, Anscombe, GEM (tr), Chicago: University of Chicago Press

Wittgenstein, L (1983) *Remarks on the Foundations of Mathematics*, Anscombe, GEM (tr), Cambridge: MIT Press

Wittgenstein, L (1980) *Culture and Value*, Winch, P (tr), Chicago: University of Chicago Press

Wittgenstein, L (1979a) *Remarks on Frazer's* Golden Bough, Miles, AC (tr), Gringley: Brynmill Press

Wittgenstein, L (1979b) *Wittgenstein's Lectures: Cambridge, 1932–1935*, Ambrose, A (ed), Chicago: University of Chicago Press

Wittgenstein, L (1978) *Philosophical Grammar*, Kenny, A (tr), Berkeley: University of California Press

Wittgenstein, L (1977) *Remarks on Colour*, McAlister, L and Schättle, M (trs), Berkeley: University of California Press

Wittgenstein, L (1975) *Philosophical Remarks*, Hargreaves, R and White, R (trs), Chicago: University of Chicago Press

Wittgenstein, L (1974) *Tractatus Logico-Philosophicus*, Pears, DF and McGuinness, BF (trs), Atlantic Highlands, NJ: Humanities Press International

Wittgenstein, L (1972) *On Certainty*, Paul, D and Anscombe, GEM (trs), New York: Harper & Row

Wittgenstein, L (1970) *Zettel*, Anscombe, GEM (tr), Berkeley: University of California Press

Wittgenstein, L (1967) *Lectures & Conversations on Aesthetics, Psychology and Religious Belief*, Barrett, C (ed), Berkeley: University of California Press

Wittgenstein, L (1965) 'A lecture on ethics', 74 *Philosophical Review* 3–12

Wittgenstein, L (1960) *The Blue and Brown Books*, New York: Harper & Row

Wittgenstein, L (1953) *Philosophical Investigations*, Anscombe, GEM (tr), New York: Macmillan

Wolcher, L (2004) 'The end of technology: a polemic', 79 Washington Law Review 331–88

Wolcher, L (2003) 'Ethics, justice, and suffering in the thought of Levinas: the problem of the passage', 14 Law and Critique 93–116

Wolcher, L (2002) 'The third mountain: a meditation on chaos and order', 15 International Journal for the Semiotics of Law 25–52

Wolcher, L (2001a) 'Language as mimesis', 5 Law • Text • Culture 187–225

Wolcher, L (2001b) 'The poetry of negligence', 23 Liverpool Law Review 187–97

Wolcher, L (1998) 'A meditation on Wittgenstein's *Lecture on Ethics*', 9 Law and Critique 3–35

Wolcher, L (1997) 'Ronald Dworkin's right answers thesis through the lens of Wittgenstein', 29 Rutgers Law Journal 43–65

Wolcher, L (1995) 'What we do not doubt: a critical legal perspective', 46 Hastings Law Journal 1783–1861

Yeats, WB (1989) *The Collected Poems of WB Yeats*, Finneran, R (ed), New York: Macmillan

Yutang, L (1955) *The Wisdom of China and India*, New York: Modern Library

Žižek, S (1999) *The Ticklish Subject: The Absent Centre of Political Ontology*, London: Verso

Index

£23·50